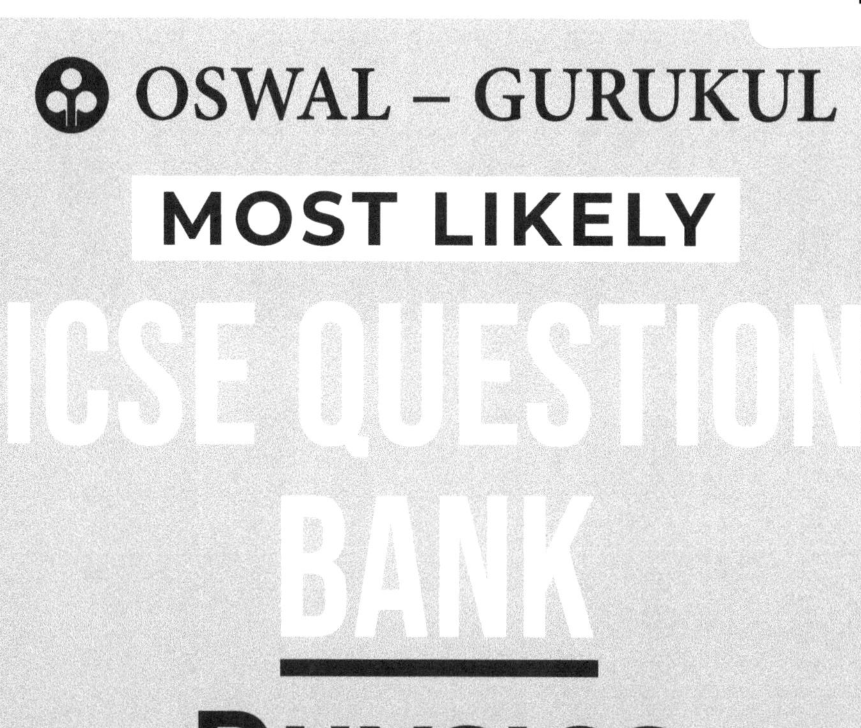

OSWAL – GURUKUL

MOST LIKELY

ICSE QUESTION BANK

PHYSICS

CLASS IX

By

PANEL OF AUTHORS

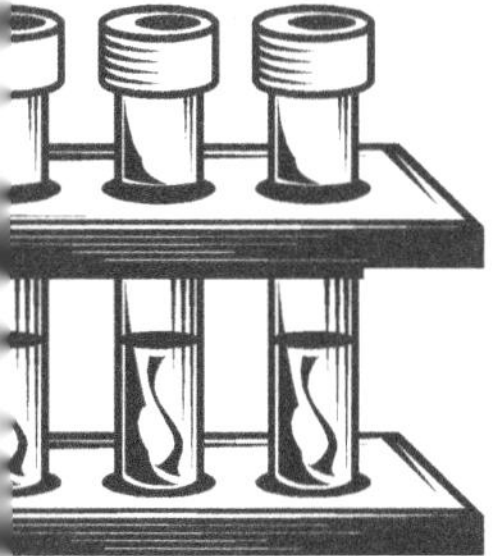

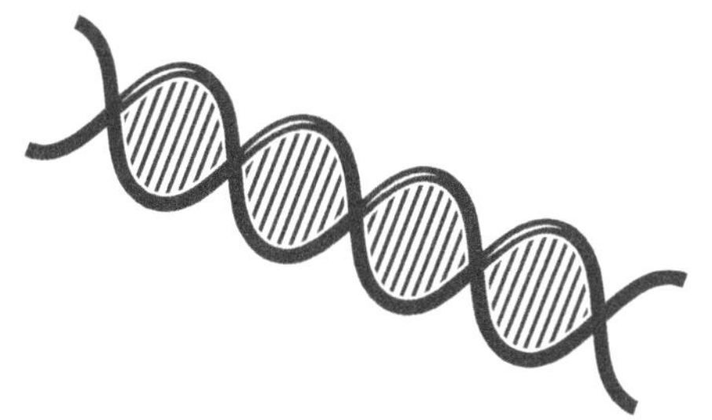

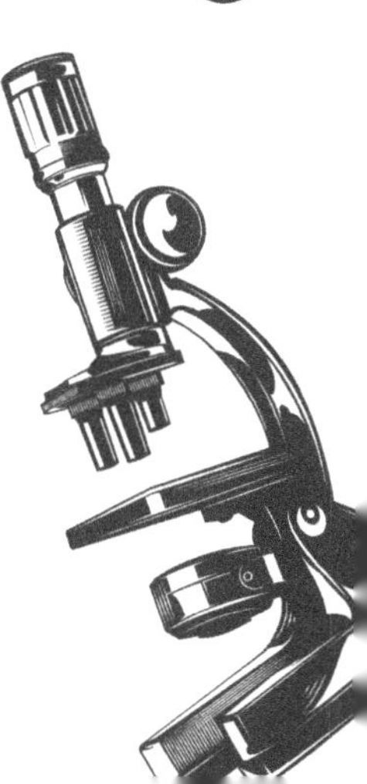

DISCLAIMER

With the ambition of providing standard academic resources, we have exercised extreme care in publishing the content. In case of any discrepancies in the matter, we request readers to excuse the unintentional lapse and not hold us liable for the same. Suggestions are always welcome.

EDITION : 2022

ISBN : 978-93-92563-81-2

PRICE : ₹ 290.00

PRINTED AT :

PUBLISHED BY

 **OSWAL PUBLISHERS**

Head Office : 1/12, Sahitya Kunj, M.G. Road, Agra - 282 002

Phone : (0562) 2527771-4

Whatsapp : +91 74550 77222

E-mail : info@oswalpublishers.in

Website : www.oswalpublishers.com

The cover of this book has been designed using resources from Freepik.com

PREFACE

It is a matter of immense pride for us to present the 'ICSE MOST LIKELY QUESTION BANK' series, especially prepared for students appearing for Board examinations in the oncoming year.

This book has been created with the specific purpose of making the students' journey of learning, understanding and revising the concepts, effortless and simple. The topical approach with ample questions for every category is adopted to reinforce the students' understanding of each chapter. The category-wise division also allows them to peruse their progress as well as keep a check on their grasp of the theory.

Meticulous care has been taken in writing the book in simple, student-friendly language without compromising with the clarity of style.

We are confident that the book will enable the candidates to develop a better understanding of the curriculum and help them organize their learning process. This book shall definitely prove to be a fruitful tool for the students and encourage them towards scholastic excellence.

Constructive suggestions for further improvement of the book are always welcome.

—Publisher

The global outbreak of the Novel Coronavirus (COVID-19) has impacted all aspects of life including the educational life at schools. Schools across the country have been shut since March, 2020 due to the pandemic. While numbers of CISCE affiliated schools have tried to adapt to this changed scenario and have tried to keep alive the teaching learning process through online classes, there has been a significant shortening of the academic year and loss of the instructional hours.

To make up for the loss in instructional hours during the current session 2020-2021, the CISCE has worked with its subject experts, to reduce the syllabi for all major subjects at the ICSE and ISC levels. Syllabus reduction has been done, keeping in mind the linear progression across classes while ensuring that the core concepts related to the subject are retained.

The following reduced syllabi, for the current Academic Year 2020-2021 have been made available on the CISCE website www.cisce.org under 'Publications':

- ICSE Reduced Syllabus for Class IX
- ICSE Reduced Syllabus for Class X
- ISC Reduced Syllabus for Class XI
- ISC Reduced Syllabus for Class XII

Heads of CISCE affiliated schools have been asked to ensure that the concerned subject teachers at the ICSE and ISC levels transact the syllabus strictly according to sequence of topics, so as to facilitate further reduction in syllabus, if required, depending on the situation of the pandemic in the country.

We at Oswal Publishers, have developed all our books on the basis of the original syllabi with complete subjective knowledge of all the subjects, so that the students have an access to the entire syllabus. However, for the examination purpose, the students are advised to structure their preparations considering the latest alterations by the Council.

Scan this to know the recent changes in Syllabus

CONTENTS

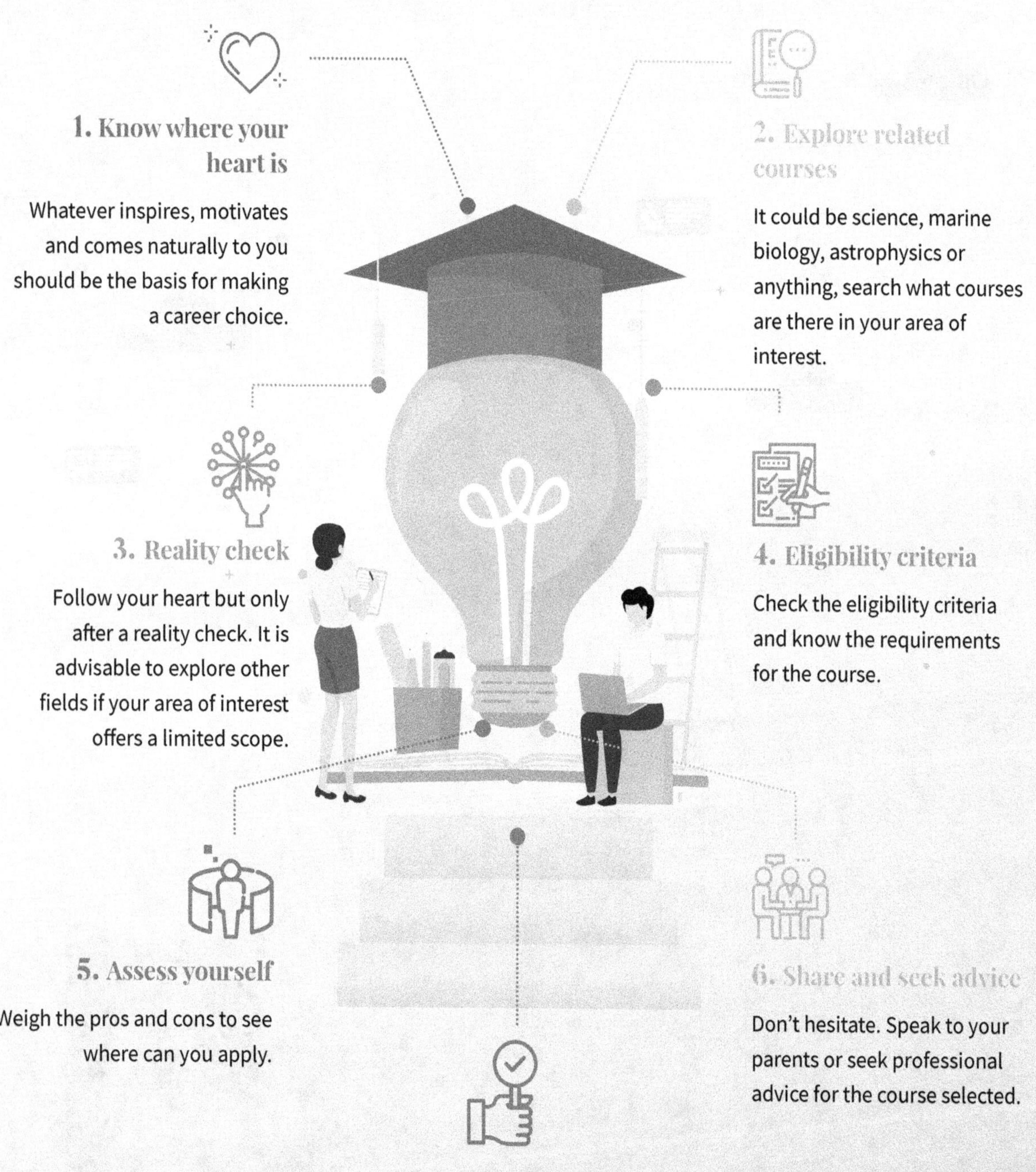

How to choose a
GREAT CAREER

1. Know where your heart is
Whatever inspires, motivates and comes naturally to you should be the basis for making a career choice.

2. Explore related courses
It could be science, marine biology, astrophysics or anything, search what courses are there in your area of interest.

3. Reality check
Follow your heart but only after a reality check. It is advisable to explore other fields if your area of interest offers a limited scope.

4. Eligibility criteria
Check the eligibility criteria and know the requirements for the course.

5. Assess yourself
Weigh the pros and cons to see where can you apply.

6. Share and seek advice
Don't hesitate. Speak to your parents or seek professional advice for the course selected.

7. The final decision
Once you are through with all the steps, you will know where you stand and will be better placed to make the right choice.

Go where your strength is, not where your friends are.

HOW TO MANAGE YOUR TIME BETTER

This is the time when you are going to be promoted to higher classes. Going a level up also means there will be more books, more syllabus, more tests & exams. We have pieced together some of the most effective tips that will surely help you stay ahead of your peers by staying organised and managing your time as well as energy in an improved manner.

• **Make a list:** Every morning, jot down all the things you have to do for the day. Arrange all your tasks according to their importance and urgency. Then, before going to bed, strike off the tasks you managed to finish, giving yourself a sense of accomplishment and helping you stay on track.

• **Segregate your time:** You should divide your day into hourly-chunks, based on your routine. For example, separate about 6-7 compulsory hours for school; then, 7-8 hours for sleep, 4-5 hours for self-study, 1 hour each for leisure and meals. You can keep the remaining hours free as they get used up in chores and other mundane tasks.

• **Improve your focus:** You must strive to finish your tasks in a decided time limit. Learn to eliminate distractions. You should give your undivided attention to their completion. This will improve your efficiency and help you finish your work on time.

• **Take little breaks:** In your study schedule, make sure to assign small breaks between long study sessions to give your brain some rest and restore your energy for another round of rigorous learning. You can have a snack or simply close your eyes and quietly meditate.

• **End procrastination:** Procrastination is the biggest hurdle in your path to success. If you have a daunting task at hand, it's better to break it into smaller chunks and work on them than just postponing it for later. Slow and steady wins the race, after all!

Follow these tips and watch your productivity increase with time. Share your experience with us at contact@oswalpublishers.com .

WEEKLY SCHEDULE

	MONDAY	TUESDAY	WEDNESDAY	THURSDAY	FRIDAY	SATURDAY	SUNDAY

GOALS

DON'T FORGET!

NOTES

Chapter 1. Measurements and Experimentation

Q. 1. What do you mean by the term measurement?

Ans. Measurement is a standard determination of the magnitude of any physical quantity or comparison between a known and an unknown quantity of the same nature.

Q. 2. Define the term unit.

Ans. Unit is a quantity of constant magnitude which is used to measure the magnitudes of other quantities of the same nature.

Q. 3. What do you understand by a physical quantity?

Ans. The quantity that can be measured directly or indirectly is termed as physical quantity.

Q. 4. What do you understand by fundamental quantities?

Ans. Fundamental quantities are the quantities which are independent of any other quantity *i.e.*, they can neither be changed nor be related to any other fundamental quantity. *e.g*: length, mass, time.

Q. 5. What do you mean by derived quantities?

Ans. Derived quantities are the quantities which are dependent on a fundamental quantity *i.e.*, they can be expressed in terms of fundamental quantities. E.g: density, area, volume.

Q. 6. Define 1 kilogram on an atomic scale.

Ans. On an atomic scale, one kilogram is equivalent to the mass of 5.018×10^{25} atoms of C-12 carbon isotope.

Q. 7. Define the following terms:
(i) One metre (ii) One kilogram (iii) One second.

Ans. (i) **One metre:** It is the length of path travelled by light in vacuum during a time interval of $\dfrac{1}{299,792,458}$ of a second.

(ii) **One kilogram:** When a force of one newton produces an acceleration of $1\ \text{ms}^{-2}$ in a body, then the mass of body is said to be one kilogram.

(iii) **One second** is the time duration of 9,192,631,770 periods of certain radiations emitted by Cesium-133 atom.

Q. 8. Define One kelvin temperature.

Ans. One kelvin is defined as the fraction $\left[\dfrac{1}{273.16}\right]$ of the thermodynamic temperature of the triple point of water.

Q. 9. What do you mean by a solar day?

Ans. The time taken by earth to complete one rotation about its own axis so that sun appears in the same position in the sky is called a solar day.

Q. 10. What do you understand by the term mean solar day?

Ans. The average of varying solar days when earth completes one revolution around the sun is called mean solar day.

Q. 11. Define the term pitch of a Vernier Calliper.

Ans. The smallest value of length or any unit which can be read directly and accurately from the main scale is called pitch.

Q. 12. What do you understand by the term least count of an instrument?

Ans. The least count of an instrument is the smallest measurement that can be taken accurately with it. E.g., the least count of a ruler is 1mm if there are 10 divisions between 0 and 1cm.

Q. 13. Define the term least count of a vernier calliper.

Ans. The least count of a vernier calliper is the difference in the value of one main scale division and the value of one vernier scale division. It is the least distance which is measured accurately with the help of a vernier. Mathematically,

Least count [L.C] =

$$\dfrac{\text{Value of smallest division on main scale}}{\text{Total number of divisions on vernier scale}}$$

Q. 14. Define vernier constant for a vernier calliper.

Ans. Vernier constant for a calliper is the difference in the value of one main scale division and the value of one vernier scale division.

Q. 15. Define the term pitch of a micrometer screw gauge.

Ans. The linear distance traversed by the screw on the main scale in one complete rotation of the circular scale is known as the pitch. It is also defined as the distance between any two consecutive threads of the screw.

Q. 16. What do you understand by zero error for vernier calliper?

Ans. When the movable jaw and the fixed jaw of a vernier are in contact and if zero of main scale and vernier scale do not coincide then it is said to have a zero error.

Q. 17. Define a simple pendulum.

Ans. A heavy bob suspended from a rigid support by an inextensible, massless string is called an ideal simple pendulum.

Q. 18. Define the following terms as applied to a simple pendulum.
(i) Amplitude   (ii) Time period
(iii) Frequency   (iv) Effective length.

Ans. (i) **Amplitude:** The maximum displacement of a pendulum on either sides of its mean position is called amplitude. It is denoted by the letter 'A' and its S.I. unit is metre.

(ii) **Time period:** Time taken by a pendulum to complete one oscillation is called time period. It is denoted by letter 'T' and its S.I unit is second.

(iii) **Frequency:** Number of oscillations performed by a pendulum in one second is called frequency. It is denoted by letter 'f' or 'n' and its S.I unit is hertz. Mathematically,

$$\text{Frequency} = \frac{1}{\text{Time period}}$$

(iv) **Effective length:** The distance between point of suspension and centre of gravity of the bob of pendulum is called the effective length of pendulum.

Q. 19. Define a second's pendulum.

Ans. A simple pendulum whose time period is two seconds is called a second's pendulum.

Q. 20. What do you mean by backlash error?

Ans. The error caused due to wear and tear of the threads of screw due to which on reversing the direction of rotation of thimble, the tip of the screw does not move but remain stationary for a part of rotation is known as backlash error.

Chapter 2. Motion in One Dimension

Q. 1. Define scalar quantities.

Ans. Scalar quantities are those quantities which are expressed only by their magnitude. E.g. mass, time, speed.

Q. 2. Define vector quantities.

Ans. Vector quantities are those quantities which are expressed by their magnitude as well as direction. E.g., displacement, velocity.

Q. 3. Define distance. State its unit.

Ans. The length of path moved by a moving body in certain interval of time is called distance travelled by the body. It is a scalar quantity. Its SI unit is metre and CGS unit is cm.

Q. 4. Define displacement. State its unit.

Ans. The shortest distance between the initial and final position of a body in a specified direction is called displacement. It is a vector quantity. Its SI unit is metre and CGS unit is cm.

Q. 5. Define speed. State its unit. Define the different types of speed.

Ans. The speed of a body is the rate of distance travelled with time. Its SI unit is m s^{-1}, while the CGS unit is cm s^{-1}.

There are four types of speed:

(i) **Uniform speed:** If a body covers equal distances in equal intervals of time, then it is said to be moving with uniform speed.

(ii) **Variable speed:** If a body covers unequal distances in equal intervals of time, then the body is said to possess variable speed.

(iii) **Instantaneous speed:** If a body is moving with continuous changes in speed, then its speed at any instant during its course of motion is known as instantaneous speed.

(iv) **Average speed:** The ratio of total distance travelled by the body to the total time taken is called the average speed.

$\therefore$ Average speed

$$= \frac{\text{Total distance travelled}}{\text{Total time taken}}$$

Q. 6. Define velocity. State its unit.

Ans. The velocity of a body is the distance travelled by the body in a specified direction in a unit time interval. It is a vector quantity. It is represented by the symbol u or v. Its SI unit is m s^{-1} and CGS unit is cm s^{-1}.

Q. 7. Define the different types of velocitys.

Ans. (i) **Uniform velocity:** If a body travels equal distances in equal intervals of time along a particular direction, the body is said to be moving with a uniform velocity.

(ii) **Non-uniform or variable velocity:** If a body moves unequal distances in a particular direction in equal intervals of time or it moves equal distances in equal intervals of time, but its direction of motion changes then the velocity of the body is said to be variable or non-uniform.

(iii) **Instantaneous velocity:** The velocity of a body at any instant of time during its course of motion is called the instantaneous velocity.

(iv) **Average velocity:** The ratio of the total distance travelled in a specified direction to the total time taken by the body to travel that distance is called average velocity.

$\therefore$ Average velocity =

$$\frac{\text{Total distance travelled in specified direction}}{\text{Total time taken}}$$

Q. 8. What do you understand by acceleration and retardation?

Ans. The rate of change of velocity with time is known as acceleration. While negative rate of change of velocity with time is called negative acceleration or retardation. Generally while moving, bodies change their velocity either in magnitude or in direction or both. If this variable velocity increases with time then it is acceleration and if it decreases then it is retardation. In other words "negative acceleration is called retardation".

Q. 9. Define:

(i) Uniform acceleration.

(ii) Variable acceleration

(iii) Acceleration due to gravity

Ans. (i) **Uniform acceleration:** The acceleration is said to be uniform when equal changes in velocity takes place in equal intervals of time.

(ii) **Variable acceleration:** If changes in velocity are not same in same intervals of time, the acceleration is said to be variable.

(iii) **Acceleration due to gravity:** The acceleration of a freely falling body, under the influence of gravity is called acceleration due to gravity. Its value changes from place to place and is constant at a given place. The average value of 'g' is 9.8 m s^{-2} in SI units and 980 cm s^{-2} in CGS units.

Chapter 3. Laws of Motion

Q. 1. Define force.

Ans. Force is that physical quantity which changes or tends to change the state of rest or motion of the body.

Q. 2. State the Newton's first law of motion.

Ans. A body continues to remain in the state of rest or in uniform motion along a straight line unless acted upon by an external unbalanced force. This is known as the first law of motion.

Q. 3. Define the term Inertia.

Ans. The inherent tendency of a body to remain in the state of rest or in uniform motion along a straight line unless acted upon by an external unbalanced force is called Inertia.

Q. 4. Name and define the different types of inertia.

Ans. Inertia is of three types:

(i) **Inertia of rest:** The inherent property of a body by virtue of which a body at rest will remain at rest unless or until an external force is applied to it.

(ii) **Inertia of motion:** The inherent property of a body by virtue of which a body in motion continues to remain in motion unless or until an external force is applied on it.

(iii) **Inertia of direction:** It is the inherent property of a body by virtue of which it is unable to change its direction of motion by itself.

Q. 5. Define the term Linear momentum.

Ans. The total quantity of motion possessed by a body due to the collective effect of mass and velocity is called linear momentum.

Q. 6. State the Newton's second law of motion.

Ans. It states that rate of change of momentum is directly proportional to the force applied and takes place in the direction of the force applied.

Mathematically,

Force = mass × acceleration.

Q. 7. Define 1 newton force.

Ans. 1 newton force is the force that acts on a body of mass 1kg producing an acceleration of $1ms^{-2}$ in it.

Mathematically, $1N = 1kg \times 1ms^{-2}$

Q. 8. Define 1 dyne force.

Ans. 1 dyne force is the force that is exerted on a body of mass 1g producing in it an acceleration of $1cms^{-2}$.

Mathematically, $1 \text{ dyne} = 1g \times 1cms^{-2}$

Q. 9. State the Newton's third law of motion.

Ans. For a system of two bodies into consideration, to every action there is equal and opposite reaction.

Q. 10. Define the gravitational unit of force.

Ans. The gravitational unit of force is kilogram force [kgf]. 1 kgf is the force that produces an acceleration of $9.8ms^{-2}$ in a body of mass 1kg.

Q. 11. State the Universal law of Gravitation.

Ans. It states that the force of attraction between any two bodies is directly proportional to the product of their masses and inversely proportional to the square of distance between them.

i.e.,

$$F \propto \frac{m_1 m_2}{r^2}$$

or

$$F = \frac{Gm_1 m_2}{r^2}$$

Where, G is universal Gravitational constant. Its value is $6.67 \times 10^{-11} \, Nm^2 \, kg^{-2}$.

Q. 12. What do you understand by: (i) contact force (ii) non-contact force (iii) resultant force?

Ans. (i) **Contact force:** The force that comes into existence due to physical contact between the two bodies is called as contact force. *e.g.*, force due to friction.

(ii) **Non-contact force:** The force that acts between two bodies kept at a distance from each other is called non-contact force. *e.g.*, magnetic force.

(iii) **Resultant force:** The net force acting on a body which produces the same effect or acceleration as produced by system of forces acting simultaneously.

Q. 13. Define gravitational constant G.

Ans. The gravitational constant G is defined as the force of attraction between two bodies of unit mass, separated by an unit distance.

Q. 14. Define the term mass.

Ans. The mass of a body is the quantity of matter contained in it.

Q. 15. Define the term weight.

Ans. The weight of a body is the force with which the earth attracts it.

Q. 16. Define the term force due to gravity.

Ans. The force with while the earth attracts a body, is called force due to gravity.

Q. 17. Define the term acceleration due to gravity.

Ans. The acceleration produced in a freely falling body due to the gravitation force, is called acceleration due to gravity.

Chapter 4. Pressure in Fluids and Atmospheric Pressure

Q. 1. Define the term thrust.

Ans. When a force is applied on the surface in a direction perpendicular to it, the force is called as thrust. Its SI unit is newton.

Q. 2. Define pressure exerted on a surface.

Ans. Pressure is defined as the thrust acting on a unit cross sectional area.

Mathematically,

$$\text{Pressure} = \frac{\text{Thrust}}{\text{Area}}$$

Its S.I unit is $N.m^{-2}$, commonly known as pascal.

Q. 3. Define 1 pascal pressure.

Ans. Pressure on a surface is said to be 1Pa when a thrust of 1N acts on a surface of area $1m^2$.

Q. 4. State the Pascal's law of transmission of pressure in case of fluids.

Ans. Pressure exerted at any point inside a confined fluid acts equally and undiminished in all directions along the same horizontal plane.

Q. 5. Define what do you understand by the term atmospheric pressure?

Ans. The thrust exerted by the column of air on a unit surface area of earth is called as atmospheric pressure.

Q. 6. What do you mean by the term fluid pressure?

Ans. The pressure exerted by a fluid in all directions due to its weight, is called as fluid pressure.

Q. 7. What is an aneroid barometer?

Ans. A barometer calibrated to read directly the atmospheric pressure is called an aneroid barometer.

Chapter 5. Upthrust in Fluids, Archimedes' Principle and Floatation

Q. 1. Define Upthrust.

Ans. The upward force exerted on a body by a fluid when partly or wholly immersed in in it, is called upthrust or buoyant force.

Q. 2. Define the term buoyancy.

Ans. The property of liquid to exert an upward force on a body, immersed in it, is called buoyancy.

Q. 3. State the Archimedes' principle.

Ans. Archimedes' principle states that when a body is immersed partially or completely in a fluid, it experiences an upthrust which is equal to the weight of the fluid displaced by it.

Q. 4. State the law of floatation.

Ans. When a body floats in a fluid, the weight of the body acting vertically downwards at its centre of gravity is equal to the weight of liquid displaced by the immersed part of the body acting at the centre of buoyancy.

Q. 5. What do you understand by the term centre of buoyancy?

Ans. Centre of buoyancy is an imaginary point, where the buoyant force due to the weight of the fluid displaced acts on a floating body.

Q. 6. Define the term volumetric density.

Ans. Volumetric density of a substance is the ratio of mass of a substance to its volume.

Q. 7. What do you understand by the term relative density?

Ans. Relative density is defined as the ratio of density of substance to the density of water at 4°C. It being a pure ratio is an unitless quantity.

Q. 8. State the principle of floatation.

Ans. According to the principle of floatation, the weight of a floating body is equal to the weight of the liquid displaced by its submerged part.

Chapter 6. Heat and Energy

Q. 1. Define heat.

Ans. On the conventional basis, heat is a form of energy which causes a sensation of warmth in us.

On the basis of kinetic model, heat is the sum total of kinetic and potential energies of all the molecules of a substance.

Q. 2. Define temperature.

Ans. On the conventional basis, temperature is the degree of hotness or coldness of a body.

On the basis of kinetic model, temperature is the average kinetic energy of all the molecules of a substance.

Q. 3. What do you understand by Superficial expansion?

Ans. If a material is in the form of a plate, such that its thickness is too small as compared to surface area and hence, can be neglected then increase in surface area on heating is called superficial expansion.

Q. 4. What do you understand by Cubical expansion?

Ans. Increase in volume of a material on heating is called cubical expansion.

Q. 5. What is an ecosystem?

Ans. A unit composed of biotic components (*i.e.,* producers, consumers and decomposers) and abiotic components (*i.e.,* light, heat, rain, and humidity, inorganic and organic substances) is called an ecosystem.

Q. 6. What do you mean by greenhouse effect?

Ans. Greenhouse effect is the process of warming of planet's surface and its lower atmosphere by absorbtion of infrared radiations of longer wavelength emitted out from the surface of planet.

Q. 7. What do you mean by global warming?

Ans. Global warming means the increase in average effective temperature near the earth's surface due to an increase in the amount of greenhouse gases in its atmosphere.

Q. 8. What is a food chain?

Ans. A food chain shows the feeding relationship between different living things in a particular environment or habitat. Often, a plant will begin a food chain because it can make its own food using energy from the Sun. In addition, a food chain represents a series of events in which food and energy are transferred from one organism in an ecosystem to another. Food chains show how energy is passed from the Sun to producers, from producers to consumers, and from consumers to decomposers.

Q. 9. What do you mean by tidal energy?

Ans. The energy possessed by rising and falling water in tides is known as tidal energy.

Q. 10. What do you mean by ocean energy?

Ans. Water in the oceans possesses energy in two forms:

(i) **Ocean thermal energy:** The energy available due to the difference in temperature of water at the surface and at deeper levels of ocean is called the ocean thermal energy.

(ii) **Oceanic waves energy:** The kinetic energy possessed by fast moving oceanic (or sea) waves is called oceanic waves energy.

Q. 11. What do you mean by geo thermal energy?

Ans. The heat energy possessed by the rocks inside the Earth is called geothermal energy.

Q. 12. What do you understand by the term anomalous expansion of water?

Ans. The expansion of water when it is cooled from 4°C to 0°C, is known as anomalous expansion of water.

Q. 13. What do you mean by thermal equilibrium?

Ans. If there is no exchange of heat between two bodies, when they are in contact, then the bodies are said to be in the state of thermal equilibrium.

Q. 14. What is carbon tax?

Ans. The tax calculated on the basis of carbon emission from industry, number of employee hour and turnover of the factory is called carbon tax.

Q. 15. Define:

(i) Renewable sources of energy

(ii) Non-renewable sources of energy

Ans. (i) The sources of energy that can be renewed or replaced, are called renewable sources of energy. E.g. water tides, sun, wind.

(ii) The sources of energy that cannot be renewed once they are consumed, are called non-renewable sources of energy. *E.g.* coal, petroleum, natural gas.

Q. 16. Define the following.

(i) Solar energy

(ii) Wind energy

(iii) Hydro energy

Ans. (i) The energy obtained from Sun is called solar energy.

(ii) The kinetic energy possessed by moving wind, is called wind energy.

(iii) The kinetic energy possessed by the flowing water, is called hydro energy.

Q. 17. Define:

(i) Nuclear fusion

(ii) Nuclear fission

Ans. (i) When two light nuclei at very high temperature and pressure, combine to form a heavy nucleus, a large amount of energy is released. This phenomenon is called nuclear fusion.

(ii) When a nucleus of a heavy radioactive atom is boarded with slow moving neutrons, it get split into two light nuclei and a large amount of energy is released. This phenomenon is called nuclear fission.

Q. 18. State ten percent law.

Ans. According to this law, ten percent of the total energy, entering a particular level, is transferred to the next higher trophic level.

Q. 19. Define the term energy degradation .

Ans. The gradual decrease of useful energy due to radiation loss, friction, etc., is called degradation of energy.

Chapter 7. Reflection of Light

Q. 1. What do you mean by light?

Ans. An invisible energy, which causes the sensation of sight is known as light.

Q. 2. What do you mean by diffused light?

Ans. When light energy spreads over vast space, due to successive reflections from rough surfaces, such that its intensity decreases is called diffused light.

Q. 3. What is reflection of light?

Ans. Reflection of light is a phenomenon of returning of light into the same medium, after striking a surface.

Q. 4. What do you mean by regular reflection?

Ans. The phenomenon, due to which a parallel beam of light, travelling through a certain medium, on striking some smooth polished surface, bounces off from it, as a parallel beam, in some other direction is called regular reflection.

Example: The reflection taking place from a plane mirror. **Use:** It is used for seeing one's face in plane mirror.

Q. 5. What do you mean by irregular reflection?

Ans. The phenomenon, due to which a parallel beam of light, travelling through some medium, gets reflected in various possible directions, on striking some rough surface is called irregular reflection.

Example: Reflection taking place from irregular surfaces, such as walls, stones, etc.

Use: It cuts the glare and hence, is helpful in seeing things around.

Q. 6. Define Spherical mirror.

Ans. A mirror, which is made from a part of hollow sphere is called spherical mirror.

Q. 7. Define Convex mirror.

Ans. A mirror, which is polished from hollow side of sphere, such that the reflection takes place from the outer surface is called convex mirror.

Q. 8. Define Concave mirror.

Ans. A mirror, which is polished from outer side of hollow sphere, such that the reflection takes place from the hollow (inner) surface is called concave mirror.

Q. 9. What do you mean by Pole of a spherical mirror?

Ans. The mid-point of a spherical mirror is called pole.

Q. 10. What do you mean by Centre of curvature of a spherical mirror?

Ans. The centre of the sphere of which spherical mirror is a part, is called centre of curvature.

Q. 11. What do you mean by Principal axis of a spherical mirror?

Ans. An imaginary line passing through the pole and centre of curvature of a spherical mirror is called principal axis.

Q. 12. What do you mean by Principal focus of a spherical mirror?

Ans. It is a point on principal axis, where a parallel beam of light after reflection either actually meets or appears to meet.

Q. 13. What do you mean by Focal length?

Ans. The linear distance between pole and principal focus is called focal length.

Q. 14. Define Radius of curvature.

Ans. The linear distance between pole and centre of curvature is called radius of curvature.

Q. 15. By drawing a neat diagram define the following:
(i)   Mirror
(ii)   Incident ray
(iii)   Reflected ray
(iv)   Angle of incidence
(v)   Angle of reflection
(vi)   Normal.
(vii) Point of incidence
(viii) Plane of incidence
(ix)   Plane of reflection

Ans. (i)   **Mirror:** A smooth polished surface from which regular reflection takes place is called mirror.

(ii)   **Incident ray:** A ray of light, which travels towards mirror (reflecting sarface) is called incident ray.

(iii) **Reflected ray:** A ray of light, which bounces off the surface of mirror (reflecting surface) is called reflected ray.

(iv)   **Angle of incidence:** The angle between incident ray and normal is known as angle of incidence.

(v)   **Angle of reflection:** The angle between reflected ray and normal is called angle of reflection.

(vi)   **Normal:** The perpendicular drawn on the point of incidence of the surface of mirror (reflecting surface) is called normal.

(viii) The point at which the incident ray strikes the reflecting surface, is called point of incidence.

(viii) The plane containing incident ray and the noraml, is called plane of incidence.

(ix) The plane countaining the reflected ray and the normal, is called plane of reflection.

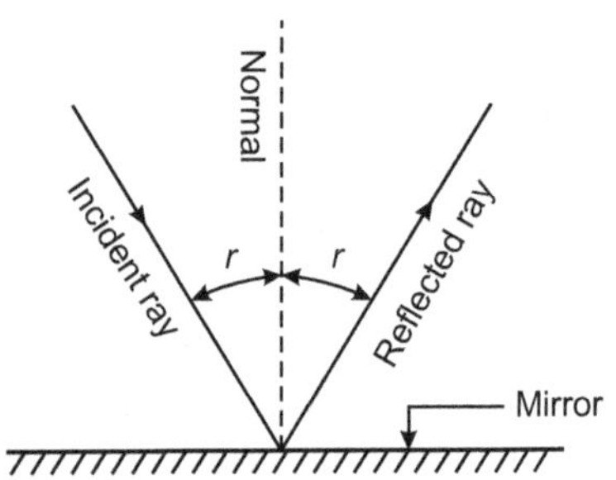

Q. 16. What do you mean by (i) real image, (ii) virtual image?

Ans. (i) When the rays of light from an object, after striking an reflecting surface, actually meet at a point, then the image formed of the object is called real image.

(ii) When the rays of light from an object, after striking a reflecting surface, do not meet but only appear to meet, then the image formed of the object is called virtual image.

Q. 17. Define principle focus of a convex mirror.

Ans. The point on the principle axis at which the light rays, incident parallel to the principle axis, appear to meet after reflection from a mirror, is called principle focus of the convex mirror.

Q. 18. What do you understand by the term lateral inversion?

Ans. The phenomenon due to which the image of an object turns through angle of 180° through a vertical axis, such that right side of object appears as left side of object and vice-versa is called lateral inversion.

Q. 19. Define the term linear magnification.

Ans. The ratio of length of the image to the length of the object is called linear magnification. It is denoted by m.

Chapter 8. Propagation of Sound Waves

Q. 1. What do you understand by the term sound?

Ans. Sound is a mechanical energy which produces sensation of hearing.

Q. 2. What do you understand by the term sonic vibrations?

Ans. The vibrations which produce sensation of hearing in human beings are called sonic vibrations.

Q. 3. What do you understand by the term infra-sonic vibrations?

Ans. The vibrations which are not perceived by human ear and have a range from 0 – 20 Hz are called infra-sonic vibrations.

Q. 4. What do you understand by the term ultra-sonic vibrations?

Ans. The vibrations which are not perceived by human ear and have a frequency range of above 20,000 Hz are called ultra-sonic vibrations.

Q. 5. Define the term wave velocity. Write its S.I. unit.

Ans. The distance travelled by a wave in one second is called its wave velocity. Its SI unit is metre per second (ms^{-1}).

Q. 6. What do you mean by wave?

Ans. The disturbance produced in a medium by the to and fro motion of its particles about their mean position is called wave.

Q. 7. Define Elastic wave.

Ans. The waves produced in a material medium are called elastic waves.

Q. 8. What do you understand by Wave motion?

Ans. The transfer of energy when the particles of a medium move about their mean positions is called wave motion

Q. 9. Define the following related to wave motion.

(i) Amplitude   (ii) Time period

(iii) Frequency   (iv) Wavelength

(v) Wave number (vi) Wave velocity

Ans. (i) The maximum displacement of the particle of medium of a wave on either side of its mean position, is called amplitude of wave.

(ii) The time taken by a particle of medium to complete one oscillation, is called time period of wave.

(iii) The number of oscillations completed by a particle of medium in one second is called frequency of wave.

(iv) The distance travelled by a wave in one oscillation is called wavelength of wave.

(v) The reciprocal of wavelength is called wave number.

(vi) The distance travelled by a wave in one second is called wave velocity.

Q. 10. Define:

(i) Longitudinal wave

(ii) Transverse wave

Ans. (i) The wave in which the particles of medium vibrate about their mean positions, in the direction of propagation of wave, is called the longitudinal wave.

(ii) The wave in which particles of medium vibrate about their mean positions, in a direction perpendicular to the direction of propagation of wave, is called transverse wave.

Chapter 9. Current Electricity

Q. 1. What do you understand by Electric circuit?

Ans. A path along which electric current flows is known as electric circuit.

Q. 2. What do you understand by Closed electric circuit?

Ans. When the path of an electric circuit starting from one terminal of the cell, ends at the other terminal of cell, without any break, then such a circuit is called closed circuit.

Q. 3. What do you understand by Open electric circuit?

Ans. When the path of an electric circuit, starting from one terminal of the cell, is broken at some point, then such a circuit is called open electric circuit.

Q. 4. What do you understand by the term electric resistance?

Ans. The obstruction offered to the passage of electric current by a material is called resistance of the material.

Q. 5. What do you understand by the term electric potential?

Ans. The amount of work done in moving a unit positive charge from infinity to a given point is called electric potential.

Q. 6. Define electric potential in terms of energy spent.

Ans. The amount of energy spent in moving a unit positive charge from infinity to a given point in an electric field is called electric potential.

Q. 7. What do you mean by quantity of electric charge?

Ans. The number of charge (electrons) which drift from lower to higher potential is called quantity of charge.

Q. 8. What do you understand by the term electric current?

Ans. The rate of flow of electric charge in an electric circuit is called electric current.

Q. 9. Define the term potential difference.

Ans. The amount of work done in moving a unit positive charge from one conductor to other conductor is called potential difference.

Q. 10. What do you understand by the term electrostatic induction?

Ans. The phenomenon due to which an insulated uncharged conductor gets electrically charged, when held near a charged body is called electrostatic induction. The charges produced on the insulated uncharged body are called induced charges.

Q. 11. What do you undertand by the term direct current?

Ans. A direct current is a current of constant magnitude, which flows in one direction only.

Q. 12. What is an electric cell?

Ans. An electric cell is a device which converts chemical enrgy, stored in it, into electric energy.

Q. 13. Define the two type of cells.

Ans. The two type of cells are:

(i) **Primary cell:** These are the cells in which electric current is produced as a result of irreversible chemical reaction.

(ii) **Secondary cell:** These are the cells in which electric current is produced as a result of reversible chemical reaction. These cells can be used again, after recharging.

Q. 14. Define 1 ampere current.

Ans. 1 ampere is the current which flows in an electric circuit where rate of flow of charge is 1 coulomb per second.

Q. 15. What is a rheostat?

Ans. A rheostat is device which is used to vary resistance in an electric circuit.

Q. 16. State Ohm's law.

Ans. According to Ohm's law, if a current of magnitude 'I' ampere flows through a wire when the potential difference across the ends of wire is V volt, then the resistance offered by the wire to the flow of current in the ratio of potential difference across it to the current flowing in it.

$$i.e., R = \frac{V}{I}$$

or V = IR

Q. 17. Define:
  (i)   Insulators
  (ii) Conductors

Ans. (i) The substances which do not allow electric current to pass through them, are called insulators. *E.g.,* Cotton, rubber, plastic.

  (ii) The substances which allow electric current to pass through them, are called conductors. *E.g.,* Iron, copper, silver.

Q. 18. Define 1 ohm.

Ans. 1 ohm is the resistance of a conductor, when 1 ampere of current flows through it and potential difference across its end is 1 volt.

Chapter 10. Magnetism

Q. 1. What is a Lodestone?

Ans. Lodestone is an ore of iron oxide (Fe_3O_4). This ore attracts small pieces of iron and it sets itself along a definite direction when it is suspended freely. It is a natural magnet which was used for the navigation by the mariners.

Q. 2. What is a natural magnet?

Ans. The pieces of lodestone found in nature are called the natural magnets.

Q. 3. What is an artificial magnet?

Ans. An artificial magnet is a magnetized piece of iron or other magnetic material.

Q. 4. Define Magnetic field.

Ans. The space surrounding a magnet within which the magnet has its influence is called magnetic field.

Q. 5. Explain the meaning of the term induced magnetism.

Ans. The temporary magnetism acquired by a magnetic material when it is kept near (or in contact with) a magnet, is called induced magnetism.

Q. 6. Define the term magnetic induction.

Ans. The process in which a piece of magnetic material acquires magnetic properties temporarily, in the presence of a magnet near it, is called magnetic induction.

Q. 7. What is a neutral point?

Ans. The points near a magnet, where the magnetic field due to magnet is equal and opposite to that of the horizontal component of Earth's magnetic field, are called neutral points.

Q. 8. What do you understand by the term magnetic field lines?

Ans. A magnetic field line is a continuous curve in a magnetic field such that tangent at any point of it gives the direction of the magnetic field at that point.

Q. 9. What is an electromagnet?

Ans. An electromagnet is a temporary strong magnet made from a piece of soft iron when current flows in the coil wound around it. It is an artificial magnet.

❑

SI Units and Correlation Between Units

Chapter 1. Measurements and Experimentation

Q. 1. Fill in the blanks to complete the given conversions of units.

(i)	1 micron	= ---------------m.
(ii)	1 angstrom	= ---------------m.
(iii)	1 nanometre	= ---------------m.
(iv)	1 fermi	= ---------------m.
(v)	1 gram	= ---------------mg.
(vi)	1 quintal	= ---------------kg
(vii)	1 kilogram	= ---------------g
(viii)	1 metric tonne	= ---------------quintal
(ix)	1 hectogram	= ---------------g
(x)	1 decagram	= ---------------g
(xi)	1 microgram	= ---------------g
(xii)	1 decametre	= ---------------m.
(xiii)	1 hectometre	= ---------------m
(xiv)	1 kilometre	= ---------------m.
(xv)	1 decimetre	= ---------------cm.
(xvi)	1 centimetre	= ---------------m.
(xvi)	1 millimetre	= ---------------cm.
(xvii)	1 micrometre	= ---------------cm.
(xviii)	1 nanometre	= ---------------cm.
(xix)	1 picometre	= ---------------cm.
(xx)	1 Mean solar day	= ---------------hour
		= ---------------min
		= ---------------sec
(xxi)	1 parsec	= ---------------m.
		= ---------------ly.

Ans.

(i)	1 micron	=	10^{-6} m.
(ii)	1 angstrom	=	10^{-10} m.
(iii)	1 nanometre	=	10^{-9} m.
(iv)	1 fermi	=	10^{-15} m.
(v)	1 gram	=	1000 mg.
(vi)	1 quintal	=	100 kg
(vii)	1 kilogram	=	1000 g
(viii)	1 metric tonne	=	10 quintal
(ix)	1 hectogram	=	100 g
(x)	1 decagram	=	10 g
(xi)	1 microgram	=	10^{-6} g
(xii)	1 decametre	=	10 m.
(xiii)	1 hectometre	=	100 m
(xiv)	1 kilometre	=	1000 m.
(xv)	1 decimetre	=	10 cm.
(xvi)	1 centimetre	=	10^{-2} m.
(xvi)	1 millimetre	=	10^{-1} cm.
(xvii)	1 micrometre	=	10^{-4} cm.
(xviii)	1 nanometre	=	10^{-7} cm.
(xix)	1 picometre	=	10^{-10} cm.
(xx)	1 Mean solar day	=	24 hour
		=	1440 min
		=	86400 sec
(xxi)	1 parsec	=	3.08×10^{16} m.
		=	3.26 ly.

Q. 2. Give the SI unit of the following:
(i) Temperature
(ii) Potential difference

Ans. (i) Kelvin (K)
(ii) Volt (V) **[November, 2019]**

Chapter 2. Motion in One Dimension

Q. 1. Convert km h^{-1} to m s^{-1}.

Ans. $1 \text{ km h}^{-1} = \dfrac{1000\,\text{m}}{3600\,\text{sec}}$

$= \dfrac{5}{18} \text{ m s}^{-1}$

Q. 2. Convert m s^{-1} to km hr^{-1}.

Ans. $1 \text{m s}^{-1} = \dfrac{1}{1000} \text{ km} \times 3600 \text{ h}$

$= \dfrac{3600}{1000} \text{ km h}^{-1}$

$= \dfrac{18}{5} \text{ km h}^{-1}.$

Chapter 3. Laws of Motion

Q. 1. State the correlation between SI and CGS unit of force.

Ans. The SI unit of force is newton and CGS unit is dyne. The correlation between the two is

$$1\,N = 10^5\ \text{dyne}.$$

Q. 2. How is the gravitational unit of force related to its SI unit ?

Ans. Mathematically, $1\ kgf = 9.8\ N$

Q. 3. What is the equivalent of CGS unit of force in gravitational unit ?

Ans. Mathematically, $1\ \text{dyne} = \dfrac{1}{980}\ gf$

Q. 4. Obtain the correlation between SI and CGS unit of force.

Ans. According to newton's second law,

$$\text{Force} = \text{Mass} \times \text{Acceleration}$$

In SI unit,
$$1N = 1kg \times 1ms^{-2}$$
$$= 1000g \times 100cms^{-2}$$
$$= 10^3\ g \times 10^2\ cms^{-2}$$
$$= 10^5\ gcms^{-2}$$

In CGS units, $1\ \text{dyne} = 1g \times 1cms^{-2}$

$$\therefore \qquad 1N = 10^5\ \text{dyne}$$

Chapter 4. Pressure in Fluids and Atmospheric Pressure

Q. 1. State the SI unit of pressure and how is it related to the CGS unit?

Ans. The S.I unit of pressure is $N.m^{-2}$, while its CGS unit is $dyne.cm^{-2}$

$$1N.m^{-2} = 10^5\ \text{dyne} \times 10^{-4}\ cm^{-2}$$
$$= 10\ \text{dyne}.cm^{-2}$$

Chapter 5. Upthrust in Fluids, Archimedes' Principle and Floatation

Q. 1. State the SI and CGS unit of density.

Ans. The SI unit of density is $kg\ m^{-3}$ and its CGS unit is $g\ cm^{-3}$.

Q. 2. State the relationship between SI and CGS unit of density.

Ans. $1\ kgm^{-3} = 10^{-3}\ g\ cm^{-3}$

Chapter 6. Heat and Energy

Q. 1. (i)   Express 350 °C into Fahrenheit scale.
(ii) Express 112 °F into Celsius scale.

Ans. (i)
$$\frac{C}{5} = \frac{F-32}{9}$$

$$\therefore \qquad F = \frac{9}{5}C + 32$$

$$= \frac{9}{5} \times 350 + 32 = 662\ °F$$

(ii)
$$\frac{C}{5} = \frac{F-32}{9}$$

$$\therefore \qquad C = 5 \times \left(\frac{F-32}{9}\right)$$

$$C = 5 \times \left(\frac{112-32}{9}\right)$$

$$= 5 \times \frac{80}{9} = 44.4\ °C$$

Chapter 8. Propagation of Sound Waves

Q. 1. Derive a relation between frequency and time period.

Ans. Consider a vibrating body, having a time period 'T' and frequency 'f'.

f vibrations are produced in 1 s.

$$\therefore\ 1\ \text{vibration is produced in } \frac{1}{f}\ \text{second.}$$

But, time required to produce one vibration is called time period 'T'.

$$\therefore \qquad T = \frac{1}{f}$$

Q. 2. Derive a relation between wave velocity; frequency and wavelength.

Ans. Consider a wave, moving with a velocity 'v', such that 'f' is its frequency, 'T' the time period and 'λ' the wavelength.

In time T, the distance covered by wave $= \lambda$.

In one second, the distance covered by

$$\text{wave} = \frac{\lambda}{T}$$

But, $$f = \frac{1}{T}$$

$\therefore$ $$v = f\lambda$$

Chapter 9. Current Electricity

Q. 1. How is potential difference related to work done and quantity of charge ?

Ans. If Q = Charge moving from one point to another in a conductor, W = Work done to move the charge Q from one point to another and V = Potential difference between two points, then work done in moving Q units of charge = W

$\Rightarrow$ Work done in moving one unit of charge

$$= \frac{W}{Q}$$

But work done in moving one unit of charge = Potential difference = V

$\Rightarrow$ $$V = \frac{W}{Q}$$

$\square$

Differentiate between | Set 3 |

Chapter 1. Measurements and Experimentation

Q. 1. Differentiate between the accuracies of a Vernier calliper and a micrometre screw.

Ans. (i) The accuracy of micrometre screw gauge is more than that of vernier calliper.

(ii) The least count of MSG is correct up to 3dp, while LC of vernier is 2dp.

Q. 2. What is the difference between positive error and negative error for a Vernier ?

Ans. On bringing the two jaws together, if the zero of vernier scale is on the right hand side of the zero of main scale, the error is said to be positive, while, if the zero of vernier scale is on the left hand side of the zero of the main scale, the error is said to be negative.

Q. 3. Distinguish between positive and negative zero error in case of a micrometer.

Ans. On bringing the flat of screw in contact with stud, if the zero of circular scale is below the reference line of main scale, the zero error is said to be positive.

While, if the zero of circular scale is above the reference line of the main scale, the zero error is said to be negative.

Q. 4. Differentiate between actual length and effective length of a pendulum.

Ans. (i) Effective length of the pendulum is the distance between point of suspension and the centre of gravity of the bob, while, actual length is the distance between point of suspension and the tip of the bob.

(ii) Effective length affects the time period of the pendulum, while actual length has no effect on the time period.

Chapter 2. Motion in One Dimension

Q. 1. Distinguish between distance and displacement.

Ans.

	Distance	Displacement
(i)	It is the length of path traversed by the object in a certain time.	It is the distance travelled by the object in a specified direction in a certain time (*i.e.*, it is the distance between the final and initial position).
(ii)	It is a scalar quantity.	It is a vector quantity.
(iii)	It depends on the path followed by the object.	It does not depend on the path followed by the object.
(iv)	It is always positive.	It can be positive, negative or zero.
(v)	It can be more than or equal to the magnitude of displacement.	Its magnitude can be less than or equal to the distance.

Q. 2. Distinguish between speed and velocity.

Ans.

	Speed	Velocity
(i)	The distance travelled by a moving object in one second is called the speed.	The distance travelled by a moving object in one second in a particular direction is called its velocity.
(ii)	It is a scalar quantity.	It is a vector quantity.
(iii)	Speed is always positive.	Velocity can be positive, negative or zero.

Chapter 3. Laws of Motion

Q. 1. Distinguish between mass and weight

Ans.

	Mass	Weight
(i)	The quantity of matter contained in a body is called mass.	The force with which a body is attracted towards the centre of earth is called its weight.
(ii)	It is measured by beam balance.	It is measured by spring balance.
(iii)	It is a scalar quantity.	It is a vector quantity.
(iv)	It remains constant at every place.	It changes from place to place.

Q. 2. Differentiate between contact and non-contact forces.

Ans.

	Contact force	Non-contact force
(i)	The force caused between two bodies due to actual physical contact is called contact force.	The force caused between two bodies separated by a distance is called as non-contact force.

(ii)	It is independent of distance of separation between the bodies.	It is inversely proportional to square of distance between the two bodies.

Q. 3. Distinguish between inertia of rest and inertia of motion.

Ans.

	Inertia of rest	Inertia of motion
(i)	A body initially at rest continues to remain at rest.	A body in motion continues to be in motion.
(ii)	It is applicable for bodies in physical contact with each other.	The bodies may not necessarily be in contact with each other.

Q. 4. Differentiate between a balanced force and an unbalanced force.

Ans.

	Balanced force	Unbalanced force
(i)	Resultant of forces acting on a body is zero.	Resultant of forces acting on a body is not zero.
(ii)	All the three type of inertias remain constant.	All three inertias vary.

Chapter 4. Pressure in Fluids and Atmospheric Pressure

Q. 1. Differentiate between Pressure in liquid column and atmospheric pressure.

Ans. (i) Pressure in liquid column is directly proportional to the depth of the point from the free surface of the liquid, while atmospheric pressure is the pressure exerted by air column of the free surface of earth.

(ii) Pressure in a liquid column depends on the density of the liquid while atmospheric pressure depends on the relative height of the point above sea level.

(iii) Pressure in liquid column is measured in pascal while atmospheric pressure is measured in mm of Hg or in cm of Hg.

Q. 2. Differentiate between Water barometer and Mercury barometer.

Ans. (i) Vertical height of water barometer should be approx. 10 m making it inconvenient to be portable while mercury barometer is smaller in size and portable (1m vertical height).

(ii) The barometric liquid used is water in case of water barometer while in case of a mercury barometer, mercury is used as barometric liquid.

(iii) Water is transparent and would stick to the glass, while mercury is shiny viscous liquid which would not stick to the glass.

Chapter 5. Upthrust in Fluids, Archimedes' Principle and Floatation

Q. 1. Distinguish between the terms density and relative density.

Ans. (i) Density of a substance is the ratio of mass of a substance to its volume, while relative density of a substance is the ratio of density of the substance to the density of water at 4°C.

(ii) The SI unit of density of a substance is kg m^{-3}, while relative density is an unitless quantity.

Chapter 6. Heat and Energy

Q. 1. Differentiate between producers and consumers.

Ans. Producers like plants and some bacteria are capable of producing their own food using the energy of sun but consumers are not capable of producing their own food. They depend on producers for food.

Q. 2. State three differences between heat and temperature.

Ans. Difference between heat and temperature

Heat	Temperature
It is a form of energy.	It is thermal condition of the body.
It flows from one body to other.	It is a quantity that indicates whether or not and in which direction heat will flow.
It is a total amount of internal energy of a body.	It is proportional to average kinetic energy of the molecules of a body.
In the transmission of heat, total amount of heat remain unchanged.	In the transmission of heat, temperature doesn't remain same.
It is a cause.	It is an effect.
Its SI unit is joule.	Its SI unit is kelvin(K).

Q. 3. Differentiate between Renewable resources and Non-renewable resources.

Ans. Difference between Renewable resources and Non-renewable resources

Renewable Energy resources	Non-renewable Energy resources
These are Energy resources which can be utilized continuously over a very long period of time.	These are resources which cannot be utilized continuously over a very long period of time.
They are the non-conventional resources.	They are the conventional resources.
These are the natural resources which will not get exhausted.	These are the natural resources which would soon deplete if they are consumed indiscriminately.
These resources can be regenerated.	These resources cannot be regenerated within a limited time period.
Examples: air, water, sunlight, etc.	Example: Coal, mineral oil, etc.

Chapter 7. Reflection of light

Q. 1. Differentiate between two kinds of spherical mirrors.

Ans. Difference between Concave and Convex mirrors :

S. No.	Concave Mirror	Convex Mirror
(i)	It converges the light rays incident on it to some point.	It diverges the light rays incident on it after reflection.
(ii)	Its bulging surface is silver coated and inner surface is reflecting.	Its bulging surface is reflecting and inner surface is coated.
(iii)	The image formed will be real or virtual depending upon the distance of object from the mirror.	In this case, image formed will be always virtual, irrespective of the distance of object from the mirror.

Q. 2. Differentiate between real image and virtual image.

Ans.

Real Image	Virtual Image
A real image can be obtained on a screen.	A virtual image cannot be obtained on a screen.
A real image is inverted with respect to the object.	A virtual image is erect with respect to the object.
A real image is formed when rays of reflected light actually meet.	A virtual image is formed wehn rays of reflected light appear to meet, when produced backwards.

Chapter 8. Propagation of Sound Waves

Q. 1. State two important differences between light and sound waves.

Ans. (i) Light waves are electromagnetic waves and hence, do not require material medium for propagation. However, sound waves are mechanical waves and, hence, require material medium for propagation.

(ii) Light waves travel in air with a speed of $3 \times 10^8 \text{ms}^{-1}$, whereas sound waves travel in air at a speed of 330 ms^{-1}.

Q. 2. Differentiate between a pulse and a periodic wave.

Ans. Differentiate between a pulse and a periodic wave.

	Pulse	Periodic wave
(i)	A pulse is a wave set up by sudden and short duration disturbances.	A periodic wave is set up by a continuous disturbances of long duration in a medium.
(ii)	It is not repetitive.	It has a basic pattern which repeats itself after a fixed interval.
(iii)	Due to a pulse, the medium oscillates for a short while and then returns to its original undisturbed position.	Due to a periodic wave, medium vibrates for a long time after it is disturbed.
(iv)	It is formed in a small portion of the medium.	It is stretched over the entire length of the medium.

Chapter 9. Current Electricity

Q. 1. Distinguish between a closed circuit and an open circuit, with the use of suitable labelled diagrams.

Ans. A circuit is said to be closed when every part of it is made of a conductor and on plugging in the key or on being complete, current flows through the circuit.

A circuit is said to be open when no current flows through it. It can happen when the key is not plugged in or when any one of its components is not made of a conductor or when the circuit is broken.

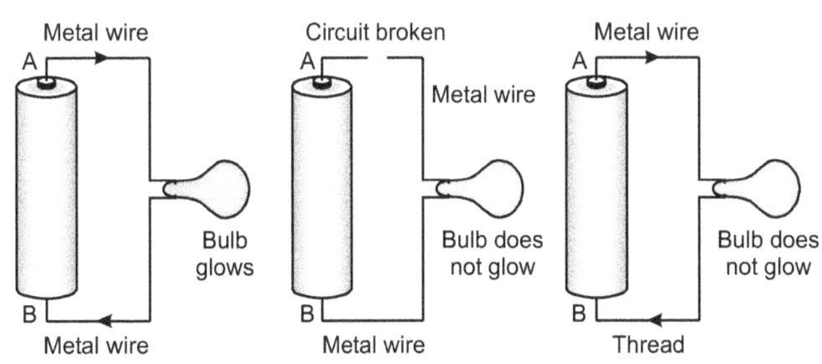

Q. 2. State two difference between a primary cell and a secondary cell

Ans.

Primary cell	Secondary cell
Chemical reaction is irreversible.	Chemical reaction is reversible.
It cannot be recharged.	It can be recharged.

Q. 3. Give three points of difference between a conductor and an insulator.

Ans.

Conductor	Insulator
They allow electric current to pass through them.	They does not allow electric current to pass through them.
They have large number of free elctrons.	They almost have no free electrons.

They offer very less resistance in the path of electric current.	They offer very high resistance in the path of electric current.

Q. 4. Distinguish between D.C. and A.C.

Ans. Direct current (D.C.) is a current of constant magnitude flowing in one direction but alternating current (A.C.) is a current which reverses its magnitude and direction with time.

Chapter 10. Magnetism

Q. 1. State two differences between an electromagnet and a permanent magnet.

Ans.

Electromagnet	Permanent magnet
It is made up of soft iron.	It is made up of steel.
The magnetic field strength can be changed.	The magnetic field strength cannot be changed.
Electromagnets of very strong field can be made.	Permanent magnets are not so strong.

Q. 2. Magnetically speaking, what is the difference between a piece of brass, a piece of soft iron and a piece of lode- stone ?

Ans. Brass is not a magnetic substance as it is not affected by magnetic field. It does not stick to a magnet. Soft iron is a temporary magnet and gets strongly attracted towards a magnet. Soft iron cannot attract other magnetic substances unless gets magnetised. Lodestone is naturally magnetized piece of mineral magnetite. It can attract other magnetic substance.

❏

Chapter 1. Measurements and Experimentation

Q. 1. Name the two parts of measurement and state the significance of each.

Ans. Measurements consist of two parts:
   (i) The unit in which the quantity is to be measured.
   (ii) The numerical value which expresses how many times the above selected unit is contained in the given quantity.

Q. 2. Why is a standard unit of measurement necessary?

Ans. A standard unit of measurement is necessary so that it does not vary from person to person and is understood by everyone.

Q. 3. How is corrected reading obtained from observed reading?

Ans. To obtain corrected reading, observation is taken and zero error is calculated. This error with proper sign is subtracted from observed reading to obtain the corrected reading.
Corrected reading = Observed reading – Zero error [with appropriate sign]

Q. 4. How would you calculate the least count of a micrometer screw gauge?

Ans. Least count of micrometer screw gauge =
$$\frac{\text{Pitch of screw}}{\text{Total number of divisions on circular scale}}$$

Q. 5. The SI unit of length is represented by the Symbol 'm'.
What is the symbol for SI unit of current?

Ans. The symbol for SI unit of current is A.

Q. 6. When is a Vernier calliper said to be free from zero error?

Ans. A Vernier calliper is said to be free from zero error if on bringing the movable jaw in contact with the fixed jaw, the zero mark on vernier scale coincides with the zero mark on the main scale.

Q. 7. Name the principle on which screw gauge works. **[February, 2020]**

Ans. A screw gauge works on the principle of a screw.

Q. 8. Draw a graph (not to the scale) representing the variation of square of time period (T^2) with the length (l) of a pendulum.

Ans. The graph representing the variation of T^2 with l of a pendulum is given below.

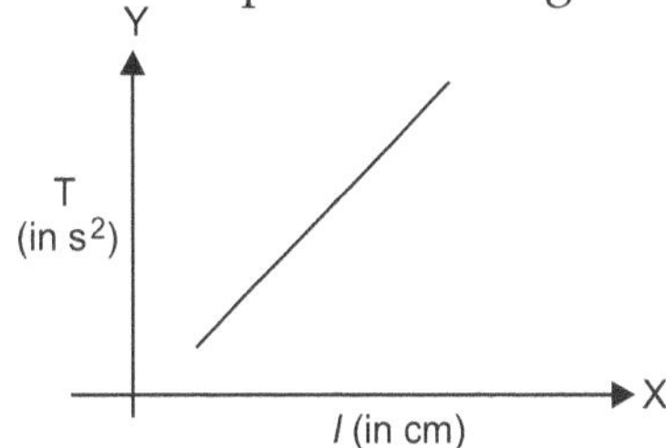

Q. 9. If the length of a simple pendulum is increased to four times the initial length how is the time period affected? **[February, 2020]**

Ans. (i)

   (ii) $$T - 2\pi\sqrt{\frac{l}{g}}$$

   i.e., $\qquad$ $T \propto \sqrt{l}$

   So, if length is increased four times, the time period will increase two times or gets doubled.

Q. 10. What is the relation between time period (T) and frequency (f) of an oscillation of a simple Pendulum?

Ans. $$T = \frac{1}{f}$$

Q. 11. What will be the effect on the time period of the pendulum if the mass of the bob is increased for the same length?

Ans. Time period remains same.

Q. 12. A screw gauge has a pitch of 1 mm and 100 divisions on the circular scale. Is it possible to increase the accuracy of the gauge arbitrarily by changing the divisions on circular scale?

Ans. If the least count of an instrument is smaller, then the accuracy of the instrument will be greater. The least count of screw gauge can be reduced by increasing the number of divisions on the circular scale only up to the extent that the divisions are visible clearly to the eye.

Q. 13. A girl is swinging in a swing in a sitting position. How will the period of the swing be affected if she stands up?

Ans. The case of a swinging girl can be considered as a simple pendulum. As the girl stands up on the swing the centre of gravity is raised up, that means the effective length of pendulum decreases, hence time period too decreases.

Q.14. Name the units which are used to measure very large astronomical distances.

Ans. (i) Astronomical unit, (ii) Light year, (iii) Parallactic second (parsec)

Q. 15. How backlash error can be avoided?

Ans. To avoid the backlash error, the screw should be rotated in one direction only, while taking the measurement.

Q. 16. Two simple pendulums A and B have equal length , but their bobs weighs 20 g and 30 g. What will be difference in their time period?

Ans. Time period of simple pendulum is independent of the mass of the bob.

Q. 17. Name the instruments used for measuring length.

Ans. (i) Ruler (ii) Screw gauge (iii) Metre scate (iv) Vernier callipers

Q. 18. What is the need of measurement?

Ans. To establish and verify physical laws, measurement is necessary.

Q.19. Write some characteristics of standard unit.

Ans. Characteristics of standard unit are as follows:

   (i) It should be easily understandable.

   (ii) It should be invariable.

   (iii) It should be easily reproducible.

   (iv) It should be of convenient size.

Q. 20. Name two factors on which time period of simple pendulum depends.

Ans. Time period of simple pendulum depends upon the effective length as $T \propto \sqrt{L}$ and acceleration due to gravity as $T \propto \dfrac{1}{\sqrt{g}}$.

Q. 21. Name two factors on which time period of simple pendulum does not depend.

Ans. The two factors on which time period does not depend are mass of the suspended bob and its amplitude.

Chapter 2. Motion in One Dimension

Q. 1. When is a body said to be at rest?

Ans. A body is said to be at rest if it does not change its position with respect to its immediate surroundings. *e.g.* A chair lying in a room is in the state of rest, because it does not change its position with respect to the surroundings of the room.

Q. 2. When is a body said to be in motion?

Ans. A body is said to be in motion if it changes its position with respect to its immediate surroundings. *E.g.*, a car changing its position with respect to trees, houses, etc is in the state Lof motion.

Q. 3. Define one-dimensional motion.

Ans. A motion is said to be one dimensional motion when a body moves along a straight path.

Q. 4. When is the magnitude of displacement equal to the distance?

Ans. The magnitude of displacement is equal to the distance when the motion is in one direction along the same straight path.

Q. 5. Give an example of motion in which average speed is not zero, but the average velocity is zero.

Ans. If Virat starts from his home goes to school and back to home after a certain time, then the displacement is zero, so the average velocity is zero, but the total distance travelled is not zero and therefore, the average speed is not zero.

Q. 6. If a stone and a pen are dropped simultaneously from the terrace of a building, which of the two will reach the ground first?

Ans. As acceleration due to gravity acting on both are same, both will reach the ground simultaneously.

Q. 7. Give an example of a body which covers a certain distance but its displacement is zero.

Ans. When a body moves along a circular path, such that it reaches the starting point after a certain interval of time, it covers a distance equal to the circumference of circular path, but its displacement is zero, because the distance between initial and final position of body is zero.

Q. 8. Explain, why velocity-time graph can never be a straight line parallel to velocity axis?

Ans. This is not possible because it would mean that velocity is increasing without increase in time *i.e.*, acceleration is infinite and infinite acceleration is practically impossible.

Q. 9. Give an example of an accelerated body, moving with uniform speed. Explain your answer.

Ans. A dust particle which lies on the circumference of a revolving rim of a bicycle has a uniform speed. However, as the direction of motion of particle continuously changes, it has a variable velocity and hence has an acceleration.

Q. 10. Does the value of acceleration due to gravity remains the same at all places of earth? Explain the answer.

Ans. No. The value of acceleration due to gravity changes from place to place. It is maximum at the poles and decreases if the body is moved towards equator.

Q. 11. Are the passengers sitting in a moving train in motion or at rest with respect to each other?

Ans. Passengers sitting in a moving train are at rest with respect to each other.

Q. 12. We are at rest as well as in motion. Justify the statement.

Ans. We are at rest as well as in motion because we are at rest with respect to a observer which is itself at rest and we are in motion with respect to a observer which is in motion.

Q. 13. A train is moving from a railway station. Is the platform at rest or in motion with respect to moving train?

Ans. As the train is moving with respect to platform, so the platform would also look in motion with respect to the train.

Q. 14. Two bodies are moving with speeds of 25 ms^{-1} due North and 25 ms^{-1} due East, respectively. Do they have the same velocity?

Ans. As their direction is different, so they don't have same velocity.

Q. 15. What does the slope of velocity-time graph represent?

Ans. The slope of velocity-time graph represent acceleration of a body.

Q. 16. Why does the velocity of a stone, thrown vertically upwards, decreases?

Ans. This is because acceleration due to gravity is acting on it in downward direction.

Chapter 3. Laws of Motion

Q. 1. What is the tendency of a body in the absence of force?

Ans. The tendency of a body in the absence of force is to remain in the state of rest or uniform motion along a straight line.

Q. 2. Can a body remain at rest position when external forces are acting on it? Justify

Ans. Yes, the body can remain in the state of rest even if more than one force is acting on it externally. This is because the net resultant force acting on it is zero.

Q. 3. If you are given four blocks of equal volume: lead block, glass block, aluminium block and plastic block, which of these have higher inertia and why?

Ans. Since mass is the measure of its inertia, greater the mass, more is the inertia. In this case, lead block will have maximum inertia because, for a given volume of block, mass of lead would be maximum amongst all the other materials.

Q. 4. Why do passengers in a bus tend to lean backwards when it starts abruptly?

Ans. When a bus starts suddenly, the lower part of the body of the passengers is in close contact with the floor of the bus. As the bus starts, the lower part of the body is set into motion along with the bus while the upper half tends to remain at rest due to inertia of rest. Consequently, the lower part of the body moves forward while upper half is left behind and the passenger tends to lean backward.

Q. 5. Why does a person have to run a certain distance after alighting from a moving train in the direction of train?

Ans. When a person jumps from a moving train, he may fall down because when his feet touch the ground, they attain the state of rest while the upper part of the body continues to be in motion due to inertia of motion. Hence the person needs to run a certain distance along the direction of the train or else he would fall down in the forward direction.

Q. 6. Why are mudguards provided over the wheels of a car?

Ans. The rotating wheels of a car throw out mud sticking to it in a tangential direction due to inertia of direction. It is for this reason that mudguards are provided over the wheels of a car so as to avoid the mud spill and splash over others.

Q. 7. Would a ball thrown vertically upward in a moving train come back into the hands of the person throwing it? Justify your answer.

Ans. Yes, the ball would return back into the hands of the same person, as the ball maintains its inertia of motion.

Q. 8. Why does an electric fan continue to rotate for some time even after the current is switched off?

Ans. The electric fan continues to rotate due to inertia of motion, until the friction in the bearings and that of air brings it to state of rest.

Q. 9. Why do dust particles fall down on beating a blanket?

Ans. On beating a blanket with a stick, the dust particles tend to remain in the state of rest while the blanket is in a state of motion. Due to inertia of rest possessed by the dust particles, they fall down by virtue of their own weight.

Q. 10. When a train starts or stops suddenly, the sliding doors of some railway compartments may open or shut. Explain this occurrence.

Ans. When a train starts or stops suddenly, the sliding doors of some railway compartments may maintain either the inertia of motion or rest, hence tend to open or shut.

Q. 11. Prove that first law of motion is contained in the second law.

Ans. According to newton's second law,
Force = mass × acceleration.
So when no external force acts on the body, acceleration would be zero. This means in the absence of any resultant force, the body would either be at rest or move with uniform velocity, which is the first law of motion.

Q. 12. Explain the combination of two forces namely action and reaction in case of recoil of a gun to justify the newton's third law.

Ans. When a bullet is fired from a gun, it moves forward with a certain force (action), the gun recoils in the backward direction with an equal and opposite force (reaction).

Q. 13. Why is it difficult to climb up a highly polished pole?

Ans. A man climbing the pole applies force on the pole downwards with his feet and the pole in turn pushes the man in upward direction with an equal force. But since the pole is highly polished, the man is not able to apply an action force on the pole properly. As a result, no reaction force would act on the man, thus making it difficult for the man to climb the pole.

Q. 14. On a sail boat, air is thrown on the sail with an electric fan attached to the boat. Would the boat start moving?

Ans. No, the sail boat would not move. The electric fan is kept on the boat so the fan pushes the sail by air and the air also pushes the fan in the opposite direction resulting in the net moment of force being zero. The sail boat would only move if an external force acts on it.

Q. 15. The earth attracts an apple. Does the apple also attract the earth? If so, why does it not move towards the apple?

Ans. Yes, the apple also attracts the earth with an equal force by which the earth attracts the apple. Since the mass of earth is too large as compared to the apple, the movement of earth towards the apple is not noticeable and acceleration produced in earth too is extremely small.

Q. 16. If you jump to the shore from a stationary boat, the boat moves in the opposite direction. Does it demonstrate a Newton's law? If yes, which law?

Ans. Yes, it demonstrates the Newton's third law of motion as the action force is the force applied by our feet on the boat (action) while the boat offers equal and opposite force on our feet (reaction).

Q. 17. How does the distance of separation between two bodies affect the magnitude of the non-contact force between them?

Ans. Force between two bodies is inversely proportional to the square of the distance between them. So when the separation between two bodies increases, magnitude of force will decrease and when the separation between two bodies decreases, magnitude of force will increase.

Q. 18. If the distance between two bodies is doubled. How is the magnitude of gravitational between them affected?

Ans. If the distance between the bodies is doubled then force between them becomes one-fourth.

Q. 19. A body is falling freely under gravity from rest and reaches the round in time *t*. Write an expression for the height fallen by the body.

Ans.
$$h = \frac{1}{2} gt^2$$

Q. 20. Choose the odd one out and give a reason for your choice:

Tension, electrostatic force, magnetic force, gravitational force.

[November, 2019]

Ans. The old one is tension because the other three forces are non-contact forces.

Q. 21. A car in motion is brought to rest by applying brakes.
(i) Name the contact force responsible in bringing the car to rest.
(ii) What is the direction of the above identified force with respect to the motion of the car? **[February, 2020]**

Ans. (i) Frictional force.
(ii) Friction acts opposite to the direction of motion of the body.

Q. 22. The change in momentum of a body is represented by $\Delta p = m\,\Delta v$.
When is this expression valid for the change in the linear momentum?

[February, 2020]

Ans. The expression $\Delta p = m\Delta v$ is valid only if mass remains constant.

Q. 23. (i) Name the property of an object by virtue of which it opposes or tends to oppose any change in its state.
(ii) What is the factor on which this property of an object depends?
[February, 2020]

Ans. (i) Inertia (ii) Mass.

Q. 24. Why does a glass vessel break when it Falls on a hard floor, but does not break when it falls on a carpet?

Ans. When a glass vessel falls from a height, it comes to rest almost instantaneously, so the floor exert a large force on the vessel and it breaks. But if it falls on a carpet, the duration of time in which the vessel comes to rest increases, so the carpet exerts less force on the vessel and it does not break.

Q. 25. Why does a cricketer pulls his hands back while catching a fast moving ball?

Ans. By doing so, cricketer increases the time of catch *i.e.,* increases the time to bring about a change in momentum hence rate of change of momentum *i.e.,* force, decreases and small force is exerted on his hands by the ball.

Q. 26. (i) Why does the electric fan rotate for some more time after the current is switched off?
(ii) What brings it to stop after some time? **[November, 2019]**

Ans. (i) The electric fan rotates for some more time after the current is switched off due to intertia of motion.
(ii) Force of friction causes the fan to stop.

Q. 27. If you drop a rubber ball on to the floor it bounces back.
Identify the force which causes the bounce.
[November, 2019]

Ans. The equal and opposite force of reaction on the ball in the upward direction due to newton's third law of motion causes the ball to bounce.

Q.28. What is the relationship between the force applied on a body and rate of change of momentum?
Is momentum a scalar or a vector quantity?
[November, 2019]

Ans. Force = Rate of change of momentum.
Momentum is a vector quantity.

Q. 29. Which of the following force diagrams (i) or (ii) can depict an object undergoing uniform motion? Give a reason of your answer. **[November, 2019]**

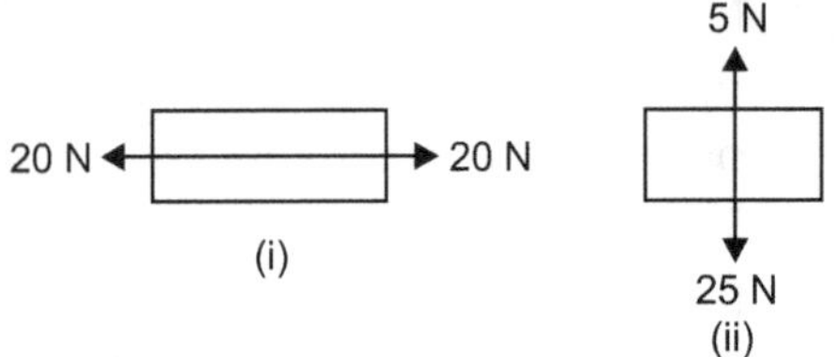

Ans. The diagram (ii) depicts an object undergoing uniform motion in the direction of 25 N force because a net force of (25 – 5) N = 20 N is acting on the body.

Chapter 4. Pressure in Fluids and Atmospheric Pressure

Q. 1. Will the pressure exerted by water on a diver at a certain depth in sea be different than in the river? If yes, explain why?

Ans. When a diver dives in deep sea water, the hydrostatic pressure acts on his body. At a certain specific depth, the pressure acting on the body due to sea water would be more than pressure acting in river water. This is on account of the density of sea water being more than density of river water.

Q. 2. Dams are build broader at the base than at the top. Why?

Ans. Pressure exerted by a confined fluid increases with the depth of the point below the free surface, so the pressure at the bottom of the dam is very large. So in order to withstand this large pressure, the area of the dam is made large indirectly reducing the thrust on the walls of the dam.

Q. 3. Pressure in case of solids is inversely proportional to area of cross section. Does this statement hold true for fluids? Justify your answer.

Ans. No, this statement is not applicable for pressure exerted in fluids as in case of fluids, pressure only depends on depth of the point inside the fluid, density of the fluid, and acceleration due to gravity hence independent of area of cross section.

Q. 4. Why are water tanks in a locality always at a higher altitude than the buildings in a locality? Explain.

Ans. Greater is the height of water tank, more will be the pressure of water in the taps of a house. Thus when water tank is situated at the highest point, the water from it can easily flow to the tallest building without the aid of any external force.

Q. 5. How does the motion of an arrow get affected by a pointed tip?

Ans. Fluid resistance offered by air is directly proportional to area of cross section of the body. The arrow with a pointed tip will experience smaller resistance and hence move with a larger velocity.

Q. 6. Fill in the blanks with appropriate words or phrases.

(i) The pressure of sea water for same depth is _______ than the river water. (less, more)

(ii) The pressure of air _______ as we move upward. (increases, decreases).

(iii) The fluid exert _______ pressure in all directions at a given point. (different, same).

(iv) The fluid pressure increases with increase in _______. (depth, area of cross-section).

Ans. (i) The pressure of sea water for same depth is more than the river water.

(ii) The pressure of air decreases as we move upward.

(iii) The fluid exerts same pressure in all directions at a given point.

(iv) The fluid pressure increases with increase in depth.

Q. 7. How does fluid pressure on balloon change when:

(i) balloon rises from height of 200 m to height of 500 m

(ii) balloon moves horizontally at height of 200 m

(iii) balloon is brought down on the surface of earth?

Ans. (i) The fluid pressure decreases as the vertical height of air column, as measured from above, decreases.

(ii) The fluid pressure remains the same as vertical height does not change.

(iii) The fluid pressure increases as vertical height of air increases.

Q. 8. What is the cause of atmospheric pressure?

Ans. It is the weight of air (thrust), which is responsible for the atmospheric pressure.

Q. 9. State the numerical value of atmospheric pressure at sea level in (i) cm of mercury (ii) Pascal (iii) bar.

Ans. (i) The atmospheric pressure at sea level is 76 cm of mercury.

(ii) The atmospheric pressure at sea level is 101300 pascal.

(iii) The atmospheric pressure at sea level is 1.013 bar.

Q. 10. Why do sea divers need special protective suit?

Ans. The sea divers need special protective suit to wear because in deep sea, the total pressure exerted on the diver's body becomes much more than his blood pressure. In order to withstand it, he needs to wear a special protective suit.

Q. 11. How does the liquid pressure on a diver change if:

(i) The diver moves to the greater depth, and

(ii) As diver moves horizontally?

Ans. (i) As pressure increases with depth, pressure on diver increases when he moves to the greater depth.

(ii) As pressure is the same at all points on a horizontal plane, the pressure does not change when the diver moves horizontally.

Q. 12. Name three applications of Pascal's law.

Ans. Three applications of Pascal's law are: Hydraulic press, Hydraulic lift, Hydraulic brakes.

Q. 13. Sense of hearing is affected while rapidly gaining or losing height. Why?

Ans. When a person rapidly, gains or loses height, the air pressure outside the ear drum change with respect to air pressure on the other side of ear drum in Eustachian tube. Thus the ear drum either bulges in or out and hence does not vibrate properly. It is on account of this reason that hearing is affected.

Q. 14. Nose of some people starts bleeding when aeroplane climbs up rapidly. Why?

Ans. When one gains height, the atmospheric pressure suddenly drops. Thus the pressure of dissolved air in blood becomes too large as compared to air outside. This difference in atmospheric pressure, at times, bursts the fine capillaries in the nose and hence bleeds.

Q. 15. A soda straw does not draw liquid, if there is a tiny hole near the upper end. Why?

Ans. If there is a hole near the upper end of soda straw, atmospheric pressure does not fall due to suction. As atmospheric pressure within the straw does not fall, hence air pressure will not force the liquid up in the straw.

Q. 16. Why do ink start leaking at higher altitudes?

Ans. As atmospheric pressure on higher altitudes decreases, the air present within tube of ink pen at higher pressure forces the ink out. Thus ink pen starts leaking.

Q. 17. Why are two holes made in oil tin to remove oil from it?

Ans. If a single hole is made, the oil will not flow out because it will be supported by atmospheric pressure. Thus in order to force out the oil, two holes are made so that air enters from one hole, exerts pressure on oil and forces it out from the other hole.

Q. 18. Why does the liquid not run out of a dropper unless rubber bulb is pressed?

Ans. It is because the liquid is supported by atmospheric pressure. However, when we press the rubber bulb, the pressure of air within the dropper becomes more than atmospheric pressure hence it forces the liquid out.

Q. 19. Why does food cook faster in a pressure cooker?

Ans. It is because the pressure inside the pressure cooker is 2 atmospheres which raises the temperature of water to 120°C. As this temperature is much higher than cooking temperature of most of food materials, food cooks faster.

Q. 20. Why does the liquid rise in a syringe when its piston is pulled up?

Ans. When the syringe is kept with its opening just inside the liquid and the plunger is pulled up in the barrel, the pressure inside the barrel below the plunger becomes much less than the atmospheric pressure acting on the liquid. As a result, the atmospheric pressure forces the liquid to rise up in the syringe.

Q. 21. Explain why water is not a suitable barometric liquid.

Ans. Water barometer will support 10.34 m of water column at sea level. It is impractical to have such a long tube. Also water vaporizes under vacuum conditions and hence water barometer will never show true atmospheric pressure.

Q. 22. State two factors which do not affect barometric height at a given place.

Ans. Barometric height is independent of:
(i) Area of cross-section of barometric tube.
(ii) Angle of inclination of barometric tube.

Q. 23. Name three factors which affect barometric height at a given place.

Ans. (i) Change in temperature
(ii) Change in humidity of air
(iii) Purity level of mercury

Q. 24. Why is the barometric pressure at a place expressed in centimetre of mercury rather than in Pascal?

Ans. The Barometric pressure of a place depends on the length of mercury column.
∴ 1 atm. pressure = 76 cm of mercury pressure

Q. 25. Why is the blood pressure in human greater at the feet than at the brain?

Ans. We know that pressure P is directly proportional to the depth (h). Pressure increases with increase in depth. As a result the blood exerts more pressure at the feet than at the brain.

Q. 26. Why does a girl on a pair of skis does not sink in snow?

Ans. The total force acting on the snow is equal to the weight of the person. On the pair of skis, the surface area is almost one twentieth times the area of the shoe, hence the pressure reduces to $\frac{1}{20}$ times the pressure that would be exerted when she would have walked through by a pair of shoes. Hence would not sink in snow.

Q. 27. State any two uses of hydraulic press.

Ans. (i) It is used for compressing straw and cotton bales.
(ii) It is used for punching holes in metal sheets.

Q. 28. State two advantages of an aneroid barometer.

Ans. (i) They are light and portable.
(ii) The zero of the scale need not be repeatedly adjusted.

Q. 29. State if:
(i) Thrust at a point in a liquid is a vector or scalar quantity.
(ii) Pressure at a point in a liquid is a scalar or vector quantity.

Ans. (i) Thrust at a point in a liquid is a vector quantity.
(ii) Pressure at a point in a liquid is a scalar quantity.

Q. 30. Two holes are drilled in a sealed oil can to remove oil from it. Explain.

Ans. In a sealed oil tin, two holes are drilled as atmospheric pressure acts through one of the hole and forces the oil to flow through the other hole.

Q. 31. Why the pressure of the atmosphere does not break glass windows?

[November, 2019]

Ans. The pressure on both sides of a glass window is same, hence the pressure of atmoshere does not break it.

Q. 32. Name the principle on which a hydraulic machine works.

Ans. A hydraulic machine works on the principle of Pascal's law.

Q. 33. Complete the following statement.
The effect of a thrust is _______ on a large area, while it is _______ on a small area.

Ans. The effect of a thrust is less on a large area, while it is more on a small area.

Q. 34. Name the two factors on which pressure exerted on a surface depends.

Ans. (i) Area on which thrust is applied.
(ii) Thrust

Q. 35. For a given thrust, how can the pressure on a surface be increased?

Ans. By decreasing the surface area.

Q. 36. Name the factors affecting pressure at a point in a liquid.

Ans. (i) Depth of the point below the free surface of liquid.
(ii) Density of liquid.
(iii) Acceleration due to gravity.

Q. 37. Write an expression for the pressure ata point inside the liquid.

Ans. $P = h\rho g$

Q. 38. Write two uses of brometer.

Ans. (i) To measure atmospheric pressure at a given place.
(ii) For weather forecasting.

Q. 39. Write is meant by the statement 'The atmospheric pressure ata place is 76 cm of Hg'?

Ans. It means that, at normal temperature and pressure, the height of the mercury column, supported by the atmoshpheric pressure, is 76 cm.

Q. 40. Write two demerits of a simple barometer.

Ans. (i) It is inconvenient to move the barometer from one place to another.

(ii) The surface of mercury in the trough is open, so there are chances that impurities may fall in and get mixed with it, thus affecting the reading.

Q. 41. It is easier to cut with a sharp knife than with a blunt one. Why?

Ans. It is easier to cut with a sharp knife because even a small thrust causes great pressure at the edges and cutting can be done with less effort.

Q. 42. If you swim beneath the surface in salt water, will the pressure be greater than in fresh water at the same depth? Give a reason for your answer. **[November 2019]**

Ans. The pressure in salt water at a certain depth will be greater than the pressure in fresh water at the same depth because density of salt water is greater than the density of fresh water.

Q. 43. Which physical quantity is expressed in the unit 'atm'? **[November, 2019]**

Ans. Atmospheric pressure.

Q. 44. An object is weighed using a spring balance in air and in vacuum. In which medium will the weight of the object be more? **[November, 2019]**

Ans. The object will weigh more in vacuum due to the absence of upthrust, which reduces the weight of an object when weighed in air.

Chapter 5. Upthrust in Fluids, Archimedes' Principle and Floatation

Q. 1. A piece of wood is suspended from the hook of a spring balance, it reads 70gf. The wood is now lowered into water. What reading would you expect in the spring balance and why?

Ans. Since the wood would float on the surface of water its apparent weight would be zero.

Q. 2. Why is a force needed to keep a piece of cork inside the water?

Ans. It is required to apply a force to keep the cork which is floating inside water as the upthrust on it due to water is more than its own weight. Hence to keep the cork immersed, the buoyant upward force due to water must be balanced by an externally applied downward force and the weight of the cork.

Q. 3. How is the buoyant force related to the volume of the solid placed inside a liquid?

Ans. Buoyant force is directly proportional to the volume of the solid immersed in liquid.

Q. 4. A ping pong ball floats half submerged in a water filled container. Will the body float or sink aboard a spaceship coasting in free space and on the surface of Jupiter?

Ans. Since the floatation of an object is independent of acceleration due to gravity, hence in free space or on surface of Jupiter, the ping pong ball will neither sink more nor rise more than its original position.

Q. 5. Why does a rotten egg float in fresh water?

Ans. Density of rotten egg is less than density of fresh water. Thus it experiences greater upthrust than its own weight, hence floats.

Q. 6. A fresh egg sinks in pure water but floats in saline water. Why?

Ans. The density of saline water is more than that of fresh water, while the density of a fresh egg is greater than the density of pure water and lesser than that of saline water. Thus, it experiences a greater upthrust in saline water than its own weight, hence floats and experiences a comparatively lesser upthrust in pure water than its own weight and hence sinks in pure water.

Q. 7. A cargo ship is loaded in sea water to its maximum capacity. What would happen if the ship is moved to river water? Give reason for your answer.

Ans. The density of sea water is greater than density of river water hence cargo ship sinks deeper in river water. Hence more volume of water is required to be displaced to balance its weight along with its cargo .

Q. 8. Why do a fish weigh less in water than in air?

Ans. In water, fishes experiences an upward buoyant force which balances the actual weight of them, acting downwards. Thus, due to upthrust, there is an apparent loss in the weight of a fish, Hence, fishes weigh less in water than in air.

Q. 9. Why does a ship being unloaded, slowly rise higher in water?

Ans. A ship floats as the weight of the ship is equal to the weight of the water displaced by its immersed part. As the ship gets unloaded, its weight decrease and thereby the weight of water displaced by it also decreases and hence it rises higher on unloading.

Q. 10. What is the significance of a plimsoll line drawn on a ship?

Ans. Each ship has a white line painted on its side known as plimsoll line which indicates the safe permissible limit for loading. A ship is not permitted to load further as it would affect the stability and equilibrium of the ship.

Q. 11. State the factors on which upthrust depend.

Ans. Upthrust is directly proportional to:
(i) Volume of solid immersed in the fluid
(ii) Density of the fluid

Q. 12. State whether Upthrust would increase or decrease if:
(i) Volume of solid increases
(ii) Density of liquid in which solid is immersed decrease.

Ans. Mathematically, Upthrust
= Volume of solid × density of fluid × acceleration due to gravity.
(i) As volume of solid increases, upthrust too will increase.
(ii) Upthrust decreases with decrease in density of the liquid.

Q. 13. When a body floats, is the weight of body greater than or equal to the upthrust?

Ans. When a body floats, the weight of the body is equal to the upthrust.

Q. 14. Will the weight of iron sinker plus cork combination in water be more or less than that of iron sinker alone in water. Explain briefly.

Ans. Weight of iron sinker in water will be more than iron sinker plus cork combined in water because in second case, increase in weight due to cork in water is less than decrease of weight due to water displaced by cork.

Q. 15. A bunch of feathers and a stone of same mass fall at different rates in air. Which of the two falls faster and why?

Ans. Stone falls faster than the bunch of feathers. As the volume of stone is less than that of bunch of feathers of the same mass, upthrust due to air on stone will be less than that of bunch of feathers.

Q. 16. Why a person cannot sit easily on the floor of a swimming pool?

Ans. The density of human body is slightly more than that of water. Thus under the surface of water, a person becomes apparently weightless on account of the upthrust offered by the water. It is on account of this large upthrust, the person cannot sit easily under water.

Q. 17. Big boulders are carried by fast moving rivers over hundreds of kilometer. Explain.

Ans. The apparent weight of big boulders is far less than their real weight, because of the upthrust due to water. It is on account of this low apparent weight that they are easily carried for hundreds of kilometers by strong water currents.

Q. 18. A swimmer can easily carry a drowning man to the shore. Explain.

Ans. It is so because the apparent weight of the drowning man is less as compared to the true weight on account of large upthrust. Thus a swimmer can easily carry the person who is drowning to the shore.

Q. 19. It is easier to lift a heavier stone under water than in air. Explain.

Ans. Upthrust acts on the heavy stone under water as a result of which the stone apparently becomes lighter in water rather than in air.

Q. 20. A body of density 'ρ' is immersed in a liquid of density 'ρ_L'. State the condition when the body will (i) float (ii) sink in liquid.

Ans. (i) $\rho = \rho_L$ or $\rho < \rho_L$
(ii) $\rho > \rho_L$.

Q. 21. A man first swims in sea water and then in river water.

(i) Compare the weight of sea water and river water displaced by him.

(ii) Where does he find easier to swim and why?

Ans. (i) The weight of sea water displaced is equal to the weight of river water displaced by him.

(ii) He will find it easier to swim in sea water than in river water. This is because, in sea water, he would experience a greater upthrust as sea water is denser than river water.

Q. 22. A dead body floats with its head immersed in water.Why?

Ans. Volume of dead body slightly increases with the decay of tissues, while the volume of the head which consist of solid bone does not increase. Thus the body displaces more weight of water than its own weight and hence floats. However the head displaces less weight of water than its own weight as a result of which it remains immersed in water.

Q. 23. Why does a ship made of iron float while an iron nail sinks?

Ans. Iron nail has a less area and volume, so it readily sinks into water, but in case of a ship, it has a large amount of void space filled with air which reduces the average density of the ship, making it much lighter. So it floats in water.

Q. 24. What is the role of swim bladder of fish?

Ans. Swim bladder is compressible due to which the fish can easily change the volume of body due to intake of air and hence in turn the average density of the body. Therefore it regulates the depth of its submersion within a specific range.

Q. 25. What do you mean by the statement, The density of silver is 10.5×10^3 kgm^{-3}?

Ans. It means that the weight of 1 m^3 of silver is 10.5×10^3 kg.

Chapter 6. Heat and Energy

Q. 1. What would have been the temperature of earth's atmosphere in absence of green house in it?

Ans. In absence of green house gases, the average temperature on earth would be –18 °C.

Q. 2. What causes the rise in atmospheric temperature?

Ans. With active industrialization, deforestation, excess burning of fossil fuel, the concentration of green house gases has increased on earth's atmosphere. This increase in the amount of greenhouse gases present in atmosphere has caused the rise in atmospheric temperature.

Q. 3. State the effect of global warming in coastal regions.

Ans. Due to global warming, the snow and ice around the poles will melt and cause flood in coastal countries.

Q. 4. How will global warming affect the sea level?

Ans. Due to melting of polar ice and glaciers, there will be rise in sea level on coastal wet lands. It would raise world wise sea level, thereby, many big cities in the coastal areas will be covered by sea water.

Q. 5. How will global warming affect the agriculture?

Ans. Global warming will cause drastic changes in the patterns of wind, rainfall, etc. Thus it will result in low agricultural yield.

Q. 6. Name three greenhouse gases.

Ans. Carbon-di-oxide, water vapour and methane are greenhouse gases.

Q. 7. Name the radiations which are absorbed by the greenhouse gases.

Ans. Infrared radiations of long wavelength are absorbed by the greenhouse gases.

Q. 8. State the effect of greenhouse gases on the temperature of earth's atmosphere.

Ans. The greenhouses gases have an average warming effect on Earth's surface of about 15.5 °C.

Q. 9. Who will pay carbon tax?

Ans. Carbon tax shall be paid by industries. This will encourage the industries to use the energy efficient techniques.

Q. 10. State one advantage of using renewable source of energy.

Ans. Renewable sources of energy are natural sources and will not get exhausted.

Q. 11. According to the law of thermodynamics, "No energy transfer is 100% efficient". Why? **[February, 2020]**

Ans. According to second law of thermodynamics, when energy transfer takes place, a part of it is always converted in unuseful form as heat. Hence, no energy transfer is 100% efficient.

Q. 12. When two bodies P and Q are kept in contact, it is found that heat gets transferred from Q to P.
  (i) Which of the two (P or Q) is hotter?
  (ii) Which physical quantity determines the direction of transfer of heat energy. **[February, 2020]**

Ans. (i) Q is hotter. (ii) Temperature

Q. 13. What is the main source of energy for earth?

Ans. The main source of energy for earth is the sun.

Q. 14. Though tidal energy is a clean source of energy, it is not a major source of energy. Why?

Ans. Though tidal energy is a clean source of energy, it is not a major source of energy because the rise and fall of sea water tides are not enough to generate electricity on a large scale and there are very few sites which are suitable for building tidal dams.

Q. 15. What is the energy transformation in a solar cell? **[February, 2020]**

Ans. In a solar cell, solar energy is converted into electrical energy.

Q. 16. What is the energy transformation in a nuclear power plant?

Ans. Nuclear Energy $\rightarrow$ Thermal energy $\rightarrow$ Mechanical energy $\rightarrow$ Electrical energy.

Q. 17. Name two components of ecosystem.

Ans. Ecosystem composed of two systems, biotic components (*i.e.*, producers, consumers and decomposers) and abiotic components (*i.e.*, light, heat, rain, and humidity, inorganic and organic substances)

Q. 18. What is the relation between joule and calorie?

Ans. 1 joule = 0.24 calorie
and, 1 calorie = 4.2 joule

Q. 19. At what temperature the density of water is maximum? State its value.

Ans. At 4°C, the density of water is maximum, *i.e.*, 1000 kgm^{-3}.

Q. 20. When do we say that two objects are in thermal equilibrium?

Ans. On keeping the two object in contact with each other, if there is no transfer of heat between them, then the two objects are said to be in thermal equilibrium.

Q. 21. What percentage of sun's energy falling on plants is converted into chemical energy during photosynthesis?

Ans. About 1 %.

Q. 22. Man is only a consumer. Justify.

Ans. Man cannot synthesis their own food, but depend on producers for food. Thus, man is only a consumer.

Q. 23. Write an equatic food chain.

Ans. Alage $\rightarrow$ Aquatic insects $\rightarrow$ Fish $\rightarrow$ Big fish

Q. 24. What is the source of enegy for all ecosystems?

Ans. Sun

Chapter 7. Reflection of Light

Q. 1. A printed card has letters SCIENCE. Show how it would appear in a mirror without showing ray diagram.

Ans. ƎƆИƎIƆƧ

Q. 2. Why are infinite images not seen when two plane mirrors are facing each other?

Ans. (i) Due to successive reflections, the images become very faint and are hardly visible.
  (ii) The eye cannot resolve very far off images as the angle subtended by them on the eye is very small.

Q. 3. State four uses of plane mirror.

Ans. Four uses of plane mirrors are:
  (i) As looking glass
  (ii) For making periscope
  (iii) In solar cookers
  (iv) For signalling purposes.

Q. 4. (i) What type of mirror can be used to obtain a real image of an object.
  (ii) Does the mirror named by you forms real image for all locations? Give reason for your answer.

Ans. (i) Concave mirror.
  (ii) No. It forms virtual image when object is between principal focus and pole.

Q. 5. Is real image always inverted?

Ans. Yes. Real image is always inverted.

Q. 6. What type of mirror is used to obtain real image?

Ans. A concave mirror is used to obtain real image.

Q. 7. Give two uses of
(a) convex mirrors
(b) concave mirrors.

Ans. (a) Uses of convex mirror:
(i) They are used as rear view mirror in automobiles.
(ii) They are used as reflectors for street light bulbs as they diverge rays of light over wide area.
(b) Uses of concave mirror:
(i) They are used as shaving mirror, as they form an enlarged and virtual image when face is between pole and principal focus.
(ii) They are used as reflectors in automobile head lights.

Q. 8. State laws of reflection.

Ans. Laws of reflection:
(i) The incident ray, the reflected ray and normal lie in the same plane, at the point of incidence.
(ii) Angle of incidence is always equal to the angle of reflection.

Q. 9. A plane mirror is used to obtain an image of an object.
Compare the size of the image formed in it to the size of the object.

Ans. Size of the image = Size of the object.

Q. 10. State the nature of the image formed in the plane mirror. **[February, 2020]**

Ans. Image formed in a plane mirror is virtual, upright, laterally inverted and of the same size as the object.

Q. 11. Why is a convex mirror preferred as a reflector in a street lamp?

Ans. Convex mirror is preferred as a reflector in street lamps because it diverges light over a larger area compared to any other type of mirror.

Q. 12. A concave mirror is used as reflectors in torches, head lights of automobiles, etc. to obtain a parallel beam of light. State the position of the source of light on the principal axis to obtain the parallel beam. **[February, 2020]**

Ans. The source has to be placed at the foccus of the concave reflector to obtain a parallel beam of light.

Q. 13. For a reflection of light on a smooth surface, what is the relation between angle of incidence and angle of reflection?

Ans. Angle of incidence = Angle of reflection

Q. 14. Write the relation between focal length (f) and radius of curuature (R) of a spherical mirror.

Ans. $f = \dfrac{R}{2}$ or R = 2f

Q. 15. If an object is placed at the focus of a concave mirror, where will the image formed?

Ans. At infinity.

Q. 16. For what position of object does a concave mirror produces real, inverted and dimineshed image?

Ans. When the object is placed beyond centre of curvature.

Q. 17. What type of spherical mirror has:
(i) Positive focal length
(ii) Negative focal length

Ans. (i) Convex mirror
(ii) Concave mirror

Q. 18. Write the spherical mirror formula.

Ans. $\dfrac{1}{f} = \dfrac{1}{u} + \dfrac{1}{v}$

Q. 19. Write down the formula of magnification produced by a spherical mirror.

Ans. Magnification $(m) = -\dfrac{\text{Image distance}}{\text{Object distance}}$

$= \dfrac{\text{Image height}}{\text{Object height}}$

Q. 20. Write the letters of english alphabet which do not show lateral inversion in front of a plane mirror.

Ans. A, H, I, M, O, T, U, V, W, X, Y.

Q. 21. You have a spherical mirror. The image of an object placed in front of the mirror is virtual. If the position of the object is changed, the image remains virtual and erect. Is the spherical mirror concave or convex? Give reason.

Ans. A convex mirror always produces a virtual and erect image irrespective of the position of the object in front of the mirror. So the given spherical mirror is convex in nature.

Q. 22. At what maximum distance the image in a convex mirror can be obtained? What will be the location of the object then?

Ans. The maximum distance at which an image in a convex mirror can be obtained is the focal length. The location of the object will be at infinity.

Chapter 8. Propagation of Sound Waves

Q. 1. State three conditions necessary for hearing sound.

Ans. (i) There must be a vibrating body.
(ii) There must be a material medium to carry sound energy.
(iii) There must be a receiver, so as to capture the sound vibrations.

Q. 2. Describe briefly an experiment to prove that vibrating bodies produce sound.

Ans. Take a tuning fork and strike it against a stationary pith ball of pith ball electroscope. It is observed that pith ball repeatedly flies outward. Thus, experiment proves that sound is produced by a vibrating body.

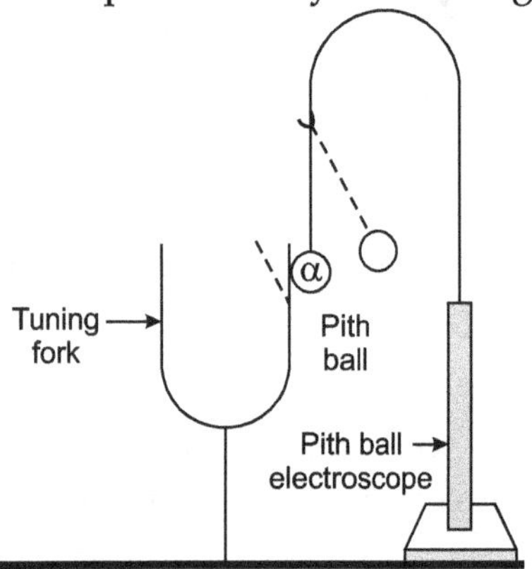

Q. 3. State the range of sonic vibrations.

Ans. Their range is between 20 Hz – 20,000 Hz.

Q. 4. Name three animals which can hear ultra-sonic range of frquencies.

Ans. (i) Bats (ii) Dogs (iii) Dolphins.

Q. 5. How do bats locate their prey during flight?

Ans. The bats emit ultrasonic vibrations during ther flight. These vibrations, on striking the prey, are echoed back to the bats. On receiving the reflected vibrations, the bats home on the target.

Q. 6. Which has the higher frequency - ultrasonic sound or infrasonic sound?

Ans. Ultrasonic sound has higher frequency.

Q. 7. State two properties of ultrasound that make it useful to us.

Ans. Two properties of ultrasound which make it useful to us are:
(i) High energy contents
(ii) High directivity

Q. 8. State two properties of medium on which the speed of sound in it depend.

Ans. The speed of sound in a medium depends upon its elasticity and density.

Q. 9. How does the speed of sound in air vary with temperature?

Ans. The speed of sound increases by 0.61 ms^{-1} for each 1°C rise in temperature.

Q. 10. What is the speed of sound in air at 0 °C?

Ans. The speed of sound in air at 0 °C is nearly 330 ms^{-1}.

Q. 11. In which medium the speed of sound is more- humid air or dry air? Give a reason to your answer.

Ans. Speed of sound is more in humid air because in presence of moisture, the density of air decreases and sound travels with greater speed.

$$v \propto \frac{1}{\sqrt{\rho}}$$

Q. 12. Arrange the speed of sound in gases V_g, solids V_s and liquids V_l in an ascending order.

Ans. $V_g < V_l < V_s$

Q. 13. Compare approximately the speed of sound in air, water and steel.

Ans. 1: 4: 15

Q. 14. How does the speed of sound change with change in (i) amplitude and (ii) wavelength, of a sound wave?

Ans. (i) Speed of sound does not change with a change in amplitude.
(ii) Speed of sound does not change with a change in wavelength

Q. 15. A sound wave emitted by a vibrator has a frequency of 40000 Hz.
(i) Name the type of wave.
(ii) Give one medical use of the wave mentioned in (i). **[November, 2019]**

Ans. (i) Ultrasonic wave
(ii) Ultrasonography

Q. 16. Two aeroplanes A and B moving at speeds 250 m/s and 350 m/s respectively. Give a special name to the speed of the aeroplane B. **[November, 2019]**

Ans. Supersonic.

Q. 17. The frequency of sound produced by a vibrating body in air is 15,000 Hz. Will the sound be audible to humans?

Ans. Yes.

Q. 18. Name the vibrations used in SONAR. **[February, 2020]**

Ans. Ultrasonic vibrations.

Q. 19. The flash of an exploding cracker is seen even before we hear the sound. Why? **[February, 2020]**

Ans. The flash of an exploding cracker is seen before we hear the sound because light travels much faster than sound.

Q. 20. In which state of matter does sound travel the fastest? **[February, 2020]**

Ans. Sound travels fastest in solids.

Q. 21. Name the factors affecting speed of sound in a gaseous medium.

Ans. Factors affecting speed of sound in a gaseous medium are:

(i) Density   (ii) Temperature

(iii) Humidity   (iv) Direction of wind

Q. 22. What is the effect of temperature of a medium on the speed of sound?

Ans. The speed of sound is directly proportional to the square root of temperature of a medium.

i.e,. $v \propto \sqrt{T}$

So, speed of increases with the increase in temperature.

Q.23. A stone is dropped on the surface of water in a lake. Name the type of waves produced.

Ans. Transverse waves.

Q. 24. In which medium does sound waves travel in the form of longitudinal waves?

Ans. Air

Q. 25. Why can we not hear each other on the moon?

Ans. Sound waves require a material medium for their propagation. On the moon, there is no atmosphere, so sound waves cannot propagate and hence we cannot hear each other.

Q. 26. Why is it possible to detect the approaching of a distant train by placing ear very close to the railway line?

Ans. Sound travels 16 times more faster in iron than in air, so we can detect the detect the approaching of a distant train by placing ear very close to the railway line.

Q. 27. To which range of frequency, are the human ears most sensitive?

Ans. 20 Hz – 20,000 Hz.

Chapter 9. Current Electricity

Q. 1. Fill in the blank spaces:

(i) _______ charges repel each other.

(ii) Opposite charges _______ each other.

(iii) A charged ebonite rod _______ tiny bits of paper.

(iv) Positive electrification is due to _______ of electrons as compared to _______.

(v) Negative electrification is due to _______ of electrons as compared to _______ .

Ans. (i) **Like** charges repel each other.

(ii) Opposite charges **attract** each other.

(iii) A charged ebonite rod **attracts** tiny bits of paper.

(iv) Positive electrification is due to **deficiency** of electrons as compared to protons.

(v) Negative electrification is due to **excess** of electrons as compared to **protons**.

Q. 2. Name four electric conductors and four electric insulators.

Ans. **Conductors:** Silver, copper, aluminium and iron.

Insulators: Plastic, nylon, dry wood and rubber.

Q. 3. Is it correct to say that a resistance wire is an insulator or a bad conductor? Explain your answer.

Ans. It is not correct to say that a resistance wire is an insulator or bad conductor. From resistance, it is implied that a given material will conduct electricity, but will also offer obstruction to the passage of electric current.

Q. 4. State two conditions necessary for a circuit, such that electric current flows through it.

Ans. For the flow of electric current through a circuit, following are the necessary conditions:

(i) Electric circuit must be closed or complete.

(ii) Every part of the circuit must be a conductor.

Q. 5. How does the proper insulation of home save energy?

Ans. By properly insulating a home, it is possible to maintain a comfortable temperature inside. It will reduce the cost of heating devices in winter and cooling devices in summer.

Q. 6. Give an example to explain that the use of modern eco-friendly technology is more efficient and less polluting.

Ans. Modern appliances like refrigerators make use of significantly less energy than older appliances as they have star rating according to their efficient use of electricity. Higher the star rating, higher is the efficiency.

Q. 7. Pick out conductors and insulators from the following list:

(i) Graphite (ii) Asbestos (iii) Mica (iv) Copper sulphate solution (v) Alcohol (vi) Copper (vii) Caustic soda solution (viii) Sulphuric acid solution (ix) Zinc (x) Lead (xi) Glass (xii) Vacuum (xiii) Benzene (xiv) Aluminium (xv) Starch.

Ans. Conductors: graphite; copper sulphate solution; copper; caustic soda solution; sulphuric acid solution; zinc; lead; aluminium.

Insulators: asbestos; mica; alcohol, glass; vacuum; benzene, starch.

Q. 8. Name two ways of charging an insulated conductor. State in which of the two ways, stated by you, charge is shared?

Ans. Two ways of charging insulated conductor are:

(i) Conduction (ii) Induction.

The charges are shared during conduction.

Q. 9. Why does the filament of an electric bulb in an electric circuit get white hot, but not the connecting wires?

Ans. Filament of an electric bulb is made up of tungsten having high resistance. Due to its high resistance, on passing electric current through it, an electrical energy changes into heat energy. So much heat is produced that filament of bulb becomes white hot and gives light. Resistance of connecting wires is very low and hence the connecting wires do not get heated.

Q. 10. On the basis of convention, which amongst the positively and negatively charged body is at a (i) higher potential (ii) lower potential?

Ans. (i) Positively charged body is at higher potential.

(ii) Negatively charged body is at lower potential.

Q. 11. Explain the concept of electric potential difference in terms of work done in transferring the charge.

Ans. Electric potential difference between two conductors is equal to the work done in transferring a unit positive charge from one conductor to other conductor.

Q. 12. State two ways to save the energy.

Ans. Two ways to save energy:

(i) Instead of fossil fuels, other renewable sources of energy such as the biogas prepared from animal dung should be used.

(ii) The use of hydroelectric energy, wind energy, etc. should be given priority.

Q. 13. The potential difference between two conductors is 1 volt. Explain the meaning of this statement.

Ans. Potential difference between two points is 1 volt, it means 1 joule of work is done in transferring 1 coulomb of charge from one point to the other point.

Q. 14. Name the factors which affect the resistance of a conductor.

Ans. Factors affecting resistance of a conductor are:

(i) The material of wire

(ii) The length of wire

(iii) The area of cross-section of wire

(iv) Temperature of the wire

Q. 15. How temperature affects the resistance of a conductor?

Ans. The resistance of a conductor increases with the increase in its temprature.

Q. 16. Give two examples of primary cells.

Ans. Deniel cell, dry cell

Q. 17. Give two examples of secondary cells.

Ans. Lead accumulator, Ni-Fe accumulator.

Q. 18. What is the purpose of using rheostat in an electric circuit?

Ans. Rheostat is used to vary resistance which in turn, control the flow of current in an electric circuit.

Q. 19. What is the purpose of ammeter in an electric circuit?

Ans. Ammeter is used to measure the magnitude of current flowing in an electric circuit.

Q.20. What is the purpose voltmeter in an electric circuit?

Ans. Voltmeter is used to measure the potential difference between two points of an electric circuit.

Q. 21. What is the purpose of galvanometer in an electric circuit?

Ans. In an electric circuit Galvanometer is used for the following two purposes.

   (i) To detect the presence of current.

   (ii) To detect the direction of flow of current.

Q. 22. How are potential differnce (V), current (I) and resistance (R) related?

Ans. $V = IR$

Q. 23. Two conductors A and B are joined by a copper wire. A is positively charged and B is negatively charged. State the direction of the conventional current.

Ans. Direction of conventional current is from conductor A to conductor B.

Chapter 10. Magnetism

Q. 1. You are provided with two similar bars, one is a magnet and the other is a soft iron. How will you distinguish between them without the use of any other magnet or bar?

Ans. A magnet when suspended freely will rest only in north-south direction, but the soft iron bar will rest in any direction.

Q. 2. Explain the mechanism of attraction of iron nails by a magnet when brought near them.

Ans. When iron nails are brought near one end of a magnet, the nearer end of iron nail acquires an opposite polarity by magnetic induction. Since unlike poles attract each other, therefore, iron nails are attracted towards the end of the magnet. Thus, the iron nail first becomes a magnet by induction and then it is attracted.

Q. 3. 'Induced magnetism is temporary.' Comment on this statement.

Ans. Induced magnetism is temporary as it lasts as long as the magnet causing induction remains in it vicinity.

Q. 4. 'Induction precedes attraction.' Explain the statement.

Ans. When a piece of magnetic material is brought near a magnet, it first becomes a magnet by induction and then it get attracted towards the magnet. Thus, we say that induction precedes attraction.

Q. 5. State two limitations of a natural magnet.

Ans. Limitations of a natural magnet are:

   (i) They are irregular and odd shaped.

   (ii) They are not magnetically very strong.

Q. 6. State two reasons for the requirement of artificial magnets.

Ans. Artificial magnets are required because natural magnets have odd and irregular shape and they are not magnetically very strong. Artificial magnets can be given desired shape and made very strong.

Q. 7. Name the material used for preparing an electromagnet.

Ans. The material used for preparing an electromagnet is soft iron.

Q. 8. How is an electromagnet made?

Ans. An electromagnet is made by winding an insulated copper wire around a soft iron core either in the shape of a solenoid or U-shape.

Q. 9. Name two factors on which the strength of magnetic field of an electromagnet depends.

Ans. The strength of magnetic field of an electromagnet depends on:

(i) The number of turns of wire wound around the coil, and

(ii) The amount of current flowing through the wire.

Q. 10. State two ways through which the strength of an electromagnet can be increased.

Ans. The strength of an electromagnet can be increased by following ways:

(i) By increasing the number of turns of winding in the solenoid.

(ii) By increasing the current, flowing through the solenoid.

Q. 11. Why is soft iron used as the core of the electromagnet in an electric bell?

Ans. The soft iron bar acquires the magnetic properties only when an electric current flows through the solenoid and loses the magnetic properties as the current is switched off. Hence, soft iron is used as the core of the electromagnet in an electric bell.

Q. 12. How is the working of an electric bell affected, if alternating current be used instead of direct current?

Ans. If an a.c. source is used in place of a battery, the core of the electromagnet will get magnetized, but the polarity at its ends will change. Since attraction of armature does not depend on the polarity of the electromagnet, the bell will still ring on pressing the switch.

Q. 13. Name the material used for making the armature of an electric bell. Give a reason for your answer.

Ans. The material used for making the armature of an electric bell is soft iron which can induce magnetism rapidly.

Q. 14. Repulsion is a surest test of magnetic condition of a body than attraction. Explain.

Ans. Repulsion is the surest test of magnetism because the attraction can be caused between two unlike poles of the two magnets or between the magnet and magnetic substance such as iron, nickel, etc. But repulsion is caused when two similar poles approach each other.

Q. 15. There are two knitting needles. One of them is magnetised. How will you find out which one is magnetised, if no other magnet is available?

Ans. When an iron bar is magnetised, it slightly increases in length due to setting of molecular magnets along straight chains. So, on precisely measuring the length of knitting needle, the knitting needle which is slightly longer in length than other is magnetised.

Q. 16. Explain, why steel is used in preference to soft iron for making permanent magnets while soft iron is used in preference to steel for making electromagnets.

Ans. Steel is used in preference to soft iron for making permanent magnets because steel acts as a magnet, even on the removal of inducing magnet and also steel has a very high retention. Soft iron is used in preference to steel for making permanent magnets because soft iron behave like magnet as long as there is an inducing magnet and also soft iron has a very poor magnetic retention.

Q. 17. What are magnetic keepers? What are they used for?

Ans. A magnetic keeper is a ferromagnetic bar made from soft iron or steel, which is placed across the poles of a permanent magnet.

Magnetic keepers are used to preserve the strength of the magnet by completing the magnetic circuit.

Q. 18. State any two properties of magnetic field lines. **[February, 2020]**

Ans. (i) Magnetic field lines are closed and continuous curves.

(ii) They never intersect each other.

Q. 19. Give any one evidence which points towards the existence of the Earth's magnetic field. **[February, 2020]**

Ans. A freely suspended magnetic needle always rests in the geographic north-south. This points towards the existence of earth's magnetic field.

Q. 20. A soft iron when brought close to a magnet is attracted towards it. Name the phenomenon.

Ans. Incluced magnetism.

Q. 21. (i) An iron piece is converted into a magnet by passing current through a wire wound around it. Name the magnet.

(ii) State any one use of the magnet given in (i).

Ans. (i) Electromagnet.

(ii) Electromagnets are used for loading furnaces with iron.

Q. 22. What is the magnitude of magnetic field at a neutral point?

Ans. Zero.

Q. 23. Why does a compass needle get deflected when brought near a bar magnet?

Ans. A compass needle gets deflected when brought near a bar magnet because the bar magnet exerts a magnetic force on the compass needle which is itself a ting pivoted magnet, capable of moving in a horizontal plane.

❑

Short Answers-II | Set 5 |

Chapter 1. Measurements and Experimentation

Q. 1. State the unit you would select to measure:
  (i) Distance between two cities.
  (ii) The volume of petrol filled in the tank of car.
  (iii) Weight of a truck

Ans. (i) Distance between two cities would be measured in kilometre.
  (ii) Volume of petrol filled in the tank of a car would be measured in litre.
  (iii) Weight of a truck would be measured in ton.

Q. 2. Name the physical quantity that the following units measure:
  (i) gram (ii) metre (iii) second

Ans. (i) Mass is the physical quantity measured in gram.
  (ii) Length is the physical quantity measured in metre
  (iii) Time is the physical quantity measured in second.

Q. 3. A simple pendulum has a hollow bob, such that its time period is T. How will the time period of the pendulum be affected if,
  (i) $\dfrac{1}{4}^{th}$ of the bob is filled with Mercury?

  (ii) $\dfrac{3}{4}^{th}$ of the bob is filled with Mercury?

  (iii) The bob is completely filled with Mercury?

Ans. (i) The time period increases because by filling $\dfrac{1}{4}^{th}$ of the bob with mercury lowers centre of gravity. This in turn increases the effective length and hence the time period also increases.

  (ii) By filling the bob with $\dfrac{3}{4}^{th}$ of mercury as it would further lower the centre of gravity, thus increasing the effective length of the pendulum and hence the time period.

  (iii) The time period remains unchanged because the centre of gravity and hence effective length remains unchanged.

Q. 4. A person standing on an oscillating swing sits down. How does the time period of a swing gets affected? What happens to its frequency of oscillations?

Ans. The time period of oscillating swing increases as the relative position of centre of gravity is lowered which in turn increases the effective length and hence the time period.
Frequency of oscillations is inversely proportional to the time period. Hence greater the time period lesser would be the frequency. Hence the swing would oscillate slower while the person sits as compared to while in a standing position.

Q. 5. Two pendulums X and Y have their lengths 1 m and 2 m respectively at a certain place. Which pendulum will make more oscillations in 1 minute? Explain your answer briefly.

Ans. We know that time period is directly proportional to square root of effective length. As the effective length of Y is twice that of X, the time period of Y will be greater than that of X. Hence pendulum X would make twice the oscillations as that of pendulum Y in the same time period of one minute.

Q. 6. Prove that effective length of a second's pendulum is approximately 1 m.

Ans. Mathematically, $T = 2\pi\sqrt{\dfrac{l}{g}}$

Since the pendulum is a second's pendulum, its time period is 2 seconds.

$$2 = 2\pi\sqrt{\frac{l}{9.8}}$$

$$4 = 4\pi^2\left[\frac{l}{9.8}\right]$$

$$l = \frac{9.8}{[3.14]^2}$$

$l = 0.99$ m [approx. 1m]

Hence the effective length of a second's pendulum is approximately 1 m.

Q. 7. (i) What is a simple pendulum?

(ii) Write an expression for the time period of a simple pendulum. **[November, 2019]**

Ans. (i) A simple pendulum is a heavy point mass suspended from a rigid support by a massless and inextensible string.

(ii) $T = 2\pi\sqrt{\dfrac{l}{g}}$ where T = time period, $l \to$ effective length, $g \to$ acceleration due to gravity.

Q. 8. (i) The figure below shows the parts of measuring scales. Which scale can measure length more accurately A or B?

(ii) Name a physical quantitiy related to the unit light year. **[February, 2020]**

Ans. (i) B

(ii) Length.

Chapter 2. Motion in One Dimension

Q. 1. What is the relation between distance and time, when:

(i) body is moving with a uniform velocity?

(ii) body is moving with variable velocity?

Ans. (i) The distance covered by a body is directly proportional to time.

(ii) The distance covered by a body is not directly proportional to time.

Q. 2. A bug is crawling on a cycle rim of radius *r*. What will be the distance and displacement of the bug in (i) half revolution (ii) one complete revolution?

Ans. (i) In half revolution, the distance travelled would be equal to half the revolution *i.e.*, π.*r*, while displacement would be equal to the diameter of the rim *i.e.*, 2*r*.

(ii) In one complete revolution, the distance travelled would be equal to the circumference of the rim *i.e.*, 2π*r*, while the displacement would be equal to zero.

Q. 3. How does the position of an object differ from its displacement?

Ans. The position of an object is expressed at a particular instant of time, while displacement of an object is defined as the object change in position in a certain interval of time.

Q. 4. What does area under a velocity–time graph indicate?

Ans. The area under velocity–time graph gives the displacement of a body.

Q. 5. (i) What will be the distance covered by the body if it moves on a circular path and reaches its original position after one complete round?

(ii) A boy while running throws a basketball high up in the air, runs and catches it. Which has more displacement, the boy or the ball? **[November, 2019]**

Ans. (i) The distance covered is equal to the circumference of the circular path.

(ii) Both will have same displacement.

Q. 6. (i) Two straight lines are drawn on the same displacement–time graph. Line 'A' making an angle of 30° with the time axis and line 'B' making an angle of 60° with the time axis. Which line represents greater velocity?

(ii) How will you calculate the displacement from a velocity–time graph? **[November, 2019]**

Ans. (i) Line B represents greater velocity.

(ii) The area enclosed between the velocity-time graph and the time axis for a certain time interval gives the displacement in that interval of time.

Q. 7. During circular motion, which physical quantity of the body

(i) remains constant,

(ii) changes continuously?

Ans. (i) Speed

(ii) Velocity

Q. 8. What can you say about the motion of a body, if:

(i) Its displacement-time graph is a straight line,

(ii) Its velocity-time graph is a straight line?

Ans. (i) In displacement graph, a straight line shows that body is at rest.

(ii) In velocity-time graph, a straight line show that the body is moving with uniform constant velocity.

Q. 9. State the types of motion represented by the following sketches below:

(i)

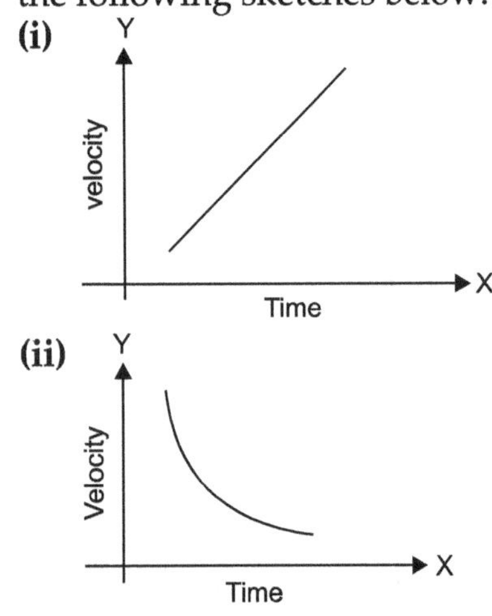

(ii)

Ans. (i) Uniformly accelerated motion e.g. motion of a body released downward.

(ii) Motion with a variable retardation e.g. a car approaching its destination.

Q. 10. The following figure shows displacement–time graph of two vehicles A and B moving in straight path. Which vehicle moves faster? Give reason.

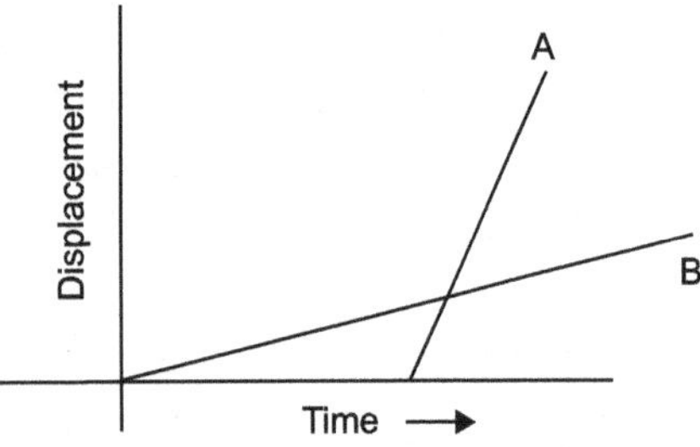

Ans. Vehicle A is moving fast.

Reason for this is that slope of line A is more than that of line B.

Q. 11. Distance-time graph of three friends A, B and C is shown in the figure. All of them moving along a straight road in a fixed direction.

(i) Is any (one or more) of them at rest? If yes, who?

(ii) When did C start moving?

(iii) Did they meet at the same time? If yes, when and where?

(iv) Who is moving the fastest?

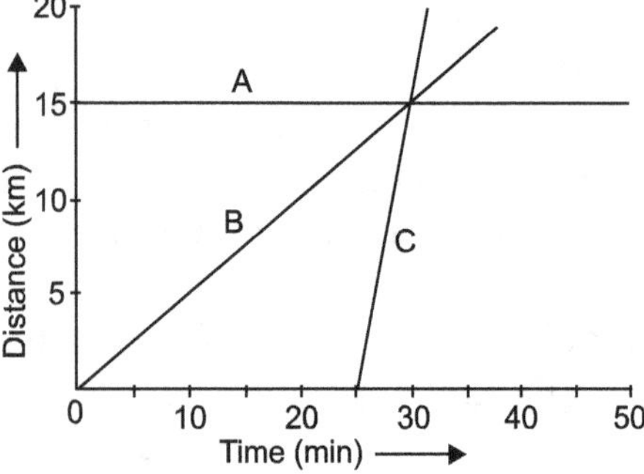

Ans. (i) Yes, A is at rest

(ii) After 25 minutes.

(iii) Yes, after 30 min and at 15 km.

(iv) C is moving the fastest.

Q. 12. The motion of a body is represented by the following displacement-time graph.

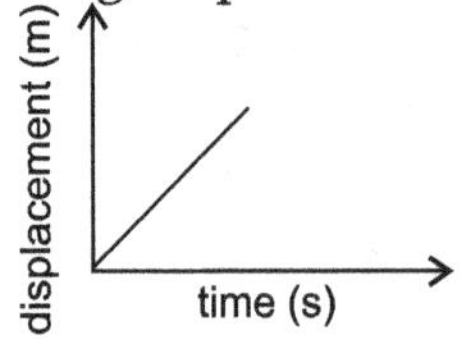

(i) State the type of motion represented in the graph.

(ii) How can the velocity of the body be determined from the above graph?

[February, 2020]

Ans. (i) The graph represents a body having uniform velocity.

(ii) Velocity can be determined by finding slope of the displacement-time graph.

Q. 13. A car travels from A to B and returns to its original position.

The distance between A and B is 2000 m.

(i) Find the total displacement of the car.

(ii) The car takes 5 min to travel from A to B but takes 8 min to travel back from B to A. Is the speed of the car greater while going from A to B or while travelling back from B to A?

(iii) When can the magnitude of distance and displacement be equal for a body in motion? **[February, 2020]**

Ans. (i) Total displacement of car = 0

(ii) Since, the car takes 5 min. to travel from A to B and 8 min. to return from B to A, the speed of car is greater while going from A to B.

(iii) The magnitude of distance and displacement can be equal for a body if motion of the body is in a straight line.

Chapter 3. Laws of Motion

Q. 1. State Newton's second law of motion both in words and equation form. Under what condition does it take the form Force = mass × acceleration?

Ans. According to the Newton's second law of motion, the rate of change of momentum is directly proportional to the force applied and takes place in the direction of force applied.

Mathematically,

$$F \propto \frac{mv - mu}{t}$$

$$\Rightarrow \quad F \propto m\left(\frac{v-u}{t}\right)$$

$$\Rightarrow \quad F \propto ma \qquad \left[\because a = \frac{v-u}{t}\right]$$

or $\qquad F = k.ma$

where, k is constant

If $\qquad k = 1,$

$\qquad F = ma$

The relation $F = ma$ hold under the following conditions:

(i) When velocity of body is much smaller than the speed of light.

(ii) When mass of body remains constant.

Q. 2. Two bodies of masses m_1 and m_2 have the same linear momenta. What is the ratio of their kinetic energies?

Ans. Given,

[Linear momentum]$_1$
$$= \text{[Linear momentum]}_2$$

Let v_1 and v_2 be the velocities of two bodies, respectively.

$$\therefore \qquad m_1.v_1 = m_2.v_2$$

Squaring both sides,

$$(m_1.v_1)^2 = (m_2.v_2)^2$$

$$\Rightarrow \quad m_1^2.v_1^2 = m_2^2.v_2^2$$

$$\Rightarrow \quad m_1.m_1.v_1^2 = m_2.m_2.v_2^2$$

$$\Rightarrow \quad \frac{1}{2}m_1.v_1^2 = \frac{1}{2}m_2.v_2^2 \times \left(\frac{m_2}{m_1}\right)$$

$$\Rightarrow \quad \frac{\text{K.E}_1}{\text{K.E}_2} = \left(\frac{m_2}{m_1}\right)$$

The ratio of their kinetic energies is the inverse ratio of their corresponding masses.

Q. 3. If a balloon is inflated by means of air such that the air exerts force on the balloon in the radially outward direction. What would be the direction of reaction force offered by the balloon? Name the law that governs the phenomenon.

Ans. The reaction force would be directed radially inwards in accordance to the Newton's third law of motion. The air blown inside the balloon acts as the action force and inflates the balloon in the outward direction. Due to the elasticity of the balloon and the atmospheric pressure outside, a reaction force is been created by the balloon inwards.

Q. 4. Mention the action and reaction forces in the following cases:

(i) A person hammering the nail in the wall.

(ii) A brick lying on the ground

(iii) A pendulum suspended from a rigid support.

Ans. (i) Person hammering a nail in the wall: Action force as applied by hammer and reaction force as applied by the wall.

(ii) A brick lying on the ground: Action force is the weight of the brick acting in the downward direction on the ground and reaction force is the normal reaction force exerted in the upward direction.

(iii) A pendulum suspended freely from a rigid support: Action force is the weight of the metallic bob acting at the centre of gravity of the bob acting downwards and reaction force is the tension in the string acting upwards towards the point of suspension.

Q. 5. Explain the motion of a rocket with the help of Newton's third law.

Ans. Newton's third law of motion states that to every action, there is an equal and opposite reaction. So, when a rocket moves is space, fuel is burnt inside the rocket and the burnt gases at every high pressure are pushed outside *i.e.*, rocket applies force on the gases in the backward direction. As a result, the gases put equal amount of force on the rocket in the opposite direction and the rocket moves in the forward direction.

Q. 6. Two spring balances, one of which is attached to a fixed support and another free, are tied to each other and pulled apart in opposite directions. Comment on the readings of the two balances and justify your observation.

Ans. The readings noted in both the balances will be the same. This is in accordance to the Newton's third law that for a system of two bodies into consideration, to every action there is an equal and opposite reaction.

Chapter 4. Pressure in Fluids and Atmospheric Pressure

Q. 1. A glass container contains a liquid of density ρ, when the height of liquid is h and acceleration due to gravity is g. If P_A is the atmospheric pressure, calculate:
  (i)   The pressure on the free surface of the liquid.
  (ii) The total pressure at the base of container.
  (iii) What is the magnitude of lateral pressure at the base of liquid, on the inner side of container?

Ans. (i) Pressure on the free surface of the liquid is P_A.
  (ii) The total pressure at the base of liquid is $P_A + h\rho g$.
  (iii) The magnitude of lateral pressure is $P_A + h\rho g$.

Q. 2. How is the barometric height of a simple barometer affected if:
  (i)   its tube is pushed down into the trough of mercury,
  (ii) its tube is slightly titled from the vertical,
  (iii) a drop of liquid is inserted inside the tube?

Ans. (i) Remains unaffected as atmospheric pressure at a place is constant.
  (ii) Remains unaffected as atmospheric pressure at a place is constant.
  (iii) If a drop of liquid gets into the tube, it will immediately change into the vapors in the vacuum space and the vapors of the liquid will exert pressure on the mercury column due to which the barometric height will decrease.

Q. 3. Why is mercury used as barometric liquid?

Ans. The vapour pressure of mercury is almost negligible under vacuum conditions. Thus mercury barometer shows true atmospheric pressure. Also mercury is the densest liquid [13.6 g cm^{-3}] at room temperature. Thus a short column of mercury can exert as much pressure as atmospheric. Mercury also does not wet the sides of glass and can be obtained in pure state.

Q. 4. An altimeter is an aneroid barometer which makes use of the change in atmospheric pressure with the change in height above the sea level (altitude).
  (i)   How does the atmospheric pressure change with increase in height above the sea level?
  (ii) Is the change in the atmospheric pressure uniform in part (i) above?
  (iii) What is the approximate value of atmospheric pressure at sea level in S.I. unit?   **[February, 2020]**

Ans. (i) Atmospheric pressure decreases with increase in height above sea level.
  (ii) No, the change of atmospheric pressure with increas in height above sea level is not uniform.
  (iii) The approximate value of atmospheric pressure at sea level in SI unit is about 10^5 Pa.

Q. 5. The figure given below, is a simplified version of hydraulic press. Answer the following questions.
  (i)   What is the pressure exerted on the piston P?
  (ii) What is the pressure throughout the fluid?
  (iii) What is the pressure exerted by the fluid on piston Q?
  (iv) What is the thrust on the piston Q?

Ans.

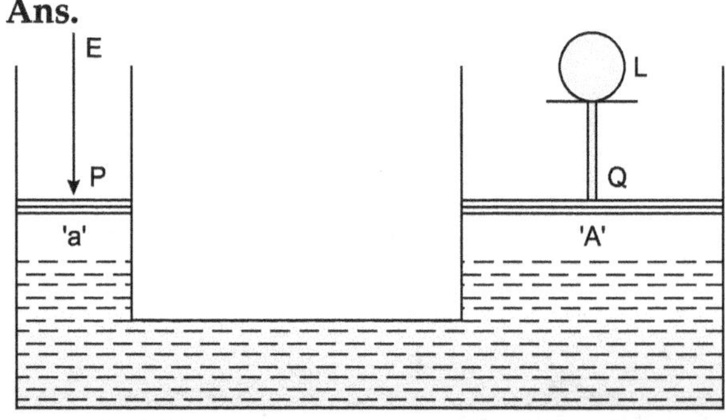

  (i) Pressure on piston P = $\dfrac{\text{Force}}{\text{Area}}$

$$= \frac{E}{a}$$

(ii) Pressure exerted by fluid

$$= \frac{E}{a}$$

[As pressure is transmitted equally]

(iii) Pressure exerted on piston Q

$$= \text{Pressure in fluid}$$
$$= \frac{E}{a}$$

(iv) Thrust [force] acting on piston Q in upward direction

$$= \text{Force} \times \text{area}$$
$$= \frac{E}{a} \times A$$

Q. 6. (i) What does fig. I tell about pressure in liquids?

(ii) What does fig. II tell about pressure in liquids?

Ans.

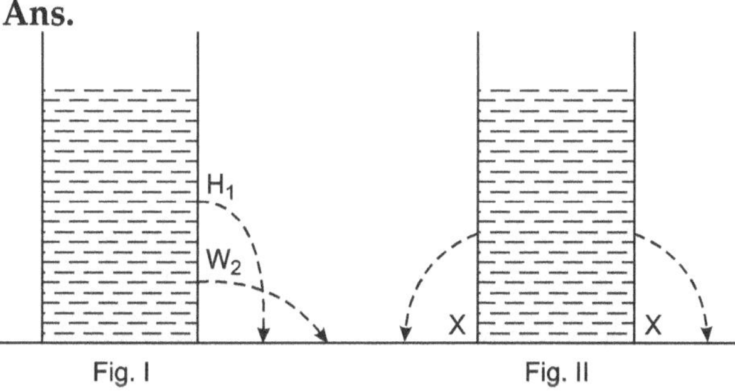

(i) It shows that fluid pressure is directly proportional to depth.

(ii) It shows that fluid pressure at a given depth is same in all direction.

Q. 7. 500 ml of water is poured into each of these vessels A, B and C. Explain, with reason, in which vessel will the pressure at the bottom of the container be the least? **[November 2019]**

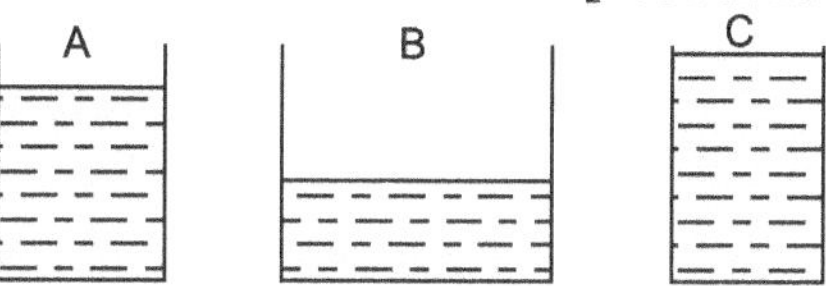

Ans. The pressure at the bottom will be least in the vessel B because pressure at a point inside a fluid is directly proportional to its depth in the fluid. Since depth of vessel B is least, so pressure at its bottom will also be least.

Q. 8. The diagram below shows the position of two divers A and B in river water at the depth of h_1 and h_2 respectively from the water surface.

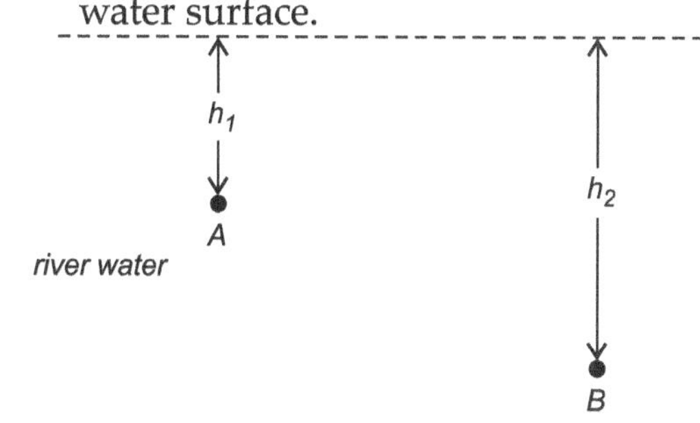

(i) Which of the two divers (A or B) will experience more pressure by the water?

(ii) The two divers were later made to dive in a sea. For the same depth, they experience more pressure in the sea compared to that in the river. Why? **[February, 2020]**

Ans. (i) Diver B will experience more pressure.

(ii) The divers experience more pressure in sea water compared to river water because density of sea water is greater than that of river water.

Chapter 5. Upthrust in Fluids, Archimedes' Principle and Floatation

Q. 1. A block of wood is so weighed that it just floats in water contained in a jar at room temperature.

(i) If water is heated what change will occur in the state of floatation of the block?

(ii) If the water is cooled to 4°C, what change will be observed in the state of floatation?

Ans. (i) When the water is heated, it would expand hence volume would increase, as a result, its density decreases. Hence block of wood will sink deeper in hot water.

(ii) When water is cooled it contracts but at a temperature of 4°C it exhibits anomalous behavior of expanding rather than contracting. Thus density again decreases and hence block of wood would sink deeper.

Q. 2. Floating icebergs in sea are dangerous for ships. Explain.

Ans. Icebergs are lighter than water. Depending upon the density of water, major fraction of the iceberg is below water while a very small part is outside the surface of water. For a sailor, it is difficult to estimate the size of the iceberg below the surface of water and hence may cause the hazards of collision.

Q. 3. Why does a hydrogen balloon rise to a certain height and then stops rising further?

Ans. As we know that density of hydrogen is much less than air, so the weight of hydrogen filled balloon is less than the weight of air displaced by it. So greater upthrust acts on the balloon rather than its own weight. As a result, it rises in air when released. After reaching a certain height, its weight becomes equal to the weight of air displaced by the balloon, which is due to the decrease in density of air with altitude. Hence, it stops rising further.

Q. 4. Figure shows the same block of wood floating in three different liquids A, B, C of densities ρ_1, ρ_2, ρ_3 respectively. Which of the liquids has highest density? Give reason for your answer.

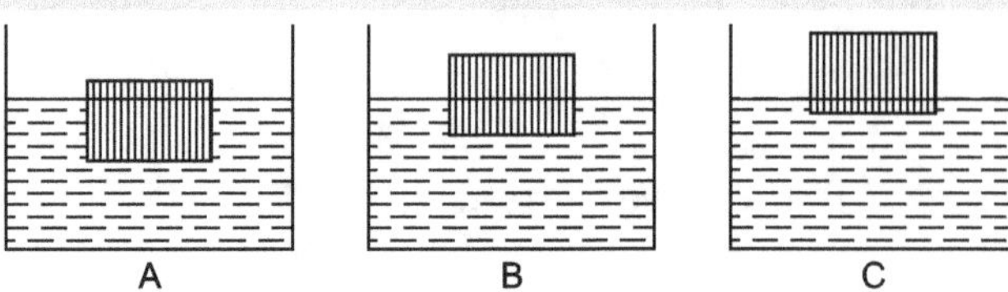

Ans. The upthrust offered by all three liquids A, B, C is same.

Upthrust = Weight of liquid displaced

= Volume submerged × ρ × g

Volume of body submerged is least in liquid C, so its density ρ_3 must be maximum.

Q. 5. If d_1, d_2 and d_3 are the densities of liquid 1, liquid 2 and a solid respectively Compare:

(i) The densities of d_1 and d_2.

(ii) The densities d_2 and d_3

[November, 2019]

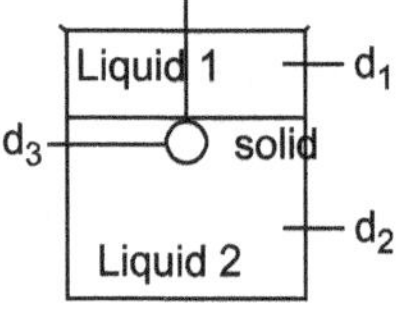

Ans. (i) $d_2 > d_1$

(ii) $d_2 = d_3$

Chapter 6. Heat and Energy

Q. 1. Why do vegetables and fruits get damaged during severe winter?

Ans. When the water in the cell sap freezes, it expands due to anomalous expansion. This expanding water breaks the cell walls, which in turn damages fruits.

Q. 2. Why are the taps left dripping in sub-zero temperatures during winter?

Ans. The dripping taps will always create some space for expansion. Thus, when water in the pipes freeze in sub-zero temperatures, due to its anomalous expansion, it expands. This expanding water always finds space for expansion as tap is dripping. Thus, water pipes do not burst.

Q. 3. Why are exposed water pipes lagged with straw in hilly regions during winter?

Ans. When the pipes are lagged, the temperature of water within the pipes does not fall below 4°C. Thus, due to anomalous expansion, water will not exert force on pipes and hence, escape bursting.

Q. 4. Why does a glass bottle filled completely with water and tightly corked, break in a freezer chamber of fridge?

Ans. When the temperature of water within the glass bottle falls below 4°C, it starts expanding due to anomalous expansion. Since, there is no space for expansion, it exerts tremendous pressure and bursts open the bottle.

Q. 5. How global warming can be reduced?

Ans. With an increase in industrial growth and population, energy consumption is increasing. This leads to global warming.

To minimise global warming following three measures should be taken.

(i) Internal combustion engines in vehicles should be replaced by electric battery vehicles to reduce carbon dioxide emission.

(ii) Reforestation and sustainable use of land should be encouraged. Forest habitats should be maintained.

(iii) Controlling population, through family planning, welfare reform and the empowerment of women. This will help in reducing population, then consumption for energy and hence will reduce global warming.

Q. 6. State four effects of global warming.

Ans. The effects of global warming on the life on earth are as follows:

(i) The variable changes in the climate in different parts of the world has created difficulty and forced the people and animals to migrate from one place to the other.

(ii) If has affected the blooming season of the different plants.

(iii) The climatic changes has shown the immediate effect on simple organisms and plants.

(iv) It has affected the world's ecology.

(v) It has increased the heat stroke deaths.

Q. 7. Name two thermometric scales, commonly used for laboratory thermometers. State the relation for converting temperature from one scale to another scale.

Ans. (i) Celsius scale or centigrade scale (C)

(ii) Fahrenheit scale (F).

Relation for converting one scale to another scale:

$$\frac{C}{5} = \left(\frac{F-32}{9}\right)$$

Q. 8. State four reasons for using mercury as thermometric liquid.

Ans. Reasons for using mercury as thermometric liquid are as follows:

(i) It has a very low specific heat capacity.

(ii) It has a uniform rate of expansion.

(iii) It has a wide range of temperature (Boiling Point is 357 °C and freezing point is 39 °C).

(iv) It dose not stick to the sides of glass capillary tube.

(v) It is a good conductor of heat.

(vi) It is opaque and shining and can be easily seen in glass.

Q. 9. Why do water pipes burst during severe frost?

Ans. When the temperature falls below zero degree Celsius, the water in the pipes expands due to anomalous expansion. However, if there is no space for expansion, then it exerts tremendous pressure on the pipes and bursts them.

Q. 10. Why are soft drink bottles not completely filled?

Ans. All soft drinks contain water. When soft drink bottles are chilled in sub-zero temperatures, the water, on account of its anomalous expansion, expands. Thus, to provide space for expanding water, soft drink bottles are not completely filled as otherwise they will burst.

Q. 11. State the functions of decomposers in an ecosystem.

Ans. The role of a decomposer is to break down dead organisms and then feed on them. The nutrients created by the dead organisms are returned to the soil to be later used by the producers. Once these deceased organisms are returned to the soil, they are used as food by bacteria and fungi by transforming the complex organic materials into simpler nutrients. The simpler products can then be used by producers. Thus, decomposers play an important role in every ecosystem.

Q. 12. State four effects, which heat energy can bring about.

Ans. Effects of heat energy are as follows:

(i) Heat brings about change in temperature.

(ii) Heat brings about change in dimensions of a body.

(iii) Heat brings about change in state of a body.

(iv) Heat brings about chemical reactions in large number of bodies

Q. 13. State the importance of green plants in an ecosystem.

Ans. Green plants absorb most of the energy falling on them and by the process of photosynthesis, they produce food for the consumers. Plants, being primary producers are of great importance in the ecosystem. They also maintain the balance of oxygen and carbon dioxide on earth.

Q. 14. The diagram below shows Hope's experimental set up. The temperature in the metallic cylinder is 10°C. The trough is packed with a freezing mixture of ice and salt.

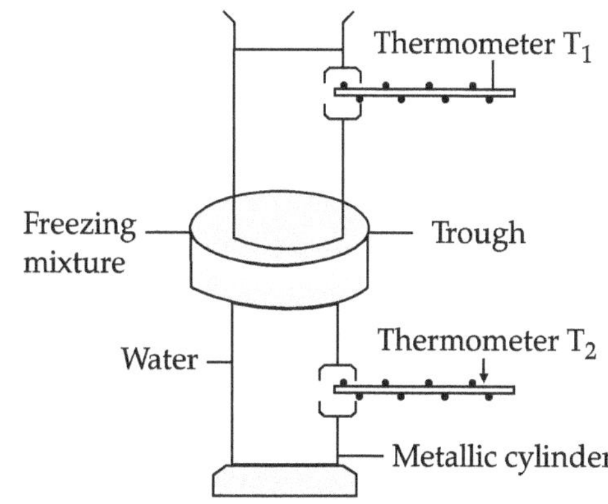

(i) Which of the two thermometer shows rapid fall in temperature initially —T_1 or T_2 and why?

(ii) After some time when ice is formed:

(a) Will it sink to the bottom of the metallic cylinder?

(b) What does it tell about density of ice in relation to density of water at the bottom?   **[February, 2020]**

Ans. (i) Initially the thermometer T_2 shows a rapid fall in temperature because the freezing mixture cools the central portion of the cyllinder, water contracts and its density increases. The cooled water sinks to the bottom and warm water rises up to take its place due to which the thermometer T_2 shows a rapid fall in temperature.

(ii) (a) After some time when ice is formed, it will not sink to the bottom of the metallic cylinder.

(b) Density of ice is less than the density of water at the bottom of the metallic cylinder.

Q. 15. What are the two laws of thermodynamics in energy flow?

Ans. First law of thermodynamic says that, 'Energy can neither be created nor can be destroyed, but can be transferred from one form to other. While, second law of thermodynamics says that, when energy is put to work, a part of it is always converted into unuseful form as heat, due to friction and radiation.

Q. 16. Why is the use of wood as a fuel not advisable although wood is a renewable source of energy?

Ans. Wood is obtained from trees. Hence, trees need to be cut down for wood to be used as a fuel. Also, burning of wood releases a lot of smoke, which pollutes the atmosphere.

Q. 17. State some characteristics of a source of energy.

Ans. (i) A source of energy should be such that it can provide adequate amount of useful energy, at a steady rate over a longer period of time.

(ii) It should be safe and convenient to use.

(iii) It should be economical and easy to store and transport.

Chapter 7. Reflection of Light

Q. 1. You are provided a convex mirror, a concave mirror and a plane mirror. How will you distinguish between them, without touching or using any other apparatus?

Ans. Hold an object (pen) close to each mirror and look for its image.

(i) If the image is erect and of same size as object, the mirror is plane.

(ii) If the image is erect and diminished, the mirror is convex.

(iii) If the image is erect and enlarged, the mirror is concave.

Q. 2. How should two plane mirrors be arranged to get an infinite number of images?

Ans. The two plane mirrors must have their reflecting surfaces parallel to each other.

Q. 3. Where should an object be placed in front of a concave mirror to obtain an image of the same size as that of the object?

Ans. The object must be placed at the centre of curvature of the concave mirror.

Q. 4. (i) Which spherical mirror will you choose if you want to see the enlarged image of your face?

(ii) What will be the position of your face to observe the enlarged image?

Ans. (i) Concave mirror.

(ii) The position of face must be between the focus and pole of concave mirror.

Q. 5. When does a ray of light falling on a plane mirror completely retrace its path?

Ans. A ray of light falling on a plane mirror completely retraces its path when the angle of incidence is $0°$ or it is incident perpendicular to the surface of the plane mirror.

Q. 6. Name the type of mirror used in the following situations:

(i) Headlights of a car

(ii) Side/rear-view mirror of a vehicle

(iii) Solar furnace

Support your answer with reasons

Ans. (i) A concave mirror, as it diverges the rays of light when bulb is between P and F.

(ii) A convex mirror, as it covers a wide field and forms a small erect image close to the eye of the driver.

(iii) A concave mirror, as it concentrates the parallel rays of sun at principal focus.

Q. 7. The diagram below image formation A'B' of an object AB kept between pole (P) and Focus (F) in a spherical mirror MM'.
Identify the spherical mirror used and state the focal length of the spherical mirror. (Do not draw the diagram.)

[February, 2020]

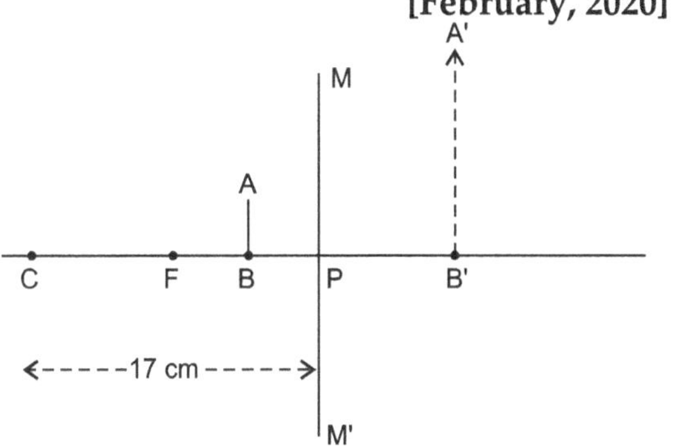

Ans. The spherical mirror used in the given diagram is a concave mirror and its focal length is $\dfrac{17}{2}$ cm = 8.5 cm.

Q. 8. The diagram below shows a light ray striking and reflecting from a plane mirror. AO is the incident ray and OB the reflected ray. The angle between the incident ray and the reflected ray is 120°.

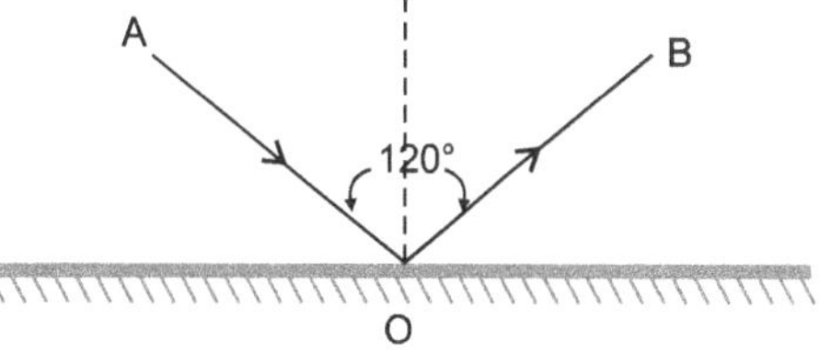

(i) What is the value of the angle of reflection?

(ii) If the image of an object is formed 5 cm behind the mirror, what is the distance between the image and the object?

(iii) If two plane mirrors are used and kept facing parallel to each other, how many images are formed if the object is kept in between them?

[February, 2020]

Ans. (i) Angle of reflection = 60°

(ii) Distance between the image and object = (5 + 5) cm = 10 cm.

(iii) Infinite number of images will be formed.

Chapter 8. Propagation of Sound Waves

Q. 1. What is Galton's whistle? To what use it can be put?

Ans. Galton's whistle is a special kind of whistle which emits ultra-sonic vibrations between 20,000 Hz to 40,000 Hz. The vibrations of this range cannot be perceived by human ears, but can be easily perceived by dogs. Thus, the dogs can be trained to perform special tasks on hearing the sound from Galton's whistle. It is very useful, if intruders enter in someone's house. On blowing the whistle, the dog will attack intruder and the intruder will not be able to hear the sound.

Q. 2. How does a bat avoid obstacles in their way when in flight?

Ans. A bat emits ultrasonic vibrations in the course of its flight. These vibrations on striking an obstacle are reflected back to form echo. On hearing the echo, the bat can locate the obstacle during flight and steers clear from it.

Q. 3. State any two characteristics of wave motion.

Ans. (i) A wave is caused due to periodic disturbance of particles of medium, and the wave by itself is periodic in nature.

(ii) It is the disturbance which travels outward and not the particles of medium. The particles of medium, simply vibrate either to and fro or up and down about their mean positions.

Q. 4. Explain, why lightning flash is seen before the crack of thunder.

Ans. Light travels at a speed of $3 \times 10^8\ \text{ms}^{-1}$ and hence, reaches instantly to an observer. However, sound travels at a very slow speed of 330 ms^{-1} and hence, reaches observer after sometime. Thus, flash of lightning is seen at once, but crack of thunder is heard later on.

Q. 5. State four practical uses of ultrasonic vibrations.

Ans. Uses of ultrasonic vibrations:

(i) These are used for dissipating fog on the runways at the airports.

(ii) These are used in the ultrasound scanning of internal organs of human body.

(iii) These are used for making dish washing machines. In these machines, water and detergents are vibrated with ultrasonic vibrator. The vibrating particles of the dissolved detergent rub against the plates and clean them.

(iv) These are used in SONAR (Sound navigation and ranging) to detect and find the distance of objects under water.

Q. 6. Why only ultrasonic sound waves are used in SONAR?

Ans. Ultrasonic sound waves are used in SONAR because of the following advantages it has over the ordinary sound waves:

(i) Ultrasonic sound waves have a very high frequency (and very short wavelength) due to which they can penetrate into sea-water to a large extent.

(ii) Ultrasonic sound waves cannot be confused with engine noises or other sounds made by the ship because they cannot be heard by human beings.

Q. 7. What is approximate value of speed of sound in iron as compared to that in air? Illustrate your answer with simple experiment.

Ans. The speed of sound in air is 330 ms^{-1} and in iron is 5100 ms^{-1}.

Ask a person to hit the rail at some predetermined time with a hammer. Put your ear on the rail. (The person must be 2 km or more from observer). You will notice that sound energy reaches very quickly to the ear through rails, however, it takes quite a lot of time before sound is heard through air.

Q. 8. State three characteristics of the medium required for propagation of sound.

Ans. Requisites of the medium for propagation of sound:

(i) The medium must be elastic.

(ii) The medium must have inertia.

(iii) The medium should be frictionless.

Q. 9. Describe a simple experiment to determine the speed of sound in air. What approximation is made in the method described by you?

Ans. The simple experiment that a person can do to calculate the speed of sound in air is that a person stands at a known distance (d metre) from the cliff and fires a pistol and simultaneously start the stopwatch. He stops the stopwatch as soon as he hears an echo. The distance travelled by the sound during the time t seconds is $2d$. So,

$$\text{speed of sound} = \frac{\text{distance travelled}}{\text{time taken}} = \frac{2d}{t}$$

The approximation made is that speed of sound remains same for the time when the experiment is taking place.

Q. 10. How do the following factors affect, if at all, the speed of sound in air:

(i) Frequency of sound,

(ii) Temperature of air,

(iii) Pressure of air and

(iv) Moisture in air?

Ans. (i) Frequency of sound has no effect on the speed of sound.

(ii) Speed of sound increases with the increase in the temperature of sound.

(iii) Pressure of sound has no effect on the speed of sound.

(iv) Speed of sound increases with the increase in presence of moisture in air.

Q. 11. Answer the following questions:

(i) Can sound travel in vacuum?

(ii) How does the speed of sound differ in different media?

Ans. (i) No, sound cannot travel in vacuum as it requires a material medium for its propagation.

(ii) Speed of sound is maximum in solids, less in liquids and least in gases.

Q. 12. Sound travels slower on a cold winter night. Give a reason. **[November, 2019]**

Ans. Density of air increases when temperature decreases, and since, speed of sound is inversely proportional to the square root of delsity, so speed of sound in air decreases with increase in density of air.

Q. 13. The figure shows a glass container filled with air and having an electric bell kept inside it. A person standing close to it can distinctly hear the bell. Now the air inside is removed slowly.

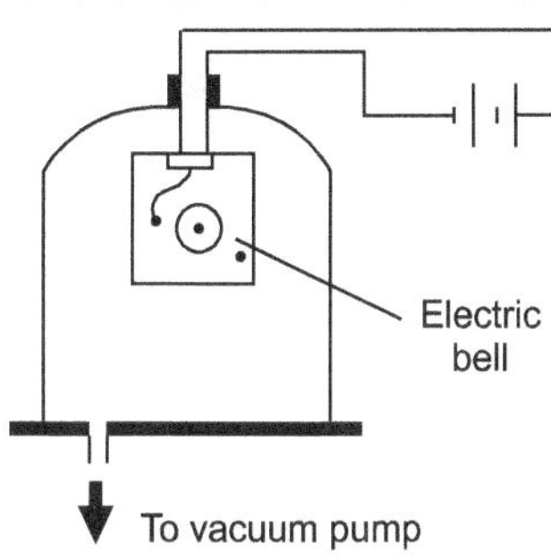

(i) Will the person be able to hear the bell after the air in the container is completely removed? Why?

(ii) How does the speed of sound get affected when there is an increase of moisture in the air? **[February 2020]**

Ans. (i) No, the person will not be able to hear the bell when the air is completely removed because sound needs a material medium for its propagation.

(ii) Due to increase in moisture in air, density of air decreases, hence speed of sound in air increases.

Chapter 9. Current Electricity

Q. 1. What do you understand by the terms

(i) conventional current

(ii) electronic current?

Which amongst the two is real current?

Ans. (i) The current which flows from positively charged body to negatively charged body when connected by some conductor is called conventional current.

(ii) The current which flows due to the drift of electrons from negatively charged body to positively charged body is called electronic current.

The electronic current is the real current because it is the electrons which drift in a conductor from negative to positive.

Q. 2. Explain why does a metal wire when connected to a cell offer resistance to the flow of current.

Ans. A metal wire has free electrons which move in random directions. When the ends of the wire are connected to a cell, the electrons start moving from the negative terminal of the cell to its positive terminal through the metal wire. During their movement, they collide with the free electrons and fixed ions of the wire. This causes them to lose their speed and change their direction. As a result, the electrons slow down and slowly drift towards the positive terminal. Thus, the wire offers resistance to the flow of current (or electrons) through it.

Q. 3. How is the current flowing in a conductor change if the resistance of conductor is doubled keeping the potential difference across it the same?

Ans. According to question,

If $R' = 2R$, $V' = V$ then, $I' = ?$

By Ohm's law, we have

$$V = IR \qquad \qquad ...(i)$$

or $\quad V' = I'R'$

$\Rightarrow \quad V' = I'(2R)$

$\Rightarrow \quad I' = \dfrac{V}{2R} = \dfrac{1}{2} \times \dfrac{V}{R} = \dfrac{1}{2} \times I = \dfrac{I}{2}$

Thus, current gets halved.

Q. 4. How is the resistance of a wire affected if its

(i) Length is doubled

(ii) Radius is halved

Ans. (i) We Know, Resistance $\propto$ Length

So, if there length of wire is doubled, then its resistance will also get doubled.

(ii) We know,

$$\text{Resistance} \propto \dfrac{1}{\text{Area of cross section}}$$

$$\Rightarrow \text{Resistance} \propto \dfrac{1}{\neq \times (\text{radius})^2}$$

$$\Rightarrow \text{Resistance} \propto \dfrac{1}{(\text{radius})^2}$$

Thus, if radius of wire is halved, its resistance will becomes 4 times of its original value.

Q. 5. Study the diagram given below and answer the question that follows.

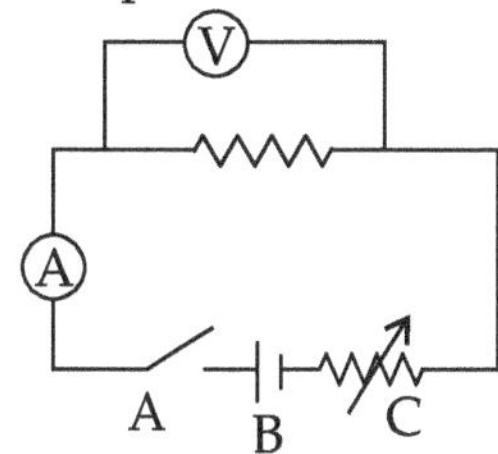

(i) Identify the electrical components labelled A, B, and C.

(ii) State whether the circuit is open or closed.

Ans. (i) A - switch, B - Cell, C - Rheostat

(ii) Since, the switch is open, so the circuit is open.

Q. 6. On the basis of electron model explain:

(i) What are conductors? Give four examples of conductors.

(ii) What are insulators? Give four examples of insulators.

Ans. (i) The substances which have a very large number of free electrons, such that they can be made to drift on the application of electric potential, are called conductors.

Examples: silver, copper, aluminium, gold.

(ii) The substances which do not have very large number of free electrons and which cannot be made to drift on the application of electric potential, are called insulators or bad conductors.

Examples: asbestos, mica, rubber, glass.

Q. 7. Describe three ways for the efficient use of energy.

Ans. Three ways to use energy efficiently:

(i) The use of compact fluorescent lights (CFL) saves 67% energy and may last 6 to 10 times longer than the incandescent lamps.

(ii) The use of advanced boilers and furnaces in industry can save sufficient amount of energy in attaining high temperatures while burning less fuel. Such technologies are more efficient and less polluting.

(iii) The fuel efficiency in the vehicles can be increased by reducing the weight of the vehicle, using the advanced tyres and computer controlled engines.

Q. 8. The diagram shows a circuit in which a bulb is connected through connecting the wires to a cell.

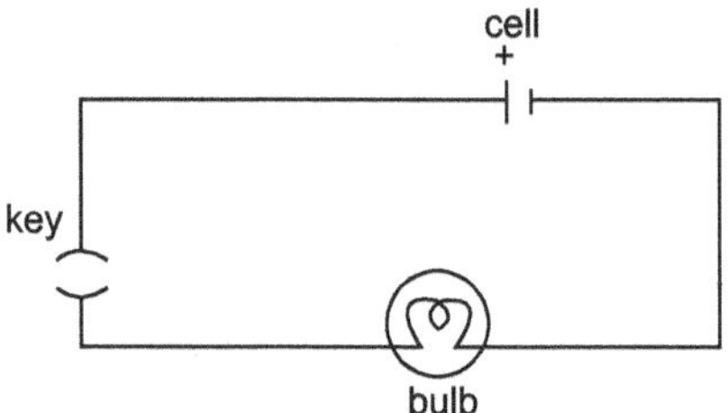

(i) The bulb in the circuit does not glow. Why?

(ii) If the bulb is glowing then what will be the direction of the conventional current in the circuit?

[February, 2020]

Ans. (i) The bulb in the circuit will not glow because the circuit is open or the key (switch) is off.

(ii) The direction of conventional current will be from positive terminal to the negative terminal of the cell in the circuit.

Chapter 10. Magnetism

Q. 1. Why do lines of magnetic field never cross? Why do they never pass through a neutral point?

Ans. No two lines of magnetic field cross each other because in that case there would be two directions of resultant magnetic field at a given point, which is not possible. Magnetic lines of force never pass through neutral point because at neutral point, magnetic field due to bar magnet is neutralised by earth's magnetic field.

Q. 2. State four properties of magnetic field lines.

Ans. (i) They are closed and continuous curves.

(ii) They are directed from North pole towards the south pole of a magnet.

(iii) Magnetic field lines never intersect each other.

(iv) They are crowded near the poles and are far separated near the middle of a magnet.

Q. 3. What are the evidences of existence of Earth's magnetic field?

Ans. (i) A freely suspended magnet always rest in geographic North-South direction.

(ii) An iron buried inside the Earth, along North-South direction, becomes a magnet.

(iii) Neutral points are obtained on plotting magnetic field lines of a magnet.

Q. 4. What are the advantages of an electromagnet over a permanent magnet?

Ans. (i) The strength of magnetic field of an electromagnet can be easily changed.

(ii) The polarity of an electromagnet can be reversed.

(iii) An electromagnet can produce a stronger magnetic field.

Q. 5. In the diagram below AB is a magnet and CD is an iron bar.

Study the diagram and determine the polarities at the ends A, B and D.

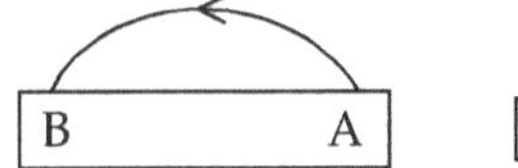
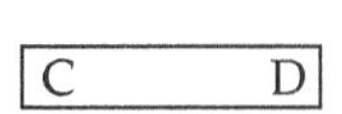

Ans. A is north pole, B is south pole and D is north pole.

Q. 6. A coil of insulated copper wire is wound around a piece of soft iron and current is passed in the coil from a battery.

(i) What name is given to the device so obtained?

(ii) Give two uses of the device mentioned by you.

Ans. (i) The device obtained is an electromagnet.

(ii) An electromagnet can be used for the following purposes:

(a) For removing pieces of iron from wounds.

(b) In electrical devices like bell, telegraph, etc.

Q. 7. The figure shows a coil wound around a soft iron bar XY.

(i) State the polarity at the ends X and Y as the switch is pressed.

(ii) Suggest one way of increasing the strength of electromagnet so formed.

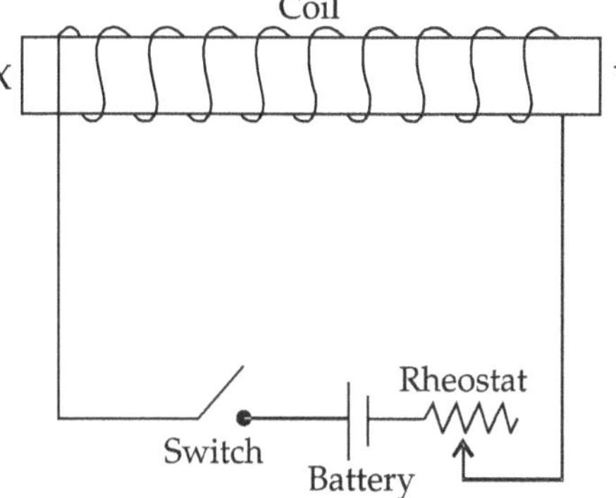

Ans. (i) X is north pole, Y is the south pole.

(ii) The strength of the electromagnet can be increased by increasing the current in the coil.

Q. 8. The diagram below shows the magnetic field lines of earth in a limited space.

The field lines are parallel and equidistant.

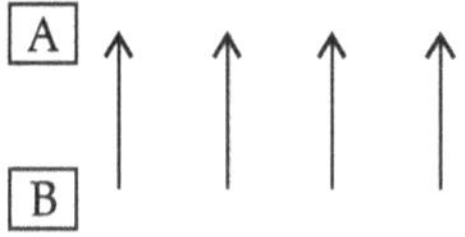

(i) Are the magnetic field lines uniform or non-uniform?

(ii) Where is the position of the geographic north, A or B?

[February, 2020]

Ans. (i) The given diagram represents a uniform magnetic field.

(ii) The position of geographic north is at A.

❑

Chapter 1. Measurements and Experimentation

Q. 1. State four characteristics of a standard unit.

Ans. The four characteristics of a standard unit are:

(i) The value of unit should not change with space and time.

(ii) It should be of a convenient size.

(iii) It should be possible to define without any ambiguity.

(iv) It should be easily reproduced.

Q. 2. Give scientific reason for the following:

(i) Pendulum clock runs faster in winter and slower in summer.

(ii) Pendulum clock runs slow when either taken to a mountain top or in a mine.

Ans. (i) Time period of a pendulum is directly proportional to square root of its length. During winter its length contracts, hence decreasing the time required to complete one oscillation. Decrease in time results in faster movement of the pendulum clock. While in summer its length expands, hence increasing the time required to complete one oscillation. Increase in time results in slower movement of the pendulum clock.

(ii) When we go on the top of a mountain or in a mine there is a minimal decrease in the value of acceleration due to gravity. Hence the period of oscillation increases and so the pendulum clock runs slow.

Q. 3. State the factors which influence the time period of oscillation for a pendulum.

Ans. Time period of a simple pendulum is given by the relation:

$$T = 2\pi\sqrt{\dfrac{l}{g}}.$$

(i) Time period is directly proportional to square root of effective length of pendulum.

(ii) Time period is independent of mass and material of bob.

(iii) Time period is inversely proportional to square root of acceleration due to gravity.

(iv) Time period does not depend on amplitude of oscillation, provided effective length is not large.

Q. 4. A simple pendulum is set up in a laboratory at sea level. How would its time period change if it is shifted to:

(i) the moon

(ii) a deep mine

(iii) top of Mount Everest

(iv) an artificial satellite of earth?

Ans. Since the acceleration due to gravity is maximum at the surface of the earth,

(i) The acceleration due to gravity on moon is almost $\dfrac{1}{6}^{th}$ that of the earth, so, the time period would increase.

(ii) Time period is inversely proportional to square root of acceleration due to gravity. Since g reduces in a deep mine effectively, the time period would increase.

(iii) On the top of Mount Everest, acceleration due to gravity decreases hence the time period indirectly increases.

(iv) In case of an artificial satellite, the acceleration due to gravity is zero hence the time period is infinite.

Q. 5. (i) Which of the following instrument is the most precise instrument for measuring length:

1. A Vernier Callipers of least count 0.01 cm.

2. A screw gauge of pitch 1 mm and 100 divisions on a circular scale.

(ii) When is a screw gauge said to be a free from a zero error?

(iii) Give one way to decrease the least count of a screw gauge.

[November, 2019]

Ans. (i) A screw gauge of pitch 1 mm and 100 divisions on circular scale is more precise for measuring length compared to a Vernier Callipers of least count 0.01 cm.

(ii) A screw gauge is said to be free from zero error if the zero mark of circular scale coincides with the zero mark on base line of main scale when the flat end of screw is brought in contact with the stud of screw gauge.

(iii) Least count of a screw gauge can be decreased by (a) decreasing the pitch, (b) by increasing the total number of division on the circular scale.

Q. 6. (i) What is a second's pendulum?

(ii) State the effective length of second's pendulum at a place where g is 9.8 ms^{-2}?

(iii) A boy is swinging on a swing. If another boy sits along with him without distrubing the motion how will the time period change?

[November, 2019]

Ans. (i) A second's pendulum is a pendulum with a time period of oscillation equal to two seconds.

(ii) Effective length of a seconds pendulum ata a place where g = 9.8 ms^{-2} is nearly 1 metre.

(iii) There will be no change in time period.

Chapter 2. Motion in One Dimension

Q. 1. Derive the following equations graphically for a uniformly accelerated motion.

(i) $v = u + at$

(ii) $S = ut + \dfrac{1}{2}at^2$

(iii) $v^2 = u^2 + 2aS$

Ans.

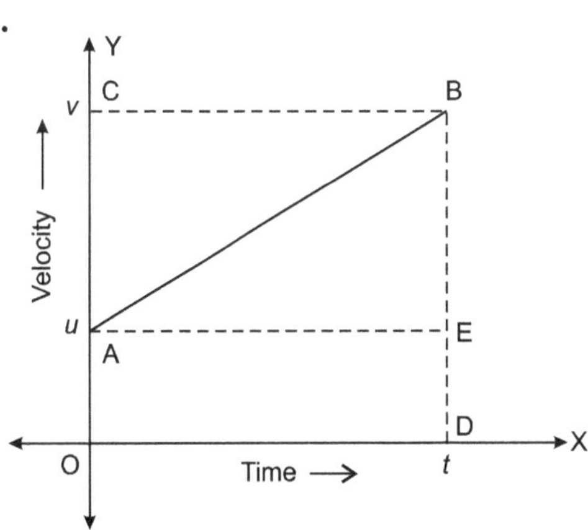

(i) Acceleration a = Slope of the line AB

$$a = \dfrac{EB}{AE}$$

$$= \dfrac{AC}{OD}$$

$$= \dfrac{OC - OA}{OD}$$

$$= \dfrac{v - u}{t}$$

$$\Rightarrow \qquad at = v - u$$
$$\Rightarrow \qquad v = u + at$$

(ii) The distance S travelled in time t

= Area of trapezium OABD

$$S = \dfrac{1}{2}(OA + DB) \times OD$$

$$S = \dfrac{1}{2}(u + v) \times t$$

But, $\quad v = u + at$

$$\therefore \qquad S = \dfrac{1}{2}(u + u + at) \times t$$

$$= \dfrac{1}{2}(2u + at) \times t$$

$$\Rightarrow \qquad S = ut + \dfrac{1}{2}at^2$$

(iii) Now, $\quad S = \dfrac{1}{2}(u + v)t$

and, $\quad t = \dfrac{v - u}{a}$

$$\therefore \qquad S = \dfrac{1}{2}(u + v)\left[\dfrac{v - u}{a}\right]$$

$$= \dfrac{1}{2}\left[\dfrac{v^2 - u^2}{a}\right]$$

$$\Rightarrow \qquad 2aS = v^2 - u^2$$
$$\therefore \qquad v^2 = u^2 + 2aS$$

Q. 2. Drive mathematically the three equations of motion.

Ans. (i) We know,

$$\text{Acceleration} = \frac{\text{Change in velocity}}{\text{Time taken}}$$

$$= \frac{\text{Final velocity} - \text{Initial velocity}}{\text{Time taken}}$$

$$\Rightarrow \quad a = \frac{v-u}{t}$$

$$\Rightarrow$$
$$\Rightarrow \quad at = v - u$$
$$v = u + at$$

Which is 1st equation of motion

(ii) Total distance covered = Average velocity $\times$ Time

$$\Rightarrow \quad S = \left(\frac{u+v}{2}\right) \times t$$

$$\Rightarrow \quad S = \left\{\frac{u+(u+at)}{2}\right\} \times t$$

$$\Rightarrow \quad S = \left(\frac{2u+at}{2}\right) \times t$$

$$\Rightarrow$$
$$S = ut + \frac{1}{2}at^2,$$

Which is 2nd equation of motion

(iii) Again,

Total distance travelled = Average velocity $\times$ Time

$$\Rightarrow \quad S = \left(\frac{u+v}{2}\right) \times t$$

From 1st equation of motion, we have

$$v = u + at$$

$$\Rightarrow \quad t = \frac{v-u}{a}$$

$$\therefore \quad S = \left(\frac{v+u}{2}\right)\left(\frac{v-u}{a}\right)$$

$$\Rightarrow \quad S = \frac{v^2 - u^2}{2a}$$

$$\Rightarrow \quad 2aS = v^2 - u^2,$$

Which is 3rd equation of motion.

Chapter 3. Laws of Motion

Q. 1. Obtain the mathematical expression of Newton's second law of motion.

Ans. Consider a body of mass 'm' kg.

Let the initial velocity be 'u'ms^{-1}.

It attains final velocity 'v' ms^{-1} in a time interval 't' sec.

Initial momentum of the body
$$= \text{'}mu\text{'} \text{ kgms}^{-1}$$

Final momentum of the body
$$= \text{'}mv\text{'} \text{ kgms}^{-1}$$

Change in momentum of the body
$$= (mv - mu) \text{ kgms}^{-1}$$

Rate of change of momentum
$$= \left(\frac{mv - mu}{t}\right) \text{ kgms}^{-2}$$

$$= m \times a$$

According to the Newton's second law,

Rate of change of momentum is directly proportional to the force applied.

Hence,

$$\text{Force} \propto m \times a$$

Substituting the proportionality constant K, we get,

$$\text{Force} = k \times m \times a.$$

When a unit force acts on a body of mass 1 kg producing in it an acceleration of 1 ms^{-2}, the value of $k = 1$.

Hence,

Force = mass $\times$ acceleration.

Q. 2. Illustrate Newton's third law of motion, giving some examples.

Ans. To illustrate Newton's third law of motion following are the examples:

(i) When a person walk on a ground, he pushes the ground in backward direction (action). The ground exerts an equal and opposite force on the person. The component of this force along the ground causes the person to move forward.

(ii) Jet aeroplanes/rockets also work on the principle of action and reaction. The hot and highly compressed gases produced due to burning of fuel escape through a jet (nozzle) at the rear end of the jet aircraft with a high speed (action). The escaping gases push the jet plane forward (reaction) with the same force. In rocket, hot gases rush out a jet at the bottom of the rocket at a very high speed thereby the downward going gases push the rocket upward with a high speed.

(iii) When a swimmer swims, he pushes the water backwards (action). The water pushes the swimmer forward (reaction) with the same force.

(iv) When a bullet is fired from a gun, it moves forward with a certain force (action), the gun recoils in the backward direction with an equal and opposite force (reaction).

(v) When two coupled spring balances, P and Q are pulled apart, balance P pulls Q towards it (action) and pulls P towards it with an equal and opposite force (reaction). Hence both the spring balances show the same reading.

Q. 3. Mention a few examples in which one body influences the other body and vice versa but they are not in contact.

Ans. For interaction, the bodies need not always be in contact. The bodies can exert force on each other from a distance also, e.g. a magnet exerts a force on the iron piece even when they are seperated by a distance. A comb rubbed in dry hair attracts bits of paper from a distance. The ball released from a height is pulled by earth, etc.

Q. 4. What exactly is the mass? Explain the relation between mass and inertia.

Ans. The mass of a body is the characteristic of that body that relates the body's acceleration to the force causing the acceleration.

Relation between mass and inertia: Let us consider two balls at rest; one cricket ball of mass m_c and the other light plastic ball of mass m_p, where $m_c > m_p$. Give a gentle blow to each ball for sometime. Due to equal force, the plastic ball attains much greater speed v_p than the cricket ball v_c. The change in velocity of plastic ball is $v_p - 0 = v_p$ and cricket ball is $v_c - 0 = v_c$ and $v_p > v_c$. It clearly shows that the ball with less mass has less resistance to change in speed or change in motion a while. The ball with greater mass has greater resistance to the change in speed or change in motion.

Similarly, if we try to stop the balls moving with the same speed or try to change their direction of motion, it is experienced that it is more difficult to stop the ball of greater mass m_c, (cricket ball) than the ball of lesser mass m_p (plastic ball). It also shows that resistance is more for greater mass and less for smaller mass. Thus, we can conclude that mass of a body is the measure of its inertia. The greater the mass, the more is the inertia.

Q. 5. Obtain the formula F = **ma** from Newton's second law of motion. In the formula, the symbols have their usual meaning.

Ans. According to Newton's second law of motion, the rate of change of momentum of a body is directly proportional to the force applied and takes place in the direction of force.

Consider a body of mass m whose velocity changes from u to v in time t on applying a force of magnitude F.

The magnitude of the initial momentum of the body $p_1 = mu$. The magnitude of the final momentum of the body $p_2 = mv$.

Change in momentum of the body $= (p_2 - p_1)$
$$= mv - mu = m(v - u)$$

Rate of change of momentum
$$= \frac{(p_2 - p_1)}{t}$$
$$= \frac{m(v - u)}{t}$$

According to Newton's second law of motion,

the magnitude of force $F \propto \dfrac{(p_2 - p_1)}{t}$

$$= \frac{k(p_2 - p_1)}{t}, \text{ where } k \text{ is constant of}$$
proportionality.

or $\qquad F = \dfrac{km(v - u)}{t}$

$\Rightarrow \qquad F = kma \qquad \qquad ...(i)$

$$\left[\because \text{acceleration, } a = \frac{v - u}{t} \right]$$

If we choose the unit of force as a unit force, then the unit force will be that force which will produce unit acceleration in a body of unit mass.

i.e., if F = 1 unit, m = 1 unit and a = 1 unit, then
$$1 = k \times 1 \times 1 \text{ or } k = 1$$

The equation (i) will be

$$F = ma$$

or

$$a \propto \frac{F}{m}$$

i.e., the acceleration produced in a body is directly proportional to the force acting on it and inversely proportional to the mass of the body, the acceleration being in the direction of the force applied.

Chapter 4. Pressure in Fluids and Atmospheric Pressure

Q. 1. State the laws of fluid pressure.

Ans. Laws of fluid pressure:

(i) Pressure in fluids at a point is directly proportional to depth (h) of the point from free fluid surface.

(ii) Pressure in fluids at a point is directly proportional to density (ρ) of the fluid.

(iii) Pressure in fluids at a point is directly proportional to acceleration due to gravity (g).

(iv) Pressure in fluids at a point is independent of the area of cross-section.

(v) Pressure in fluids at a point is same in all directions.

Q. 2. Obtain an expression for the pressure at a depth inside a liquid.

Ans.

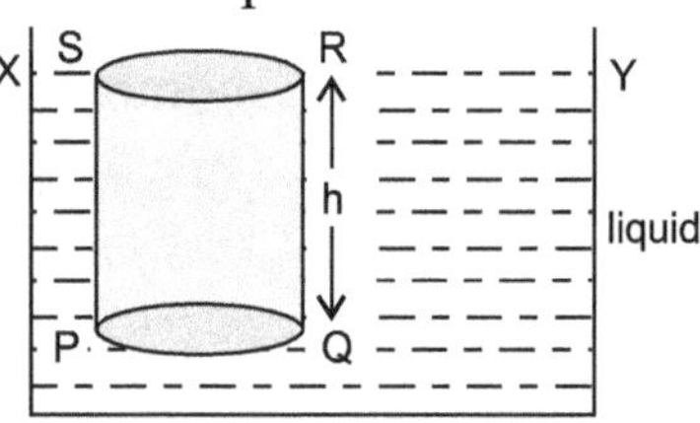

Pressure at a depth inside a liquid

Consider a vessel containing a stationary liquid of density ρ in which a cylinder PQRS of height h with PQ as its base and top face RS lying on the free surface XY of the liquid.

Thrust exerted on the surface PQ

= Weight of the liquid column PQRS

= Volume of liquid column PQRS × density × g

= (Area of base PQ × height) × density × g

= (A × h) × ρ × g = A$h\rho g$

$$\text{Pressure} = \frac{\text{Thrust}}{\text{Area}} = \frac{Ah\rho g}{A}$$

$$\therefore \quad P = h\rho g$$

Q. 3. State the weather forecast in the following situations:

(i) Air is hot and dry and atmospheric pressure falls suddenly.

(ii) Air is humid and barometric pressure falls suddenly.

(iii) Barometric pressure falls rapidily.

(iv) Barometric pressure rises steeply.

(v) Barometric pressure falls gradually over number of days.

Ans. (i) The forecast is dust storm

(ii) The forecast is rain storm

(iii) The forecast is dry weather with strong anticyclonic winds.

(iv) The forecast is fair weather.

(v) The forecast is that weather gradually changes from fair to windy over number of days.

Q. 4. Explain how aneroid barometer is used

(i) For forcasting weather

(ii) As an altimeter?

Ans. (i) If the barometric height on a particular day is less than normal height, it shows fall in pressure. If fall in pressure is steep it could mean dust storm or rain. However, if there is gradual drop in pressure, it means that weather will change from normal to windy. If there is no change in height, it is fair weather. If there is a rise in barometric height it means dry or anticyclonic weather.

(ii) Altimeter: It has been established that for a vertical rise of 105 m, the barometric height drops by 1 m. This fact is used in the construction of altimeter, where fall in height of mercury column is calibrated as height of a place.

Q. 5. How will you set up a simple barometer in a laboratory?

Ans. Take a tube 1 m long, closed at one end. Fill it completely with mercury. By placing thumb on the open end of tube, invert the tube in the bowl of mercury and then remove the thumb. It is seen that fairly large length of mercury is supported in the tube. On measuring the length of mercury from its level in tube to the level of mercury in the bowl, it is found to be 76 cm at sea level. This length is equivalent to atmospheric pressure.

Q. 6. State the precautions for the use of a simple barometer.

Ans. (i) The barometer tube should be perfectly clean and dry.

(ii) The mercury should be pure and dry

(iii) No air bubbles should be left inside the tube filled with mercury.

(iv) Record the vertical height of mercury column in the tube, by holding the tube in an upright position.

Q. 7. Draw a simple diagram of a hydraulic jack and explain how it works.

Ans.

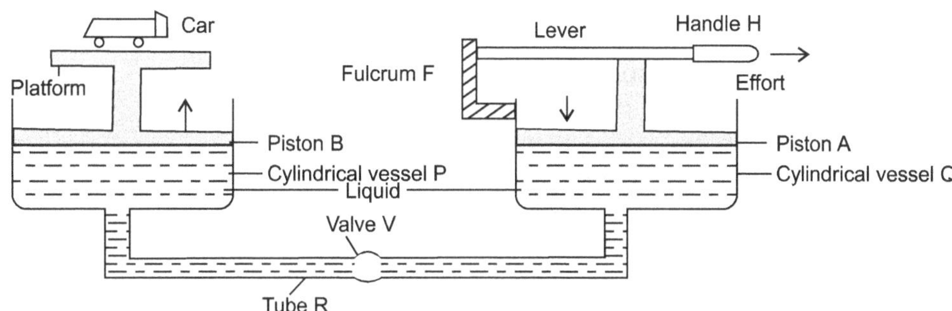

Working:
(i) When the handle H of the lever is pressed down by applying the effort, the valve opens because of increase in pressure in the cylinder P.
(ii) The liquid runs out from the cylinder P to the cylinder Q.
(iii) As a result, the piston B rises up and it raises the car placed on the platform.
(iv) When the car reaches the desired height, the handle H of the lever is no longer pressed.
(v) The valve gets closed so that the liquid may not run back from the cylinder Q to the cylinder P.

Q. 8. Describe an experiment to demonstrate that air exerts pressure.

Ans. Take a thin tin can fitted with an airtight stopper.

(i) Initially the shape of the thin tin container is maintained as the pressure inside the can is the same as the air pressure outside.

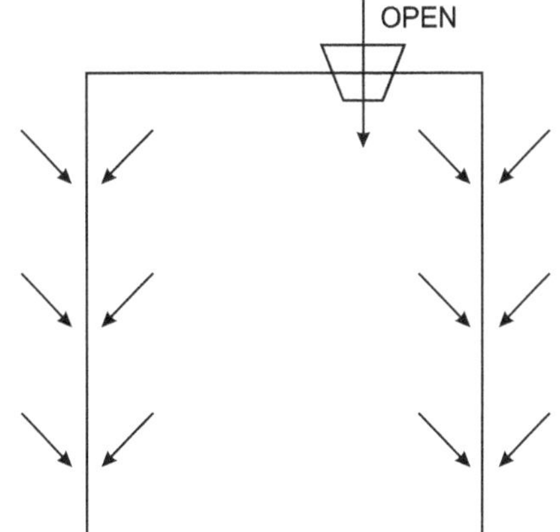

(ii) Water is filled in the can and boiled. This drives out much of the air. The pressure of the steam still equals that of the air outside.

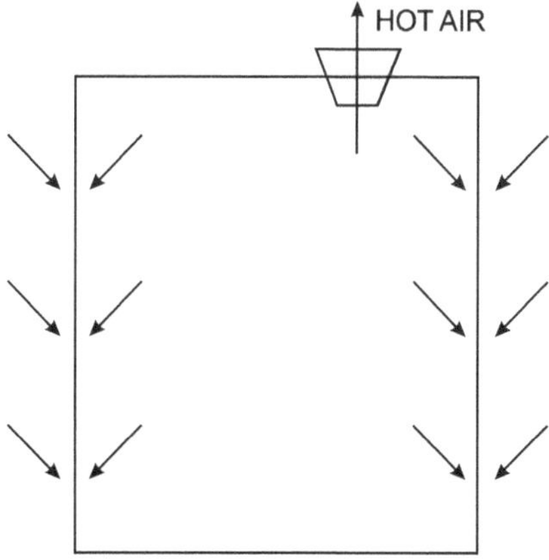

(iii) Replacing the cap prevents entry of air. As the steam cools and condenses to water, a partial vacuum is created.

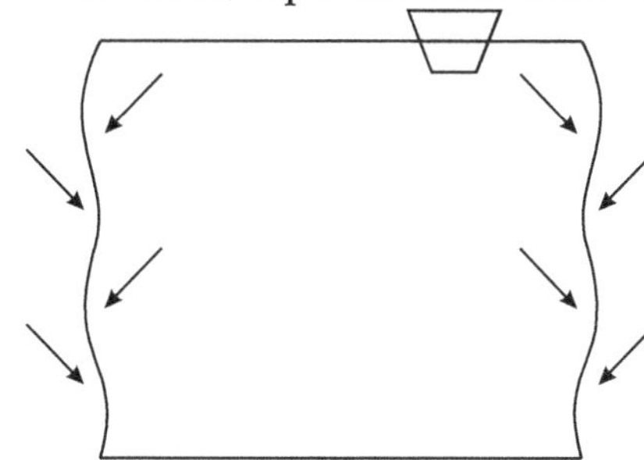

(iv) The pressure outside is now greater than the inside pressure and the excess atmospheric pressure outside causes the can to collapse.

Above experiment demonstrates how the atmosphere exerts pressure inwards at any surface.

Q. 9. (i) State the principle of working of an altimeter.

(ii) How is barometric height altered when a drop of water is introduced in a mercury barometer tube?

Ans. (i) Altimeter is a device with a scale directly indicating altitude in metres instead of atmospheric pressure. It is also known as an aneroid barometer. The variations in the atmospheric pressure make the sides of a partially evacuated corrugated box, move inwards or outwards.

This movement is magnified by a system of gears and levers and transmitted to a fine chain wrapped around the spindle of a pointer. The chain is kept stretched by means of a hair-spring attached to the spindle. The chain moves the pointer on a suitably graduated scale clockwise when the pressure increases and anticlockwise when the pressure decreases.

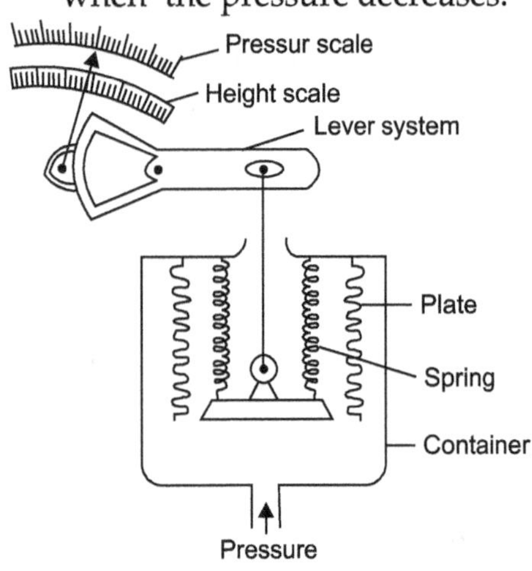

(ii) The drop reaching the Torricellian vacuum vaporizes and the vapour exerts pressure. Hence the barometric height decreases.

Q. 10. Why and how does the atmospheric pressure vary with altitude? Draw a graph to illustrate it.

Ans. As we go to higher altitudes, the atmospheric pressure is found to decrease due to (i) decrease in height h of the air column and (ii) the decrease in air density ρ.

The decrease in atmospheric pressure with altitude is not linear. It decreases by nearly 1.0 cm of mercury height for 102 m ascent. The variation of atmospheric pressure with altitude is shown in the figure.

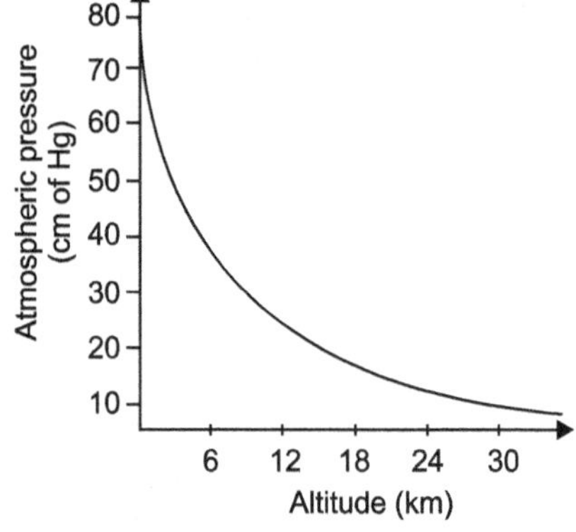

Q. 11. Draw a diagram illustrating the principle of the hydraulic press and explain briefly its action.

Ans. Hydraulic press: It is used to compress the soft materials like cotton, cloth, paper, etc. into compact bales. Its working is based on Pascal's law.

The hydraulic press is shown in the figure given below.

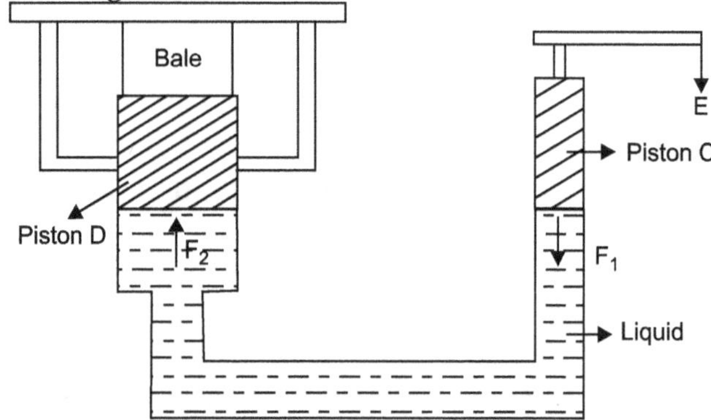

The pistons C and D fit tightly inside the vessels filled with liquid as shown in figure. A small effort F_1 is applied through the small piston C of area A_1. A pressure $P = F_1/A_1$, will be transmitted to the large piston D of area A_2. The thrust on this piston $F_2 = P \times A_2 = F_1 \times \dfrac{A_2}{A_1}$. So, an effort F_1 applied on the smaller piston C is multiplied to compress the bale.

Q. 12. Name the instrument used for measuring atmospheric pressure and describe it.

Ans. To measure the atmospheric pressure, barometer is used.

A simple barometer was constructed by Torricelli in 1643. It consists of a glass tube of uniform bore of one metre length closed at one end. Fill the whole tube with pure and dry mercury taking care that no air or water droplet remains inside the tube. Close the open end of tube tightly with your thumb and invert the tube inside the pure and dry mercury contained in a trough. Now remove the thumb keeping the end of the tube inside the mercury trough. Hold the tube as shown in the figure.

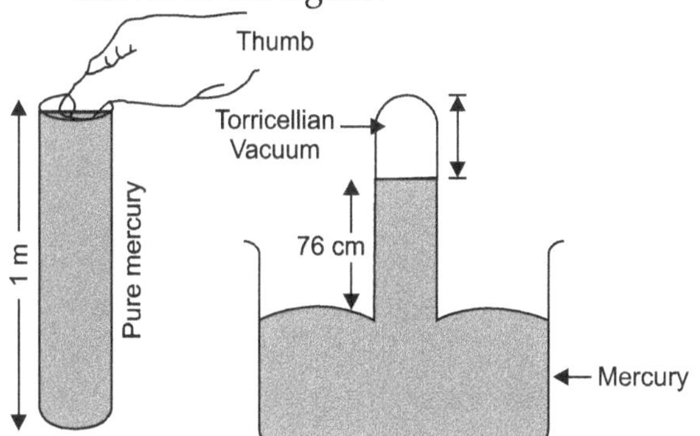

It is observed that the mercury in the tube firstly falls and becomes stationary at a particular position, thereby creates an empty space which is known as Torricellian vacuum. It is found that the height of the level of mercury in the tube at the sea level is nearly 76 cm above the free level of mercury in the trough. In equilibrium state, the pressure exerted by 76 cm vertical height of mercury column is equal to the pressure exerted by 76 cm vertical height of the trough. In other words, the vertical height of mercury column, from the mercury surface in trough to the level in tube, is a measure of atmospheric pressure.

Chapter 5. Upthrust in Fluids 'Archimedes' Principle and Floatation

Q. 1. (i) A cargo ship is loaded in sea water to maximum capacity. What will happen if this ship is moved to river water? Give a reason for your answer.

(ii) A body of mass 100 g is floating in water. What will be its apparent weight ? Justify your answer.

Ans. (i) The density of river water is lower than the density of sea water.

If a cargo ship loaded in sea water to maximum capacity, is moved to river water, it sinks deeper because river water is less denser than sea water. Hence, the more volume of river water is required to be displaced to balance its weight along with its cargo.

(ii) If a body of mass 100 g is floating in water, it will experience an upthrust due to water displaced by immersed part of the body. For a floating body, upthrust is equal to the weight of the body. Therefore, the apparent weight *i.e.*, the weight of the body in air- upthrust of a floating body is zero.

Q. 2.

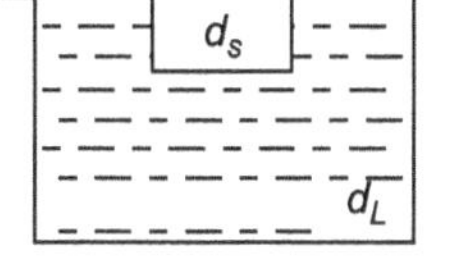

The figure above shows a solid of density d_s floating in a liquid of density d_L.

(i) What is the relation between d_s and d_L in the above case?

(ii) What is the apparent weight of the floating body?

(iii) The same solid floats in water with $3/5^{th}$ of its volume immersed in it. Calculate the density of the solid. (density of water = 1 g cm^{-3}).

[February, 2020]

Ans. (i) $d_s < d_L$

(ii) Zero.

(iii) Let the volume of the solid be V and its density be ρ.

∴ Volume of submerged part of solid

$$= \frac{3}{5} V$$

Applying principle of floatation:
Weight of floating body = Weight of water displaced by the immersed part of the body

$$\Rightarrow \quad V\rho g = \frac{3}{5} V \times 1 \times g$$

[∵ density of water = 1 g cm^{-3}]

$$\Rightarrow \quad \rho = \frac{3}{5} \text{ g cm}^{-3}$$

$$= 0.6 \text{ g cm}^{-3}.$$

Chapter 6. Heat and Energy

Q. 1. What is solar energy? How is the solar energy used to generate electricity in a solar power plant?

Ans. The energy obtained from Sun is called solar energy. A solar power plant is a device in which heat energy of Sun is used to generate electricity. It consists of a large number of concave reflectors, at the focus of which there are black painted water pipes. The reflectors concentrate the heat energy of the sun rays on the pipes due to which water inside the pipes starts boiling and produces steam. The steam, thus produced is used to rotate a steam turbine which drives a generator, producing electricity.

Q. 2. State two advantages and two disadvantages of producing electricity from solar energy.

Ans. **Advantages of producing electricity from solar energy:**
(i) It is suitable for producing electricity in remote and inaccessible places, where electricity power lines cannot be laid.
(ii) It is does not cause any pollution.
Disadvantages of producing electricity from solar energy:
(i) The initial cost of entire set up is sufficiently high.
(ii) The efficiency of conversion of solar energy to electric energy is low.

Q. 3. What important consequences follow the peculiar property of water? Discuss the importance of this phenomenon in nature.

Ans. The peculiar property of water *i.e.,* anomalous expansion of water, helps in preserving the aquatic life during the very cold weather. In winters, when the temperature falls, the top layer of water in a pond contracts, becomes denser and sinks to the bottom. A circulation is thus set up until the entire water in the pond reaches its maximum density at 4°C. If the temperature falls further, then the top layer expands and remains on the top till it freezes. Thus, even though the upper layers are frozen, the water near the bottom is at 4°C and the fishes can survive in it easily.

Q. 4. What is hydro energy? Explain the principle of generating electricity from hydro energy. How much hydroelectric power is generated in India?

Ans. The kinetic energy possessed by flowing water is called the water or hydro energy. Principle of a hydroelectric power plant is that the water flowing in high altitude rivers is collected in a high dam (or reservoir). The water from the dam is then allowed to fall on a water turbine which is located near the bottom of the dam. The shaft of the turbine is connected to the armature of an electric generator or dynamo.
At present only 23% of the total electricity is generated by the hydro energy.

Q. 5. State two advantages and two disadvantages of producing hydro-electricity.

Ans. **Advantages of producing the hydro-electricity:**
(i) It does not produce any environmental pollution.
(ii) It is a renewable source of energy.
Disadvantages of producing hydro-electricity:
(i) Due to the construction of dams over the rivers, plants and animals of that place get destroyed or killed.
(ii) The ecological balance in the downstream areas of rivers gets disturbed.

Q. 6. What is nuclear energy? Explain the principle used for producing electricity using the nuclear energy.

Ans. When a heavy nucleus is bombarded with slow neutrons, it splits into two nearly equal light nuclei with a release of tremendous amount of energy. In this process of nuclear fission, the total sum of masses of products is less than the total sum of masses of reactants. This lost mass gets converted into energy. The energy so released is called nuclear energy.
Principle: The heat energy released due to the controlled chain reaction of nuclear fission of uranium-235 in a nuclear

reactor is absorbed by the coolant which then passes through the coils of a heat exchanger containing water. The water in heat exchanger gets heated and converts into steam. The steam is used to rotate the turbine which in turn rotates the armature of a generator in a magnetic field and thus produces electricity.

Q. 7. State two advantages and two disadvantages of using nuclear energy for producing electricity.

Ans. Advantages of using nuclear energy:

(i) A very small amount of nuclear fuel can produce a tremendous amount of energy.

(ii) Once the nuclear fuel is loaded into nuclear power plant, it continues to release energy for several years.

Disadvantages of using nuclear energy:

(i) It is not a clean source of energy because very harmful nuclear radiations are produced in the process.

(ii) The waste obtained from nuclear power plants causes environmental pollution.

Q. 8. Describe an experiment to show that water has maximum density at 4°C.

Ans. Hope's experiment:

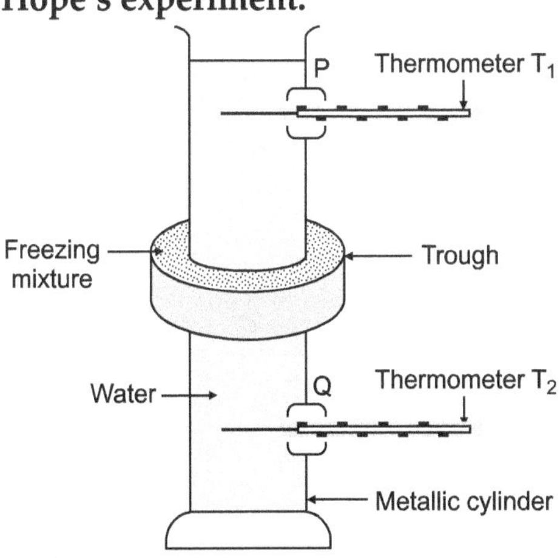

Hope's apparatus consists of a tall metallic cylinder provided with two side openings P and Q, fitted with thermometers T_1 and T_2 in them. The central part of the cylinder is surrounded with a cylindrical trough containing a freezing mixture of ice and salt. The cylinder is fitted with pure water at room temperature.

Observations:

(i) Initially, both thermometers T_1 and T_2 are at the same temperature.

(ii) First, the temperature recorded by the lower thermometer T_2 starts decreasing and finally it becomes steady at 4 °C, while the temperature recorded in the upper thermometer T_1 remains almost unchanged during this time.

(iii) Then, the temperature recorded by the lower thermometer T_2 remains constant at 4°C and upper thermometer T_1 records a continuous fall in temperature up to 0 °C and then it becomes steady.

Thus, finally, the temperature recorded by the upper thermometer is 0 °C and that by lower thermometer is 4 °C.

Explanation: As the freezing mixture cools water in the central portion of the cylinder, water contracts and its density increases, consequently it sinks to the bottom, thereby causing the reading of the lower thermometer T_2 to fall rapidly. The reading of the upper thermometer T_1 does not change as the temperature of water in the upper part does not change. This continues till the entire water below the central portion reaches 4°C. On cooling further below 4°C, due to anomalous expansion, water of the central portion expands, so its density decreases and hence it rises up. As a result, reading of the upper thermometer T_1 falls rapidly to 0°C and water freezes to form ice at 0°C near the top. At this stage, the lower thermometer T_2 shows 4°C at which water has the maximum density. This proves that water has maximum density at 4°C.

Q.9. Figure shows a hard glass test tube containing coloured water, such that level of water is up to point A. The test tube is placed in a large beaker containing boiling hot water. It is observed that level of coloured water first drops to B and then rises up to C.

Long Answers

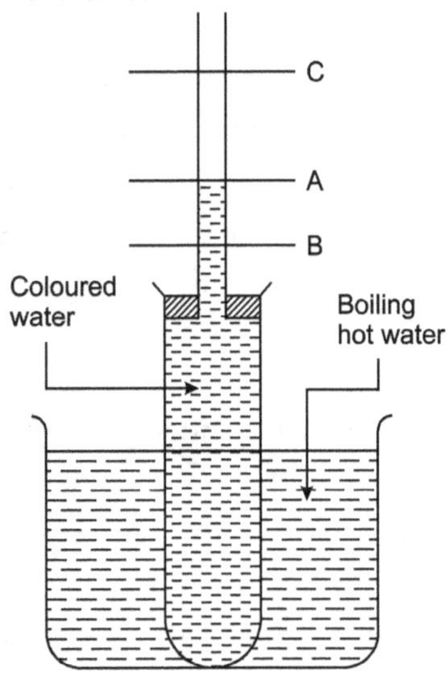

Answer the following questions:

(i) Why is there a drop in the level of water?

(ii) Why does the level of water start rising after some time?

(iii) State two important deductions which can be made regarding the action of heat on liquids from the above observations.

(iv) If the test tube is placed in ice cold water, instead of boiling hot water, state your observations with reasons.

Ans. (i) The test tube expands first, but not the coloured water. Due to the increase in volume of test tube, the level of water drops from A to B.

(ii) It is because liquid after gaining heat expands and hence, level of liquid rises to C.

(iii) (a) Liquids expand on heating.

(b) Liquids expand more than solids (glass).

(iv) Initially, the level of liquid rises in glass tubing and then falls down. It is because initially the test tube contracts but not coloured water. Thus, level of water rises up. However, when coloured liquid contracts, the level falls down.

Q. 10. Describe the energy flow in an ecosystem.

Ans. Ecosystems maintain themselves by cycling energy and nutrients obtained from external sources. At the first trophic level, primary producers (plants, algae, and some bacteria) use solar energy to produce organic plant material through photosynthesis. Herbivores animals that feed solely on plants make up the second trophic level. Predators that eat herbivores comprise the third trophic level. If larger predators are present, they represent still higher trophic levels. Decomposers, which include bacteria, fungi, etc. break down wastes and dead organisms and return nutrients to the soil.

On an average, about 10 percent of net energy production at one trophic level is passed on to the next level. Processes that reduce the energy transferred between trophic levels include respiration, growth and reproduction, defecation, and non-predatory death.

The low rate of energy transfer between trophic levels makes decomposers generally more important than producers in terms of energy flow. Decomposers process large amounts of organic material and return nutrients to the ecosystem in inorganic forms, which are then taken up again by primary producers.

Q. 11. What do you mean by a pyramid of energy? Can the pyramid of energy be inverted? If not why?

Ans. An energy pyramid indicates the amount of energy available at each trophic level as well as role played by the organisms at each level. The figure shows that the maximum energy available at the producer level and the energy available at each successive level, *i.e.*, primary, secondary and tertiary consumer level goes on decreasing. Therefore, the pyramid of energy can never be inverted.

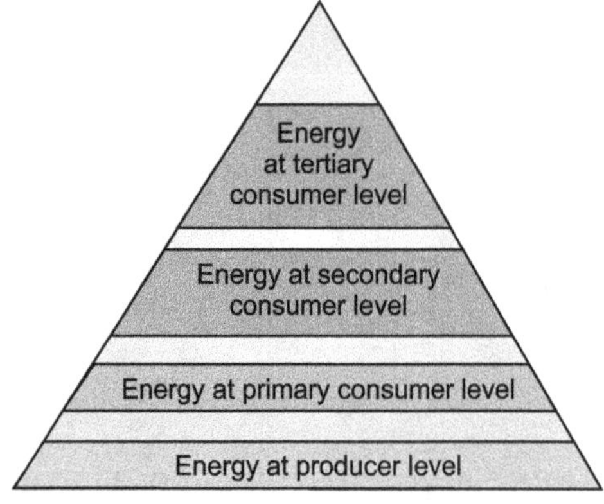

Pyramid of energy

Q. 12. State five advantages of biogas.

Ans. (i) A biogas plant can be built in rural India. A small plant using dung from 3 to 4 heads of can is capable of supplying biogas for about 6 hours daily.

(ii) It is a clean fuel that burns without smoke and leaves no ash.

(iii) Its main constituent gas, methane has higher calorific value (~ 55 kJ/g) than that of coal (17 kJ/g) or petrol (50 kJ/g).

(iv) The spent slurry is a good manure because it is rich in nitrogen and phosphorus.

(v) By using biogas, firewood is saved and this reduces the cutting of forests.

Q. 13. State some measures to conserve natural resources.

Ans. In order to conserve natural resources, the following measures should be taken:

(i) Non-renewable resources such as coal, petroleum, minerals and natural gas should be used sparingly as possible so that these can last for a longer period of time.

(ii) The projected life spans of various minerals should be extended by recycling, substitution and synthesis.

(iii) The alternative of the energy sources should be discovered so that existing non-renewable resources can be conserved.

(iv) Renewable natural resources should be used only at the rate at which they are being replenished in nature. For example, groundwater should be used in proportion to its natural accumulation through rains.

Q.14. Biomass fuel is of three types: solid liquid and gas. Which biomass fuels are included in the category of solid, liquid and gas?

Ans. The solid biomass includes fuels such as wood charcoal, fuelwood and animal dung.

The liquid biomass includes fuels such as methanol and ethanol. This liquid biomass can be used in the engine of automobiles.

The gas biomass includes biogas which is obtained from animal dung. It is a mixture of mainly 60% methane and 40% carbon dioxide.

Q. 15. Define wind. What is wind energy? State the source, nature and use of wind energy.

Ans. The motion of air along the surface of the earth is called wind.

The kinetic energy possesed by air due to its velocity is called wind energy.

Solar energy is the main factor responsible for the movement of air in the atmosphere. It is renewable source of energy. Wind energy can be utilized for performing mechanical and electric works, *i.e.*, to pump the water and generate electricity.

Q. 16. What is biogas? How is it obtained? State its composition.

Ans. Biogas is a mixture of gases produced by anaerobic degradation of biomass in the presence of water and in the absence of oxygen. It is a renewable source of energy because it is produced from continuously available organic wastes. It is mainly composed of methane up to 75% and carbon dioxide up to 25% and traces of nitrogen and hydrogen gases. Methane has a high calorific value of 55 kJ/g.

Q. 17. What is an anaerobic degradation?

Ans. Anaerobic microorganisms called anaerobic bacteria survive in the absence of oxygen. These bacteria decompose the biomass which contains carbon compounds, *i.e.*, carbohydrates, proteins and fats through a complex series of reactions into a mixture of gases which is called biogas. On producing biogas, the manurial value of the biomass is not reduced. Instead the spent slurry is an enriched manure because it has a higher content of nitrogen, phosphorus and potassium.

Q.18. Write a brief note on mineral resources and its conservation.

Ans. The core of earth is composed of various types of rocks which contain a mixture of different minerals. The mineral stores of earth fulfil the demand of energy, requirement of nutrients for living organisms and other economical requirements. The quantity of minerals is limited and unevenly distributed. The minerals being non-renewable resources, should be judiciously cconsumed so that their reserves may last long. For this, the objects should be used again and again as far as possible; the discard objects must be recycled to get new products and the more available minerals should be used in place of less available minerals.

Q.19. What is the reason of increase in carbon dioxide's share of atmosphere? What is its result?

Ans. Since the beginning of the industrial revolution, carbon dioxide in the atmosphere is increased nearly 40% *i.e.*, nearly from 280 parts per million volume to more than 380 parts per million volume. It is mostly due to anthropogenic (man-incluced) factors. *i.e.*, burning of fossil fuels, deforestation and, industrial production. The increasing amount of carbon dioxide in the atmosphere enhances greenhouse effect and subsequently climate change.

Q. 20. What is a greenhouse effect? Explain.

Ans. A greenhouse is an enclosure made of glass or polythene to grow plants during all seasons. A glass or polythene allows light and the short wavelength heat radiations to enter into the enclosure, various plants absorb these radiations readily. Thus, they get heated in this process and emit heat radiations of comparatively longer wavelength. The glass or polythene being opaque to heat radiations of its wavelength, does not allow to pass them out and thus, keep the inside of the greenhouse warm. Hence, the temperature inside the greenhouse is maintained for the proper growth of plants.

Q. 21. Why does the interior of a car become too hot when parked in the Sun as compared to the temperature outside?

Ans. The interior of a car parked in the Sun becomes too hot because windowpanes allow the wavelength (infrared) radiations to enter inside the car where they are absorbed by the seat cover. Now the inside accessories emit the heat radiations of longer wavelength, which are not allowed to go out of the car. Thus, the interior of the car becomes too hot.

Q. 22. State some ways for the judicious use of energy.

Ans. Following measures must be taken for the judicious use of energy.

(i) Cutting of trees must be banned and planting of trees should be encouraged.

(ii) Wastage of energy should be avoided.

(iii) Efforts must be made to make use of energy in community.

(iv) Efforts should be made to obtain more and more energy from renewable sources.

Chapter 7. Reflection of Light

Q. 1. Compare the characteristics of an image formed by a convex mirror and a concave mirror, when object is beyond centre of curvature, but not at infinity in case of concave mirror and in between pole and infinity in case of convex mirror.

Ans.

S. No.	Concave mirror	Convex mirror
(i)	Image is real.	Image is virtual.
(ii)	Image is inverted.	Image is upright.
(iii)	Size of image is highly diminished.	Size of image is highly diminished.
(iv)	Image is formed between principal focus and centre of curvature.	Image is formed between pole and principal focus.

Q. 2. State the rules for obtaining images formed by a concave mirror.

Ans. Following are the rules for obtaining images by a concave mirror.

Rule 1. A ray passing through (or directed towards) the centre of curvature of a concave mirror, is reflected back along its own path.

Rule 2. A ray incident parallel to the principal axis, after reflection from a concave mirror passes through focus.

Rule 3. A ray either incident from the focus after reflection from a concave mirror becomes parallel to the principal axis.

Q. 3. State the rules for drawing geometric images in convex mirrors.

Ans. Rules for drawing geometric images in convex mirrors:

(i) Any ray of light, travelling parallel to the principal axis of convex mirror, after reflection, appears to pass through the principal focus of the mirror.

(ii) Any ray of light travelling along the principal focus of convex mirror, aftrer reflection, travels parallel to the principal axis.

(iii) Any ray of light travelling along the centre of curvature of a convex mirror, after reflection, retraces its path.

Q. 4. State five characteristics of image formed in plane mirror.

Ans. Characteristics of image formed in plane mirror are as follows:

(i) Image formed by a plane mirror is virtual.

(ii) Image is erect.

(iii) Image is of same size as object.

(iv) Image is laterally inverted.

(v) Image is formed as far behind the mirror, as the object is in front of it.

Q. 5. State three ways, in which image formed in plane mirror differs from image formed in pin hole camera.

Ans.

Image formed in plane mirror	Image formed in pin hole camera
Virtual	Real
Same size as object	Diminished
Laterally inverted but erect.	Inverted

Q. 6. Prove experimentally that images are formed as far behind in a plane mirror as the object is in front of it.

Ans.

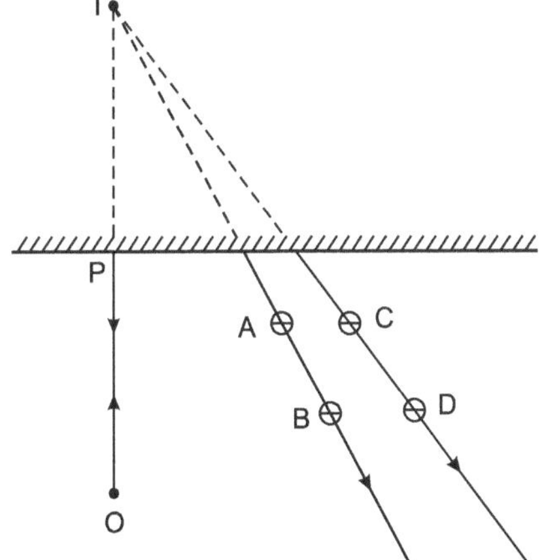

Place a plane mirror strip in an upright position on a white sheet of paper, which is mounted on a wooden board and hold it by a mirror stand.

Fix a pin at point 'O' in front of mirror and look for its image I. Looking at the image, fix two pins A and B, such that these pins and the image I are in same straight line. Remove the pins and draw small circles around the pin points A and B. Similarly, fix two pins C and D in line with the image I. Remove the pins and draw small circles around the pin points C and D. Join AB and CD and produce them backward to meet at I. Thus, I is the image of O. Join OI, such that it cuts the mirror line at P. Measure PO and PI.

It is seen that PO = PI.

Thus, in a plane mirror, image is formed as far behind the mirror as the object in front of it.

Q. 7. Why do automobile drivers prefer convex mirror as a rear view mirror? Illustrate your answer.

Ans. Automobile drivers prefer convex mirror as a rear view mirror because, it can cover a very wide field behind the driver and hence enables him to see the traffic behind him without turning his head backward.

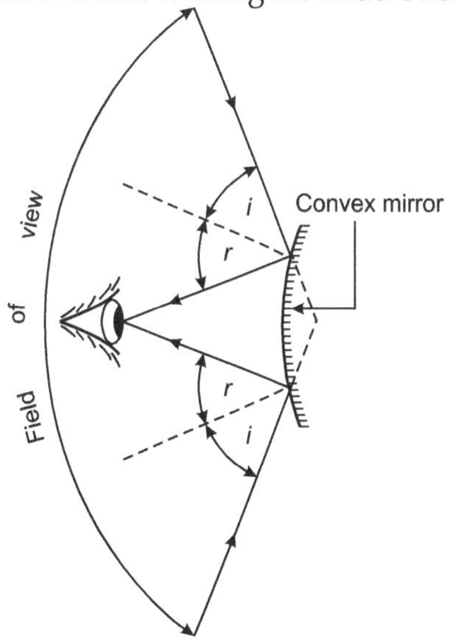

Chapter 8. Prorogation of Sound Waves

Q. 1. Explain with an example, the propagation of sound in a medium.

Ans. Take a vertical metal strip with its lower end fixed and upper end being free to vibrate as shown in fig (i). As the strip is moved to right from a to b as shown in Fig (ii), the air in that layer is compressed (compression is formed at C). The particles of this layer compress the layer next to it, which then compresses the next layer and so on. Thus, the disturbance moves forward in the form of compression without the particles themselves being displaced from their mean positions.

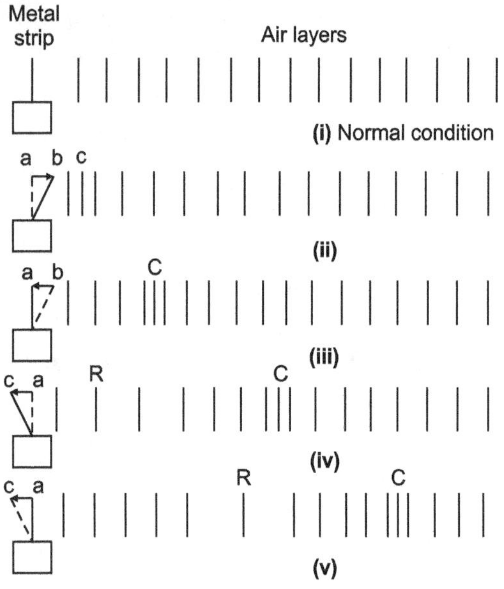

As the metal strip returns from b to a as shown in Fig (iii) after pushing the particles in front, the compression C moves forward and particles of air near the strip return to their normal positions.When the strip moves from a to c as shown in Fig (iv), it pushes back the layer of air near it towards left and thus produces a low pressure space on its right side *i.e.*, layers of air get rarefied. This region is called rarefaction (rarefaction is formed at R).When the strip returns from C to its mean position a in Fig (v), the rarefaction R travels forward and air near the strip return to their normal positions.Thus, one complete to and fro motion of the strip forms one compression and one rarefaction, which together form one wave. This wave through which sound travels in air is called longitudinal wave.

Q. 2. Draw a curve showing density or pressure variations with respect to distance for a disturbance produced by sound. Mark the position of compression and rarefaction on this curve. Also define wavelengths and time period using this curve.

Ans. The curve showing density or pressure variations with respect to distance for a disturbance produced by sound is shown below:

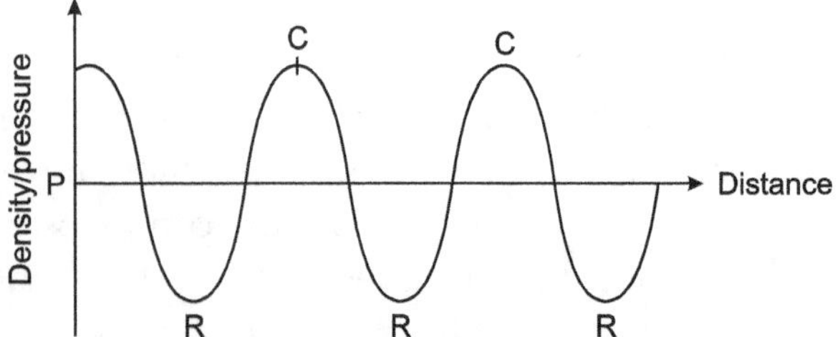

Wavelength: It is defined as the distance between two successive compressions or two successive rarefactions.

Time period: It is defined as the time taken by the disturbance to travel between two successive compressions or between two successive rarefactions.

Q. 3. Describe an experiment to prove that material medium is necessary for the propagation of sound.

Ans. An electric circuit consisting of a battery, a switch, an electric bell is arranged inside a bell jar, which is placed on the platform of an evacuated pump as shown in diagram below. The switch of the electric circuit is pressed in, when a clear sound of bell is heard. Air is now removed from the bell jar by evacuating the pump. It is noticed that intensity of sound gradually decreases. When the bell jar is completely evacuated, it is noticed that no sound is heard when the hammer of bell is striking the gong.

Thus, experiment clearly proves that material medium (in the present case, air) is necessary for the propagation of sound energy.

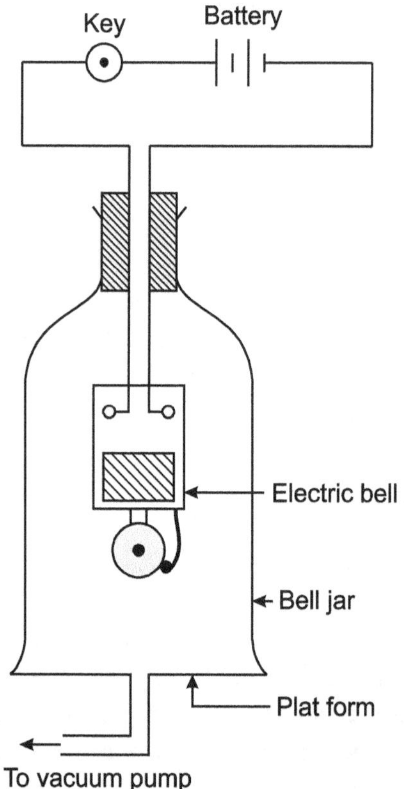

Chapter 9. Current Electricity

Long Answers

Q. 1. Sphere A is positively charged and sphere B is negatively charged. Both the spheres A and B are brought in electrical contact by a copper wire.

Answer the following questions:

(i) Which sphere is at higher potential before electrical contact on the basis of convention?

(ii) Which sphere is at lower potential before electrical contact on the basis of convention?

(iii) In which direction conventional current flows?

(iv) In which direction electronic current flows?

(v) What is potential of the spheres after electrical contact?

Ans. (i) On the basis of convention, positively charged sphere A is at higher potential before electrical contact.

(ii) On the basis of convention, negatively charged sphere B is at lower potential before electrical contact.

(iii) Conventional current flows from sphere A to sphere B *i.e.*, from a body at higher potential to the body at lower potential.

(iv) Electronic current flows from sphere B to sphere A *i.e.*, from a body at lower potential to the body at higher potential.

(v) After electrical contact, both the spheres will be at same potential.

Q. 2. How electric current flows in (i) solids, (ii) liquids?

Ans. (i) In solids, the positive charges are associated with atomic nuclei. As the nuclei are firmly packed and closely held by inter-atomic forces, therefore, positive charges cannot drift. On the other hand, negative charges (electrons) are not held firmly. Thus, when a potential difference, however small, is applied they start drifting from lower to higher potential. The continuous drift of electrons, through the body of a solid conductor constitutes an electric current.

(ii) Within a liquid, no electrons move. However, when a negatively charged and a positively charged electrodes are placed in a liquid, it sets up an electric field. Under the influence of the electric field, the positively charged ions migrate towards the negatively charged electrode and vice versa. At the negatively charged electrode, the positively charged ions gain electrons. At the positively charge electrode, the negatively charged ions lose same number of electrons. Thus, in a way, number of electrons given by the negatively charged electrode is equal to the number of electrons accepted by the positively charged electrode. Thus, we can say that simultaneous movement and discharge of positive and negative ions in the opposite directions constitutes the current in the liquids.

Q. 3. In the electric circuit shown in Fig. label the parts A, B, C, D, E, and F. State the function of each part. Show in the diagram the direction of flow of current.

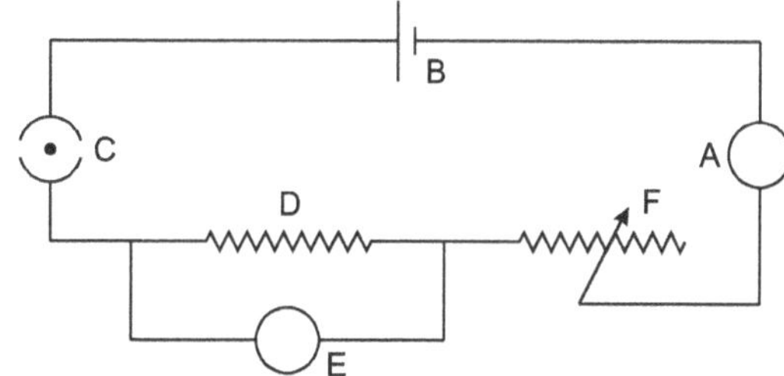

Ans. A: Ammeter: It measures the current flowing through the circuit.

B: Cell: It acts as a source of direct current for the circuit.

C: Key: It is used to put the current on and off in the circuit.

D: Load: It is an appliance connected in a circuit. It may just be a resistance (*e.g.*, bulb) or a combination of different electrical components.

E: Voltmeter: It is used to measure the potential difference between two points of a circuit.

F: Rheostat: It is used to control the current in the circuit.

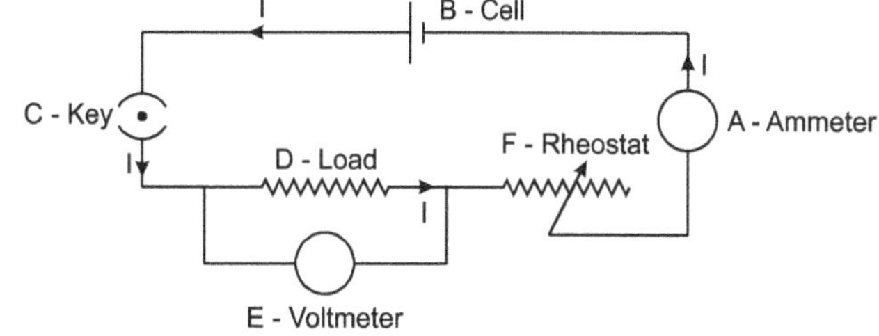

Chapter 10. Magnetism

Q. 1. How do you account for the following facts?

(i) Iron becomes magnetised when placed in a coil carrying direct current.

(ii) Bar magnets lose their magnetism when heated strongly.

(iii) Steel makes better permanent magnet than soft iron.

(iv) Soft iron keepers help to prevent the magnets from losing their magnetic properties.

Ans. (i) Iron is a magnetic substance and hence its each atom behaves as a tiny magnet. When iron piece is placed in a coil carrying direct current, then all the north poles of all the atoms of iron will align themselves in one direction and all the south poles of all the atoms of iron align themselves in a direction opposite to that to which their north poles point. As a result, iron piece gets magnetised.

(ii) Bar magnets lose their magnetism when heated strongly. Due to heat energy, the kinetic energy of the molecules of a bar magnet increases. Thus from straight line molecular chains, they form closed molecular chains and hence, magnetism is lost.

(iii) Steel makes better permanent magnet than soft iron because on magnetising steel, steel retain their magnetic behaviour for longer time even after the removal of source which is magnetising the steel. While the soft iron retains the properties of magnetism only so long as the current is passing through the coil *i.e.*, as long as the source which is magnetising the soft iron is present.

(iv) In magnets, external fields like earth's magnetic field can randomize the domains. Perhaps stray fields caused by owing currents in nearby electric circuits can also disturb the alignment of domains lying inside a magnet. Given enough time, such magnets may end their domains randomly oriented and hence their net magnetisation may get lost. A keeper for magnets is just a strong permanent magnet that keeps all the domains pointing the same way and realign those that may have gone stray and hence magnet, can retain its magnetism for a long time.

Q. 2. (i) Explain the mechanism by which unmagnetised iron nails get attracted to a magnet when brought near it.

(ii) State any two properties of magnet.

Ans. (i) Every atom of an iron nail behaves as a tiny magnet. Due to the random orientations of these tiny magnets, iron nail does not behave as a magnet. But when iron nail is placed near a magnet, then due to induced magnetism, all the atoms (tiny magnets) align themselves in a particular direction. As a result, the end of the iron nail nearer to magnet acquires the opposite polarity and hence get attracted towards the magnet.

(ii) **Properties of a magnet:**

(a) Freely suspended magnet always align itself in the geographic North-South direction.

(b) Like poles of magnets repel each other while unlike poles attract each other.

Q. 3. Describe two methods of determining other the arrangement of the lines of force in the field close to a bar magnet. Give a brief explanation of each method.

Ans. First method: Place a card board on the top of a bar magnet and scatter some iron filings uniformly over the whole of card board. Now tap it with a pencil. The filings are magnetised by induction and arrange themselves in curved lines as shown in figure. The curved lines are called the magnetic lines of force which may be defined as the lines in a magnetic field along which free magnetic poles tend to be driven if free to do so.

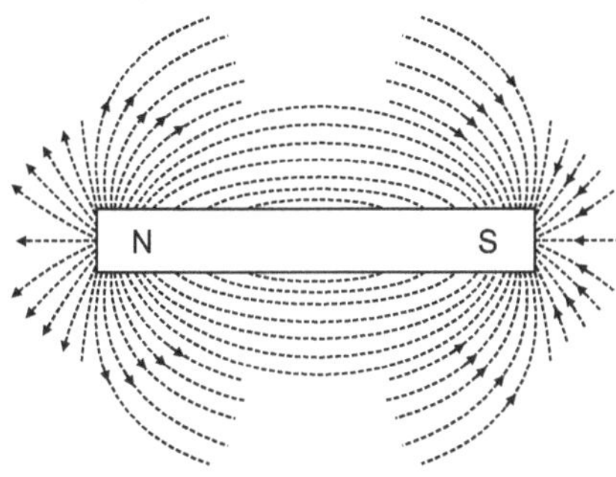

Second method: Lines of force can be traced on a paper by using tracing needle or small magnetic compass needle. The bar magnet is placed on a sheet of paper and its boundary is drawn with a sharp pencil. A point X is marked along the boundary towards the north of the magnet. The tracing needle is then placed at point X in such a way that its one end points towards the point X. With the help of pencil, the direction of other end of needle is marked on paper. Let it be point Y. Now, shift the needle from the point X and place it in such a way that its one end points towards the point Y. The direction of other end of needle is marked by pencil. Let it be point Z. The process is continued till a closed curve is obtained. This curve is called magnetic line of force.

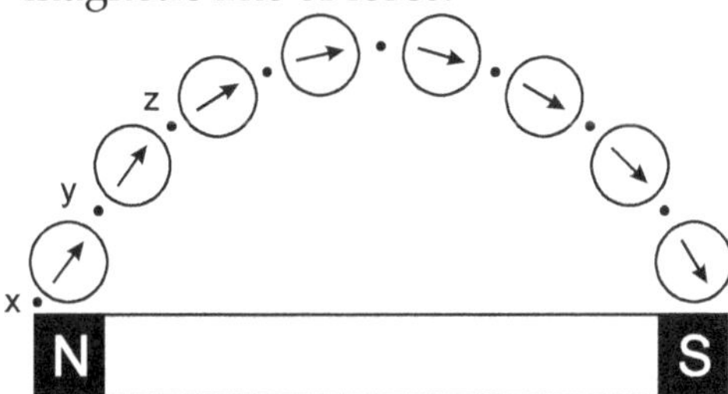

If we plot a number of such curves around the magnet, starting from different points then the space so enclosed is called magnetic field.

Q. 4. Give short account of the earth's magnetic field.

Ans. When a bar magnet is suspended freely, then it aligns itself along geographical North-South direction *i.e.*, North pole of the magnet points towards the geographical North and South pole of the magnet points towards geographical South direction. William Gilbert suggest that earth itself behaves as a huge magnet. It was assumed that:

1. A huge magnet is buried at the centre of earth.

2. The South end of earth's magnet is towards the earth's geographic North and vice-versa.

3. The axis of earth's magnet is not in line with the geographical axis, but makes a small angle with it. The diagram below show the earth as a magnet and the magnetic lines of force around it.

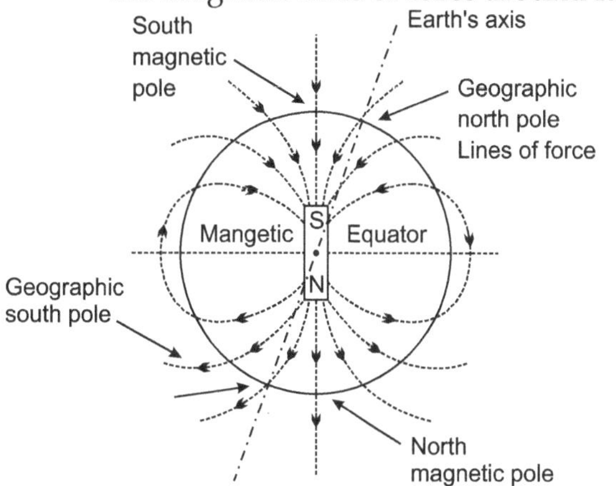

Q. 5. Explain the following:

(i) When two pins are hung by their heads from the same pole of a magnet, their pointed ends moves apart.

(ii) Several soft iron pins can cling, one below the other, from the pole of a magnet.

(iii) The north end of a freely suspended magnetic needle gets attracted towards a piece of soft iron placed a little distance away from the needle.

Ans. (i) When two pins are hung by their heads from the same pole of a magnet, they acquire same polarity. Because like poles repel each other, their pointed ends move apart.

(ii) Several soft iron pins can cling one below the other from the pole of a magnet because the magnet induces magnetism in an iron nail which gets attracted by the magnet and clings to it. This magnetized nail magnetizes the other nail near it by magnetic induction and attracts it. This process continues until force of attraction on first nail is sufficient to balance the total weight of all nails in chain.

(iii) When a piece of soft iron is placed a little distance away from the needle, the needle induces magnetism to the piece of soft iron. Thus, soft iron piece starts behaving like a magnet and it attracts the magnetic needle towards it.

Q. 6. (i) Draw the magnetic field lines around a bar magnet when the north pole of the bar magnet is placed facing the geographic south pole of the earth along the magnetic axis of the earth.

(ii) Indicate the position of neutral points by marking X.   **[November, 2019]**

Ans. (i) Magnetic field lines around a bar magnet when the north pole of the bar magnet is facing the geographic south pole of the earth is given below.

(ii) The position of the two neutral points have been marked in the diagram below.

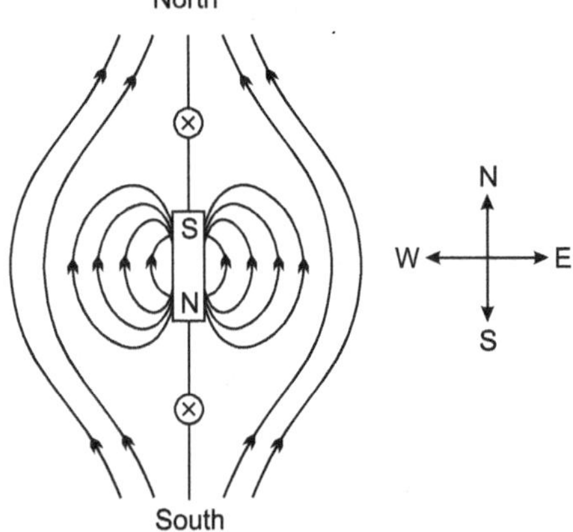

Q. 7. State briefly (i) the molecular theory of magnetism, (ii) the modern views on magnetism.

Ans. (i) Ewing suggested the molecular theory of magnetism as follows:

(a) Each molecule of a magnetic substance, whether it is magnetised or unmagnetised, is an independent magnet.

(b) In a magnetised substance, the molecules are arranged in an order so as to produce an external effect. In this order, all the north poles of the molecules of the magnetised substances point to one direction and all their south poles point to a direction opposite to that to which their north poles points.

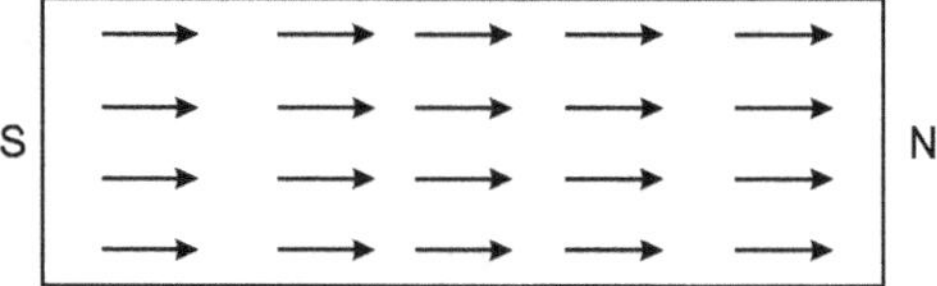

Magnetised substance

(c) In an unmagnetised substance, the molecules are not arranged in any order, so they neutralise the magnetic forces of each other.

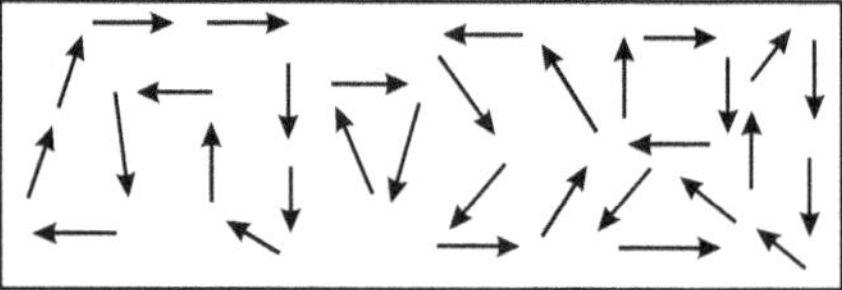

Unmagnetised substance

(ii) The molecular theory of magnetism was a considerable step forward but later there came an electrical explanation for the magnetism of atoms. Atoms consist of negatively charged particles (electrons) which revolve around the positively charged nucleus. Electrical current loops are formed in an atom due to the circulation of these electrons. Each current loop behaves a magnetic dipole and hence produce magnetic field. Also electrons are also spinning like tops and this adds further magnetism to the atom.

❑

Diagram based

Chapter 1. Measurements and Experimentation

Q. 1. Show the variation of effective length of a pendulum to its time period graphically.
Ans.

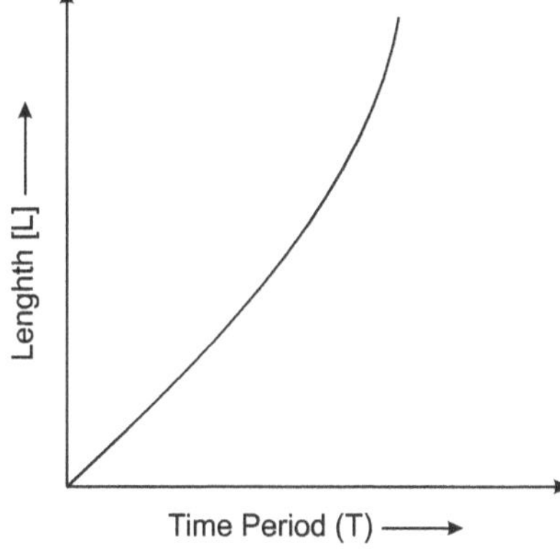

Q. 2. Draw a graph of length of pendulum to [time period]^2 to express its variation.
Ans.

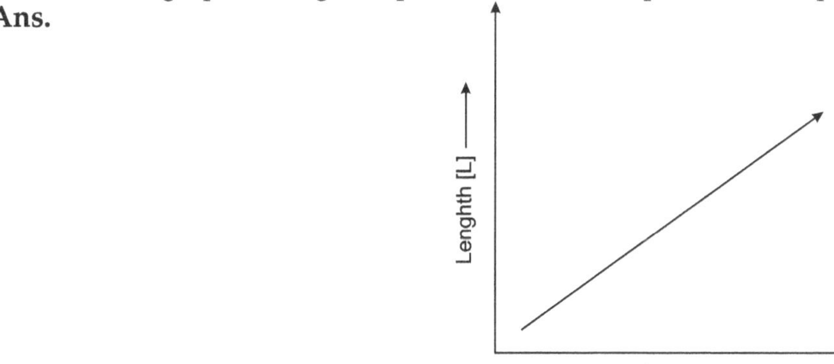

Q. 3. Draw a labelled diagram of vernier caliper.
Ans.

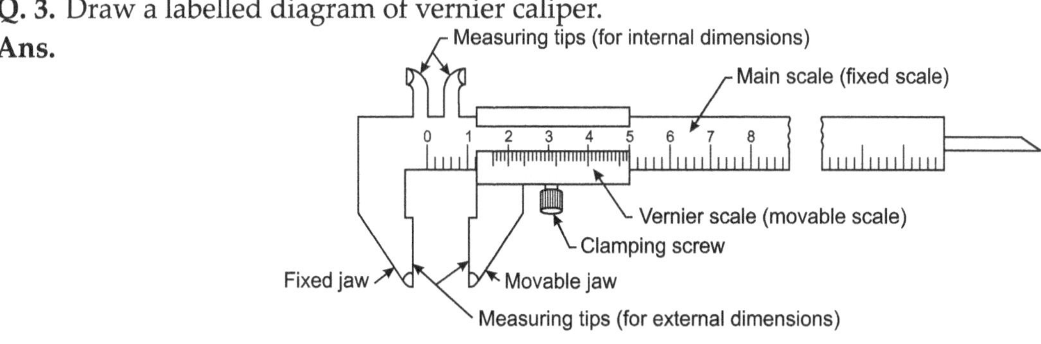

Chapter 2. Motion in One Dimension

Q. 1. Draw the displacement–time graphs for the following cases:
(i)   When a body is stationary.
(ii) When a body is moving with uniform velocity
(iii) When a body is moving with variable velocity
(iv) When a body moves with constant acceleration or a freely falling body.

Ans. (i) When the body is stationary:

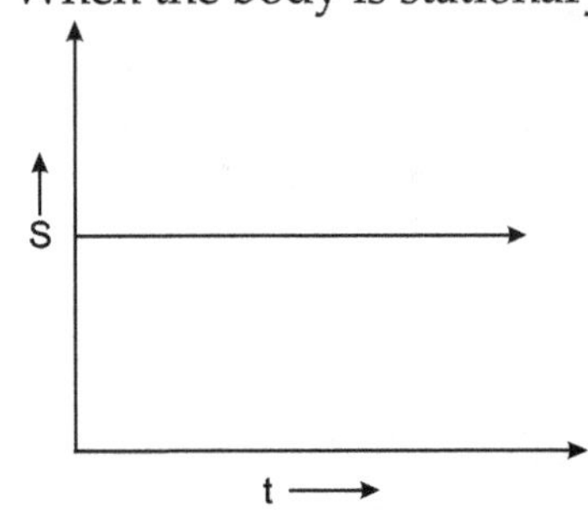

(ii) When the body is moving with uniform velocity

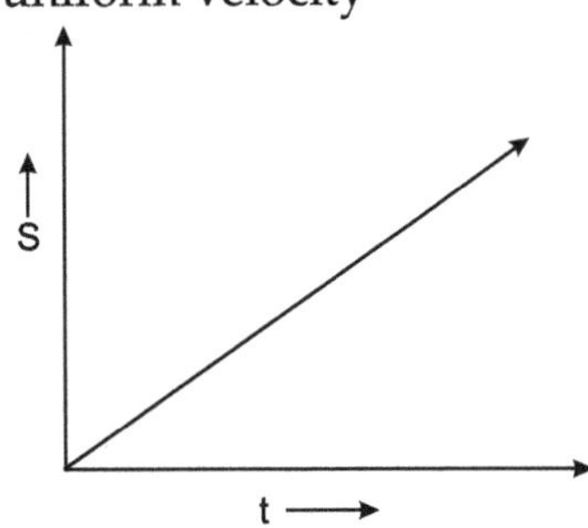

(iii) When the body is moving with variable velocity

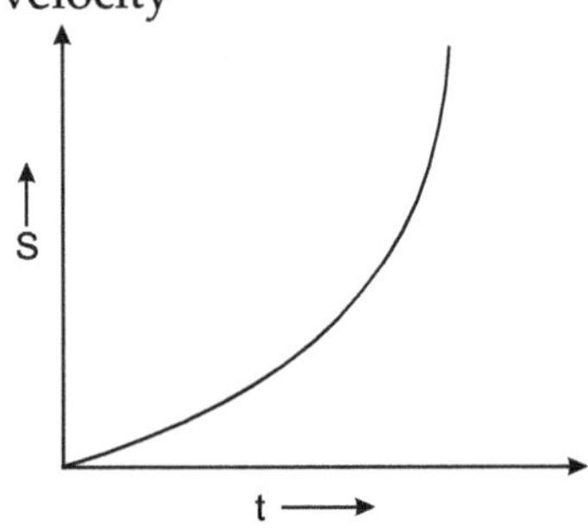

(iv) When a body moves with constant acceleration or a freely falling body.

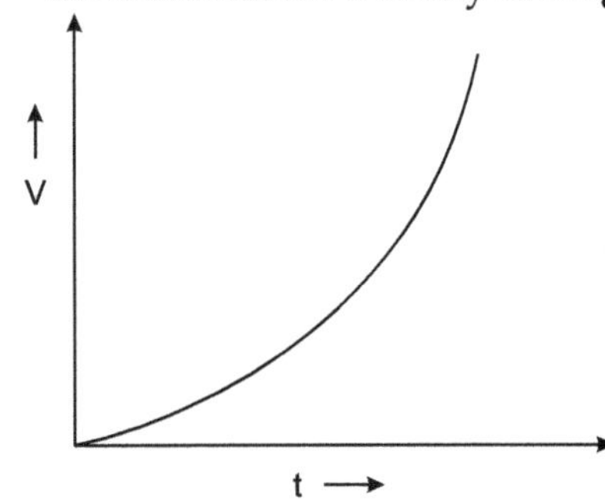

Q. 2. Draw the velocity-time graph for the following cases:

(i) If the body is in motion with uniform velocity.

(ii) If the body is in motion and acceleration is zero.

(iii) Moving body with uniform acceleration.

(iv) Initially the body is moving with some velocity and then uniformly retards.

Ans. (i) If the body is in motion with uniform velocity.

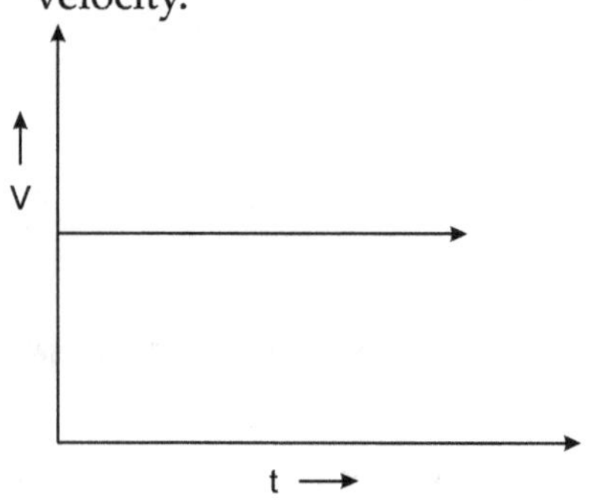

(ii) If the body is in motion and acceleration is zero.

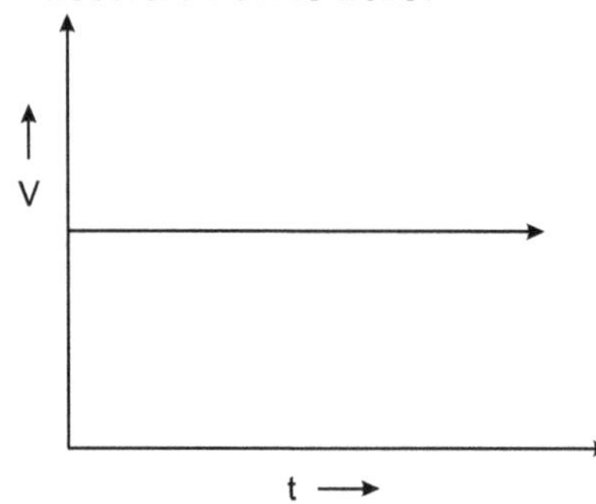

(iii) Moving body with uniform acceleration.

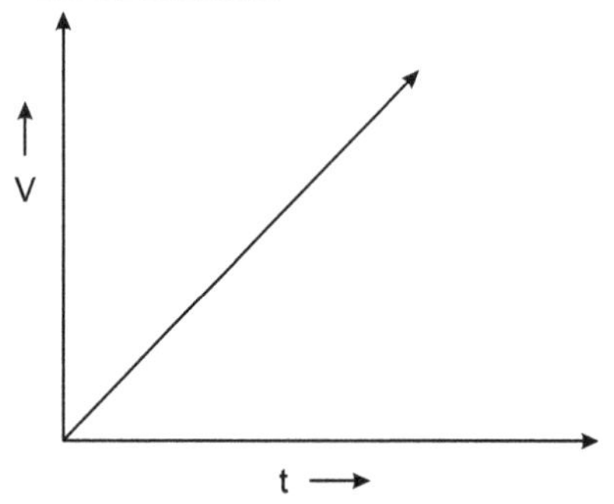

(iv) Initially the body is moving with some velocity and then uniformly retards.

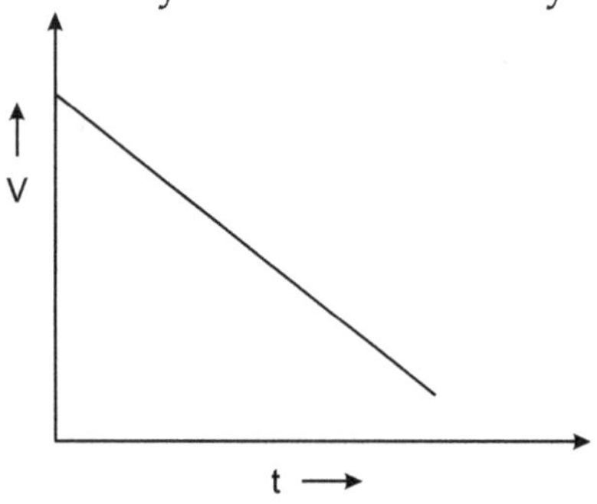

Q. 3. Show how the velocity–time graph can be used to find:

(i)   the acceleration of a body.

(ii) the distance travelled by the body in a given time, and

(iii) the displacement of the body in a given time.

Ans. (i) Acceleration = Slope of v–t graph

Retardation = Slope of v–t graph

(ii) Distance travelled by the body in given time = Area of triangle formed by straight line of v–t graph.

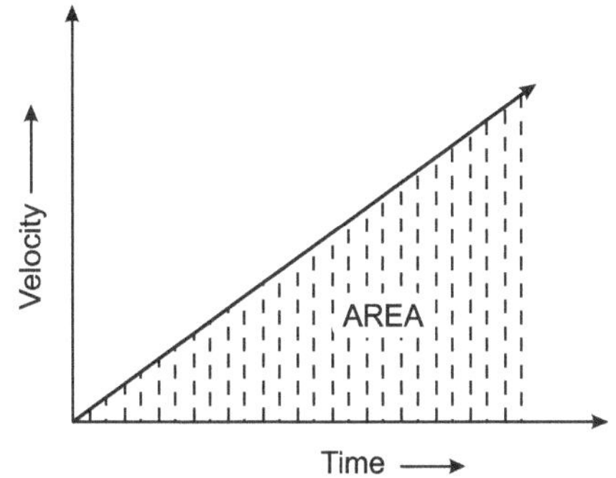

(iii) Displacement of the body in the given time = the area enclosed between in the v–t graph .

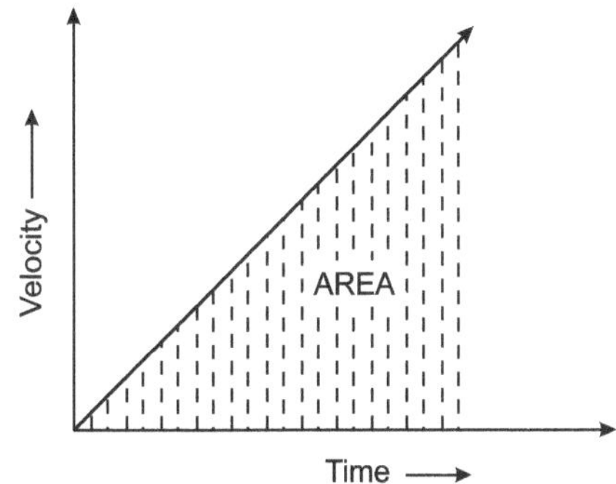

Q. 4. The figure given below shows the velocity–time graph for two objects A and B moving in same direction. Which object has the greater acceleration? Why?

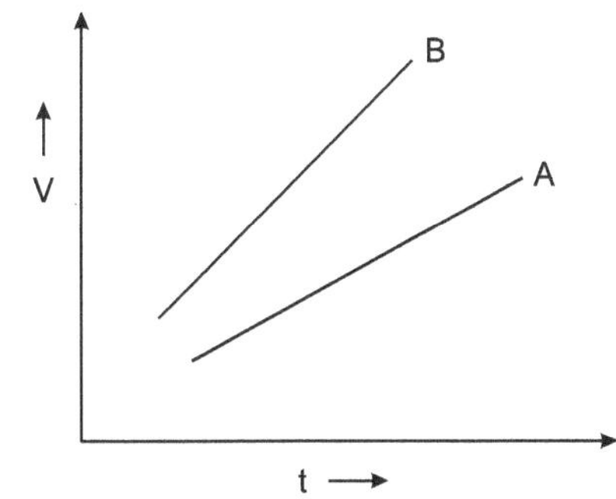

Ans. Object B has greater acceleration than A. This is because slope of line B is more than that of line A.

Q. 5. For a freely falling body, draw

(i) Acceleration–time graph

(ii) Velocity–time graph and

(iii) Displacement–time graph

Ans. (i) Acceleration–time graph:

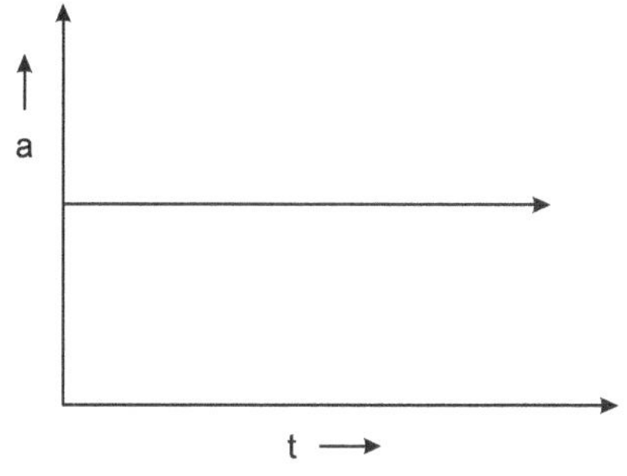

(ii) Velocity–time graph:

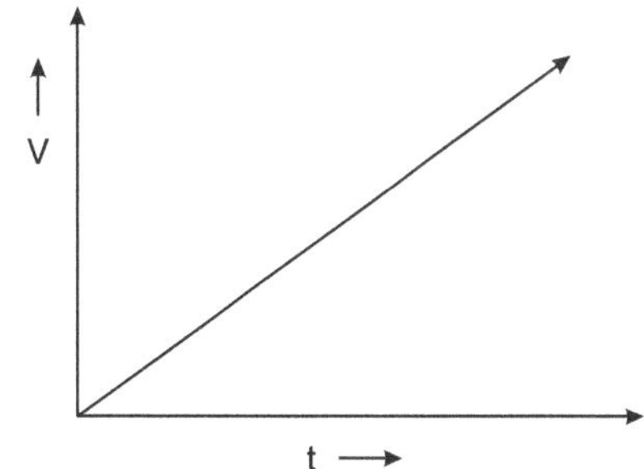

(iii) Displacement–time graph:

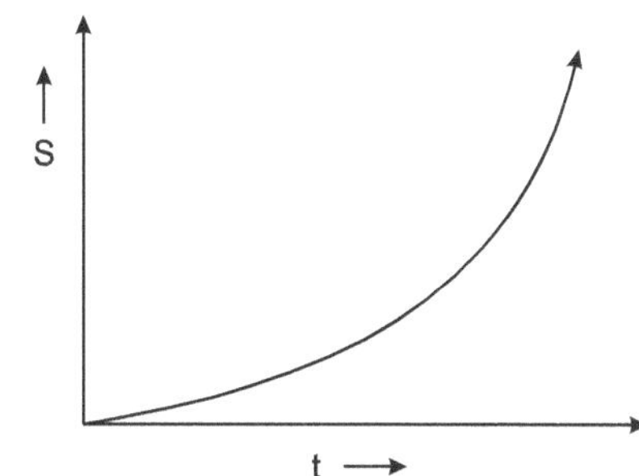

Q. 6. A body falls freely downward from a certain height. Show graphically the relation between the distance travelled and square of time. How will you determine 'g' from this graph?

Ans.

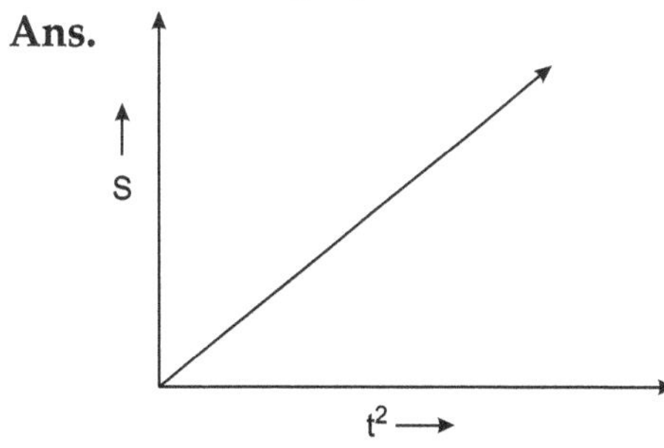

Acceleration due to gravity (g) = Twice the value of slope of above graph.

Q. 7. If the position of a body doesn't change then draw the graphical representation with respect to time for the concept regarding this problem.

Ans. If the position of the body doesn't change with time then graphical representation of this can be depicted as:

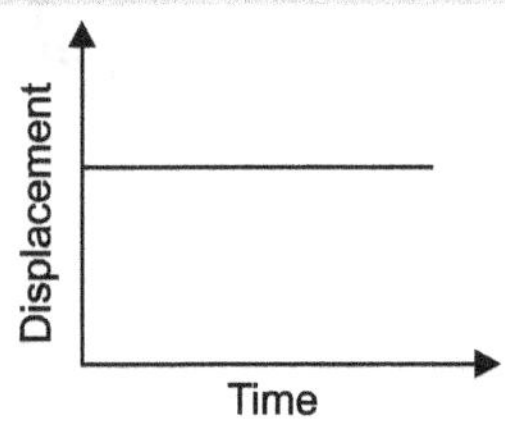

Q. 8. Draw a diagram for a motion with constant speed but with variable velocity.

Ans.

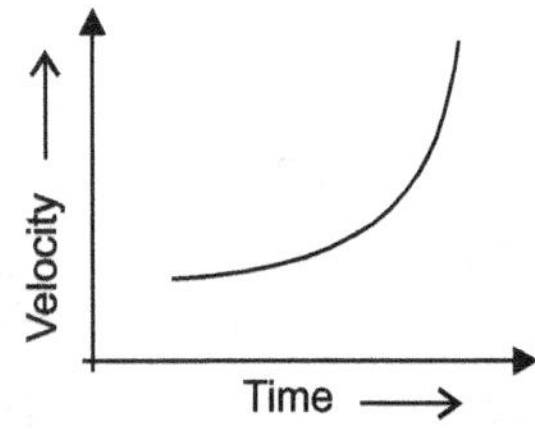

Q. 9. Draw a graph of displacement-time graph with positive and negative slopes.

Ans. The graph of displacement-time graph with positive and negative slopes is

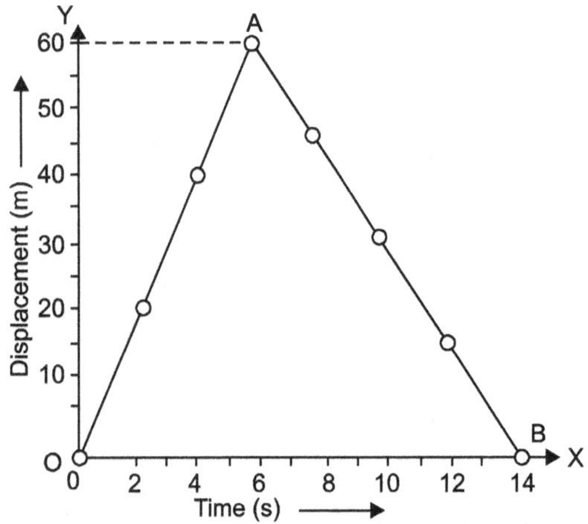

Q. 10. What happens when velocity–time graph is a curve? Represent this with the help of diagram.

Ans. Motion will be non uniform. Graph between velocity and time is shown below:

Q. 11. A person throw one stone vertically upwards with an initial velocity of 40 ms^{-1}, taking $g = 10$ ms^{-2} draw velocity– time graph of the motion of stone till it comes back to the ground.

Time (in s)	Velocity in ms^{-1}
0	40
1	30
2	20
3	10
4	0
5	–10
6	–20
7	–30
8	–40

Ans.

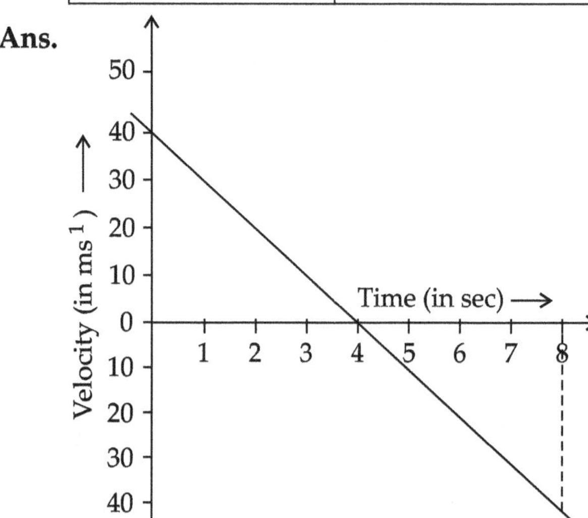

Q. 12. Draw the graph of velocity-time graph for free fall and rise of a body.

Ans. The graph of velocity-time graph for free fall and rise of a body is

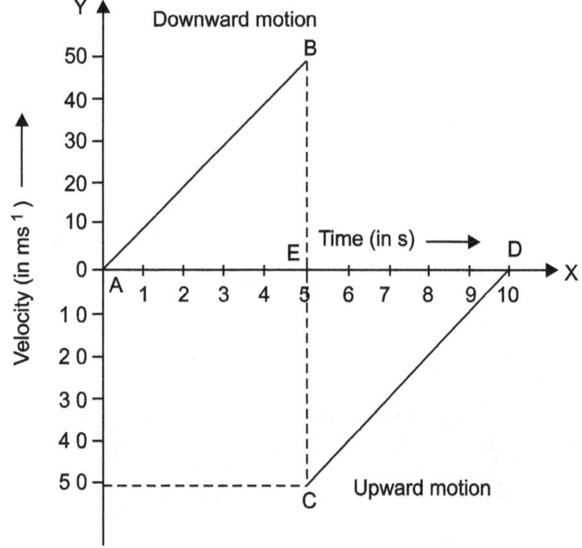

Q. 13. Draw the graph which depict the displacement-time graph of a book for which displacement at different instant is given in the table below:

Time (in s)	Displacement (in metre)
0	0
2	10
5	30
6	50

Ans.

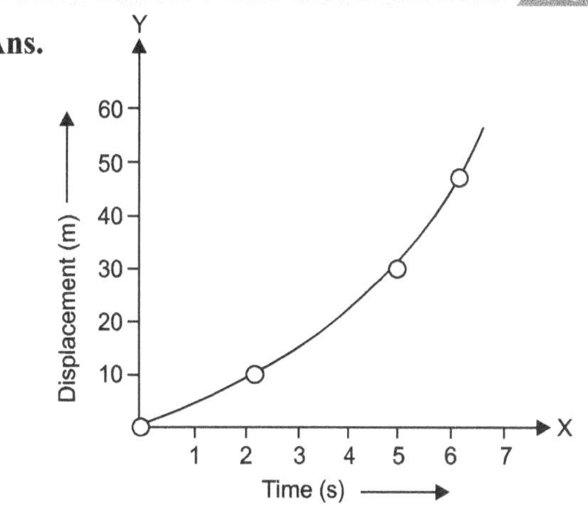

Chapter 3. Laws of Motion

Q. 1. If force is constant, then draw a graph to show the acceleration variance with mass.

Ans. Graph between mass and acceleration is shown below:

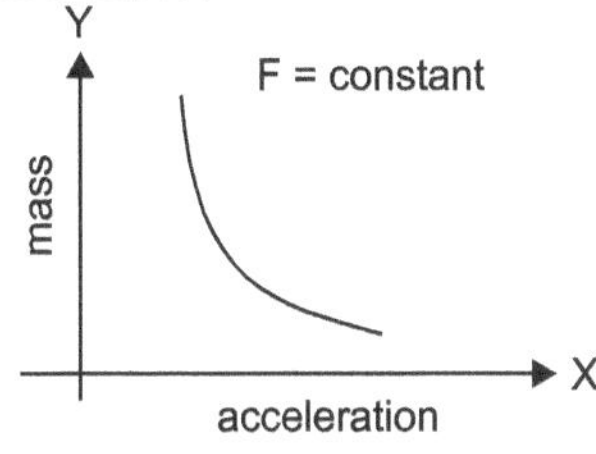

Q. 2. A block of wood is placed at a table. Write the name of force acting on the block and draw a free diagram.

Ans. Since wooden block is kept on the table, then normal force will be acting on the block vertically upwards and corresponding force due to gravity will be acting downwards.

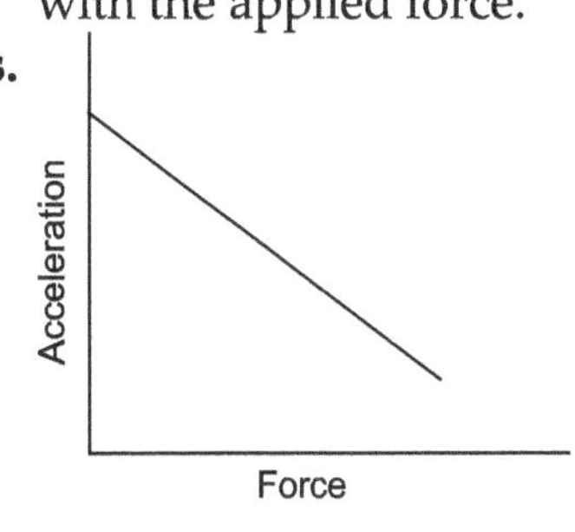

Q. 3. Depict a graph showing the motion of a body where the acceleration decreases with the applied force.

Ans.

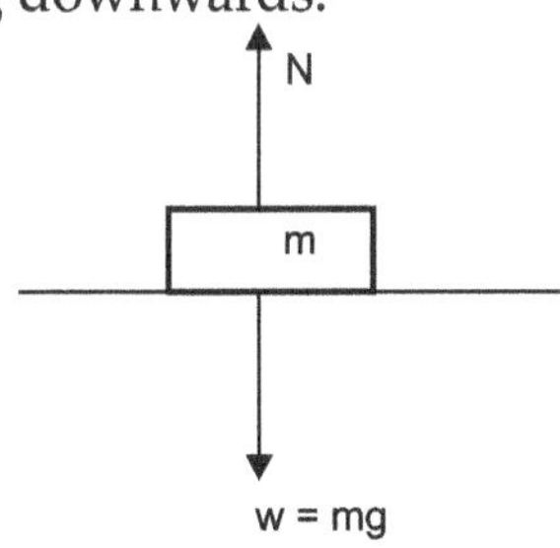

The graph showing the motion of some body where the acceleration decreases with the applied force is,

Q. 4. (i) A book is kept on the table as shown in the diagram. Copy the diagram and mark the action reaction forces with their directions.

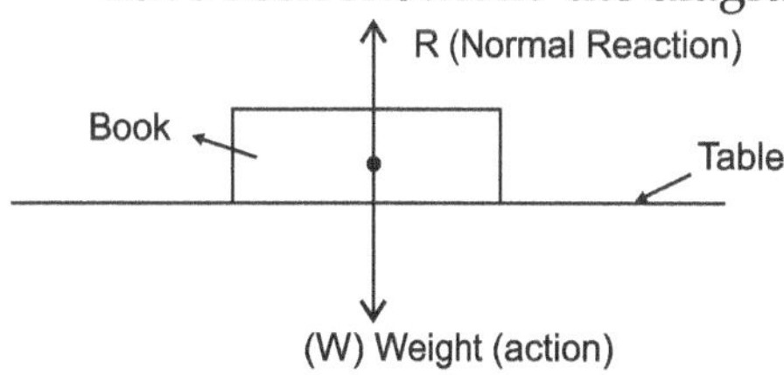

(ii) Do these forces act on the same body or on two different bodies?

[February, 2020]

Ans. (i) The action and reaction with direction have been shown in the diagram.

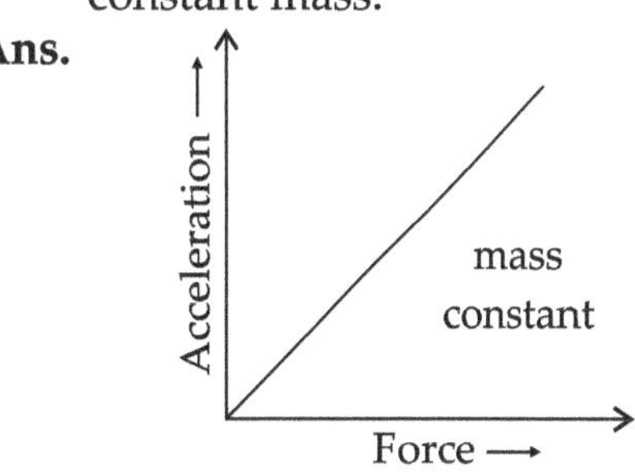

(ii) Action and reaction never act on the same body. They act simultaneously on two different bodies.

Q. 5. Draw a graph showing relationship between acceleration and force for a constant mass.

Ans.

Q. 6. Draw a graph showing relationship between force and mass for constant acceleration.

Ans.

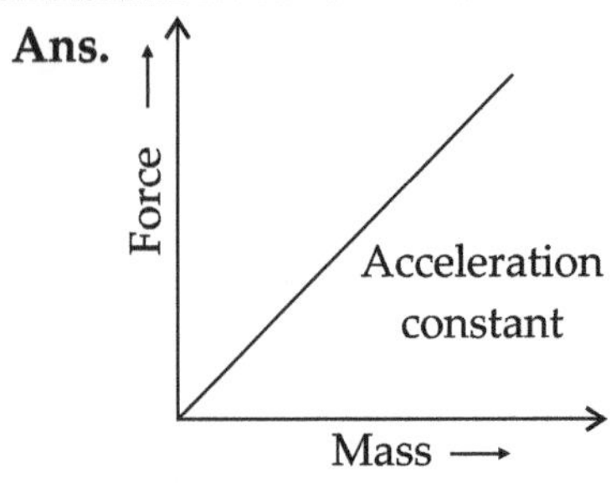

Q. 7. Draw a diagram which clearly demonstrates action and reaction (experimental demonstration of Newton's third law).

Ans. Demonstration of action reaction pair:

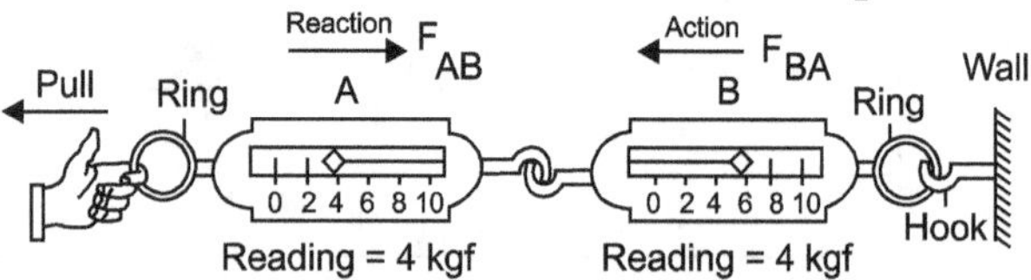

Chapter 4. Pressure in Fluids and Atmospheric Pressure

Q. 1. What is a fortin barometer? Draw its labelled diagram.

Ans. Fortin barometer is a modified form of a simple barometer that also uses mercury as the barometric liquid to measure atmospheric pressure.

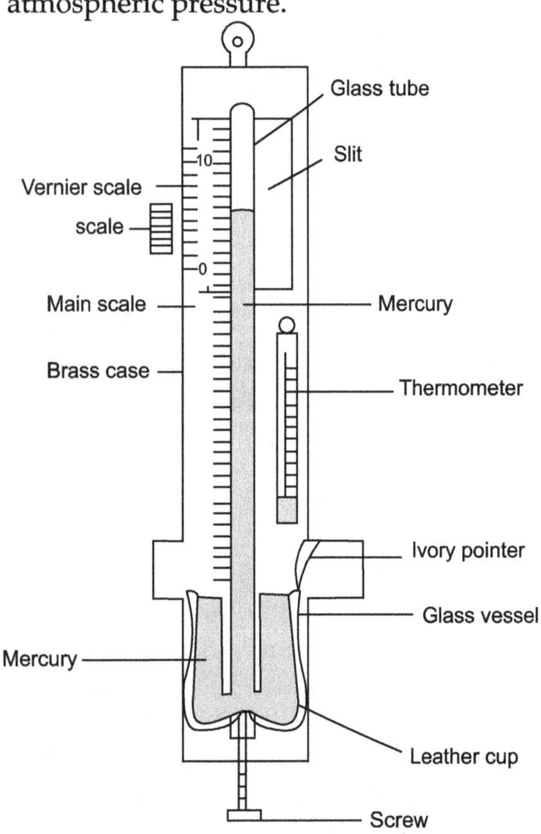

Q. 3. Draw a diagram of wall of a dam with its thickness increasing towards the bottom.

Ans.

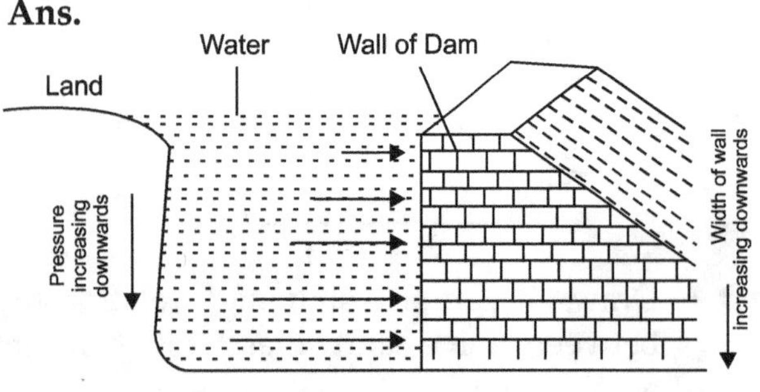

Q. 2. Draw a systematic diagram for the demonstration of Pascal's law.

Ans. Demonstration of Pascal's law is depicted below.

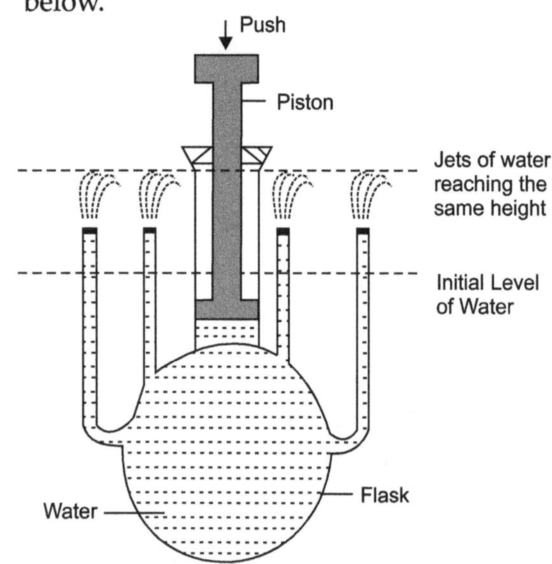

Q. 4. Draw a diagram which represents a device which uses the principle of transmission of pressure.

Ans. Device that makes use of the principle of transmission of pressure is shown below:

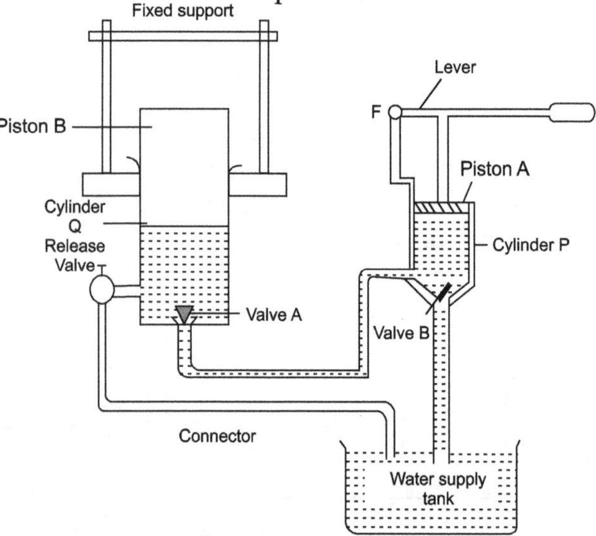

Chapter 5. Upthrust in Fluids, Archimedes' Principle and Floatation

Q. 1. Mark the forces acting on a body placed inside a liquid.

Ans.

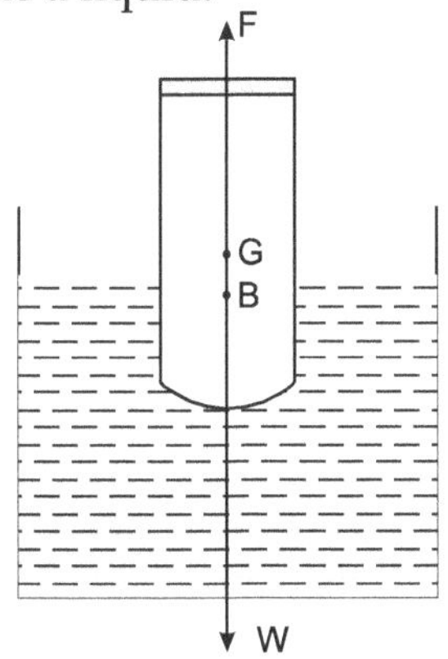

Two forces distinctly visible are:

(i) Weight of the body (W) acting vertically downwards at the centre of gravity (G) of the body. Due to this force, the body has a tendency to move downwards towards the centre of earth.

(ii) Buoyant force exerted by the liquid, acting vertically upwards at the centre of buoyancy (F).

Chapter 6. Heat and Energy

Q. 1. Draw a simple diagram showing a food chain.

Ans.

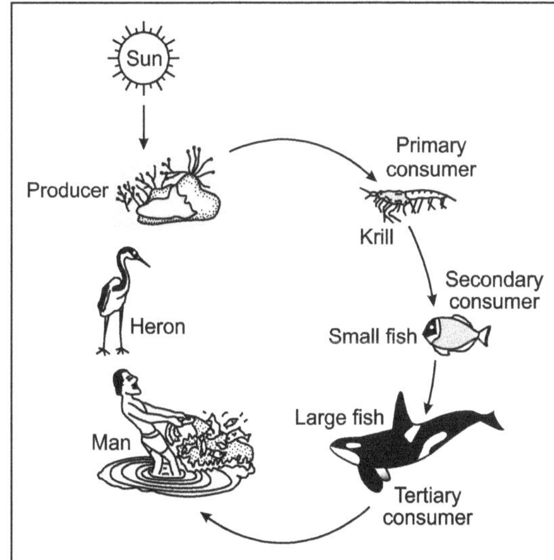

Q. 2. Draw a diagram showing the temperature of various layers of water in an ice covered pond.

Ans.

Q. 3. Draw the diagram for the variation in density of water with temperature in range 0°C to 10°C.

Ans. Variation in density of water with temperature in range 0°C to 10°C is depicted below:

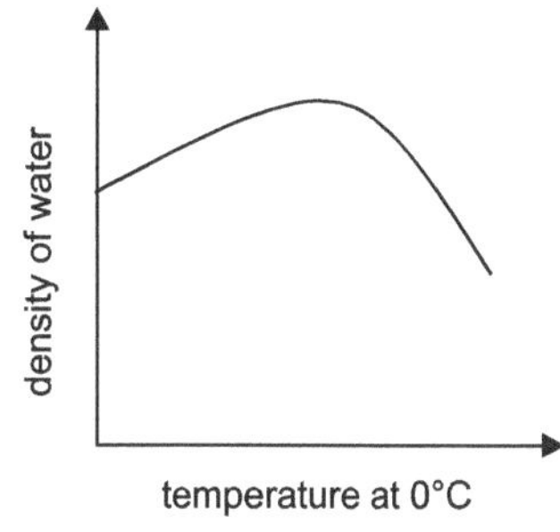

Q. 4. Diagrammatically show the flow of energy and cycling of minerals in an ecosystem.

Ans. In an ecosystem two functional aspects are: (i) flow of energy and (ii) cycling of minerals.

The flow of energy is unidirectional, *i.e.,* the energy available at a trophic level does not revert back to the previous level. In a mineral cycling, a cyclic path way operates.

Both can be depicted as follows:

Energy flow

Mineral movement ⟶

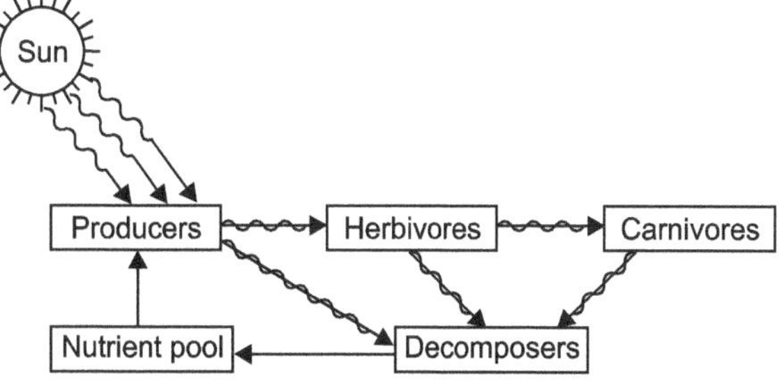

Q. 5. Depict a diagrammatic representation of 'greenhouse effect'.

Ans.

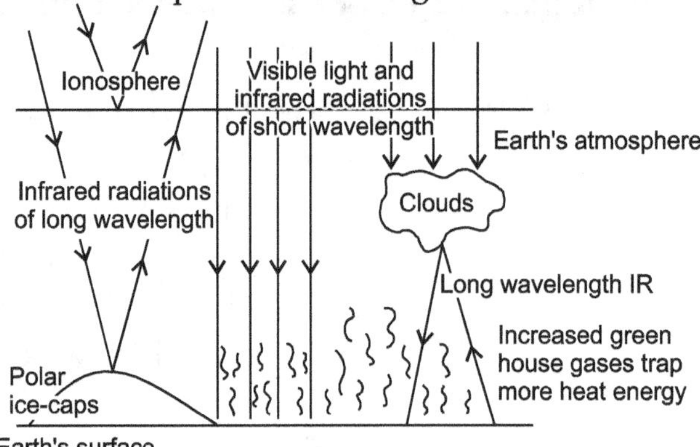

Q. 6. How can electricity be produced from nuclear energy? Draw a labeled diagram of it.

Ans. Electricity can be produced from nuclear energy by the controlled chain reaction of nuclear fission of a radioactive substance like uranium-235. This setup is called nuclear power plant.

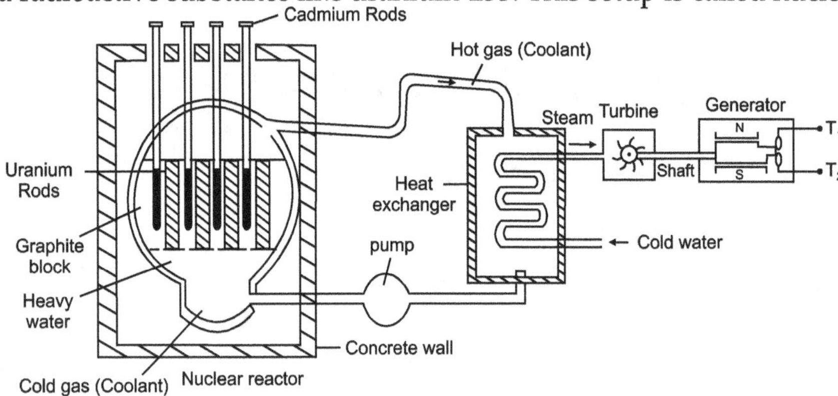

Q. 7. Draw and label a diagram of a hydroelectric plant.

Ans. The figure for hydroelectric plant is

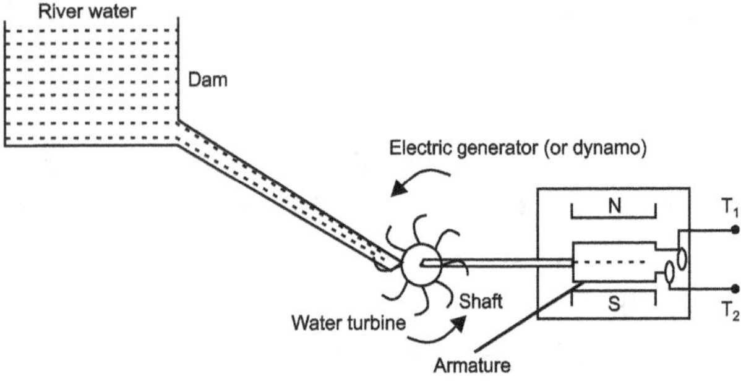

Q. 8. Draw a neat and clean diagram of wind generator. What are the advantages and disadvantages of using wind energy?

Ans.

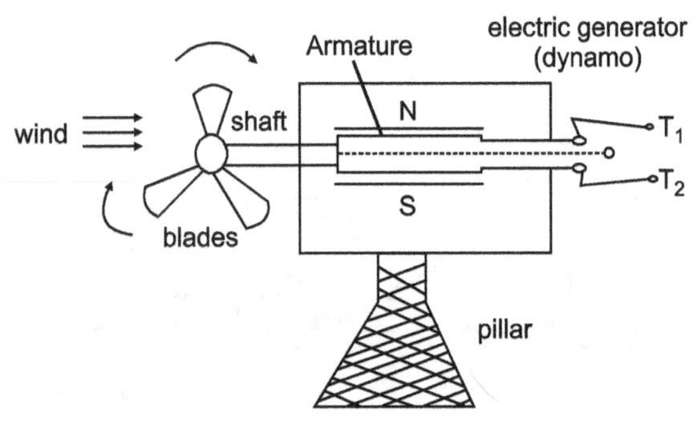

Advantages of using wind energy are:

(i) It doesn't cause any kind of pollution.

(ii) It is an everlasting source.

Disadvantages of using wind energy are:

(i) The wind farms can be established only at places near the coastal areas where wind blows around the year steadily with a speed not less than 15 kmh^{-1}.

(ii) A large area of land is needed for the establishment of a wind farm.

Q. 9. Draw a neat and clean diagram of solar panel used for running a water pump.

Ans. Diagram for solar panel used for running water pump is shown below:

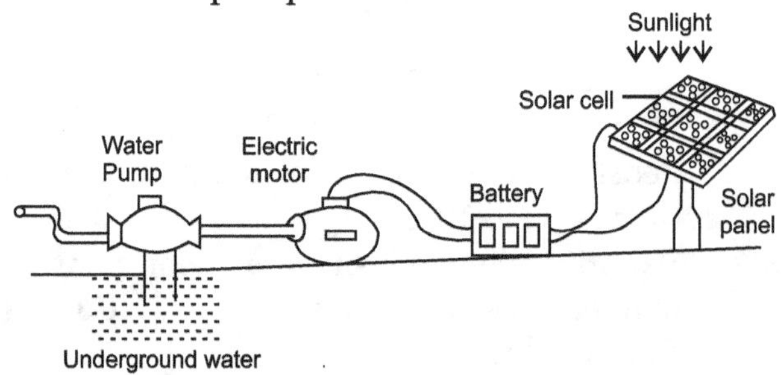

Chapter 7. Reflection of Light

Q. 1. Complete the path of ray of light after reflection at the mirror in the given diagram.

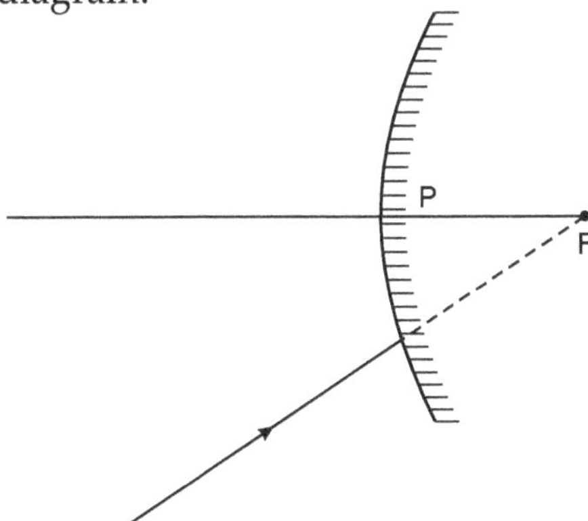

Ans.

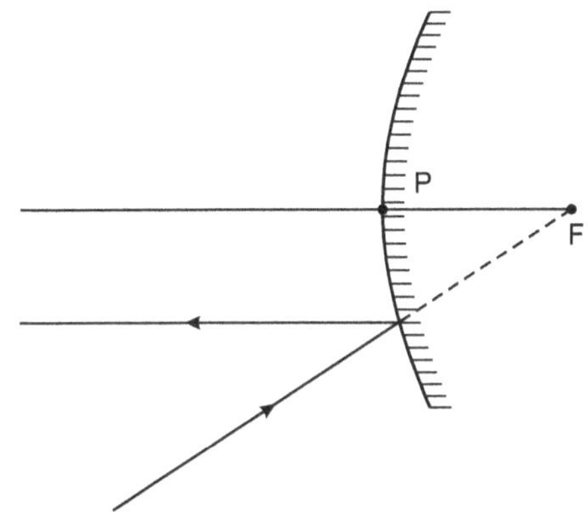

Q. 2. Copy the diagram in your note book and show the formation of the light ray after reflection.

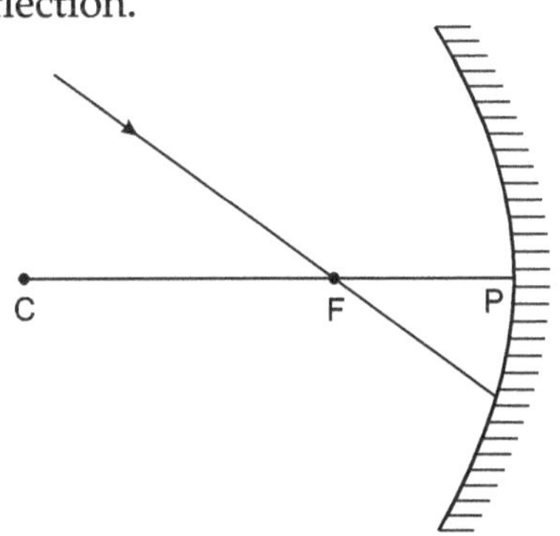

Ans. The reflected ray travels parallel to the principal axis of the mirror as shown in the diagram.

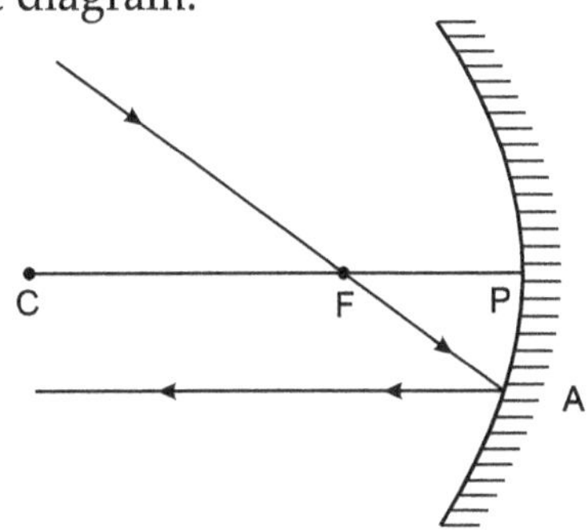

Q.3. Copy the figure. By taking two rays from point A, show the formation of image. State four characteristics of the image formed.

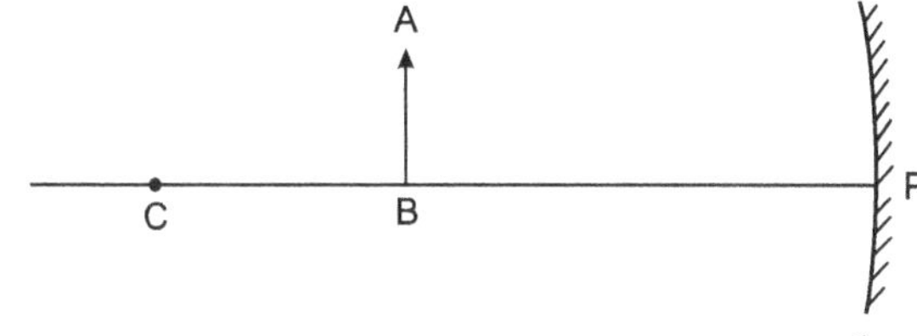

Ans.

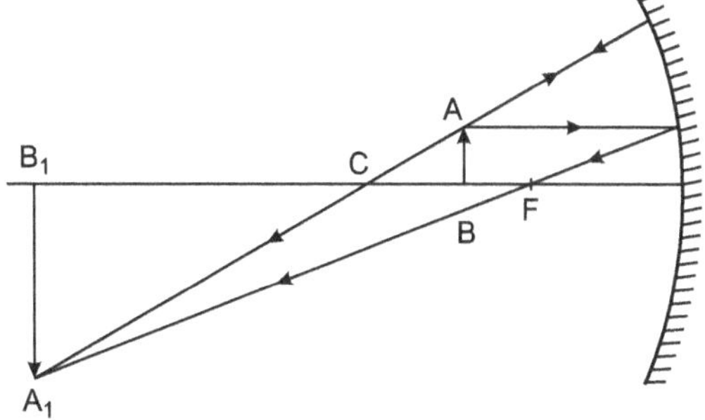

Four characteristics of image are as follows:

(i) Image is real.

(ii) Image is inverted.

(iii) Image is magnified.

(iv) Image is formed beyond centre of curvature.

Q. 4. Copy the figure. By taking two rays from point A, show the formation of image. State four characteristics of the image formed.

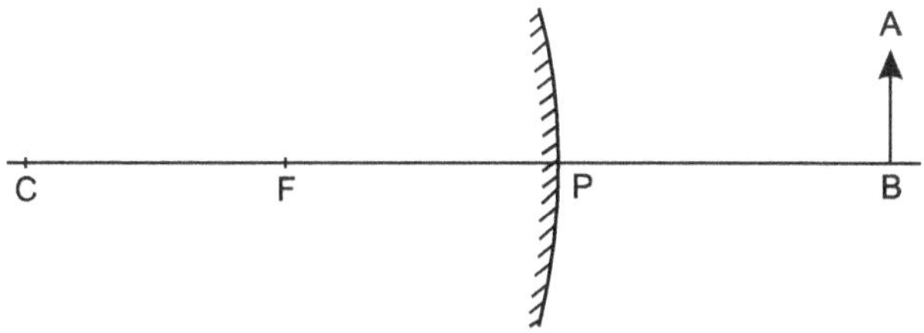

Ans.

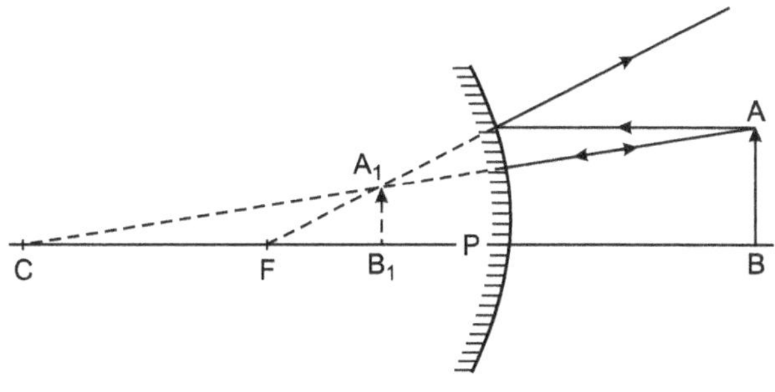

Characteristics of Image formed are as follows:

(i)   Image is virtual.

(ii) Image is erect.

(iii) Image is diminished.

(iv) Image is formed between pole and principal focus of convex mirror.

Q. 5. Copy the fig (i) and (ii) and complete them by drawing two ray diagram.

(i)

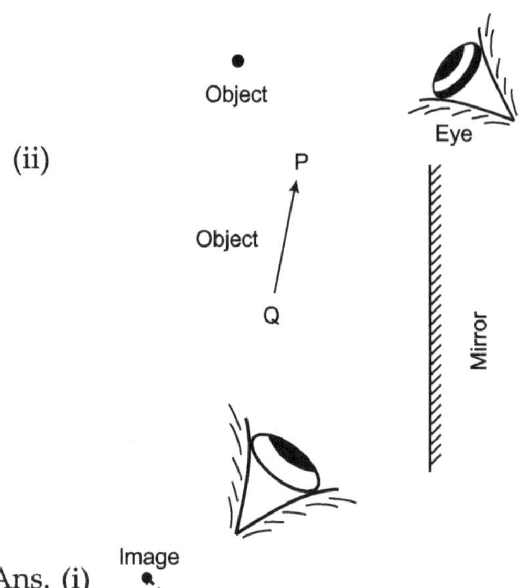

(ii)

Ans. (i)

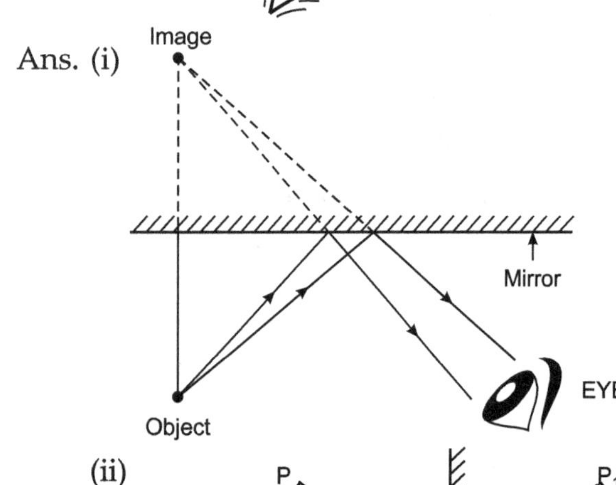

(ii)

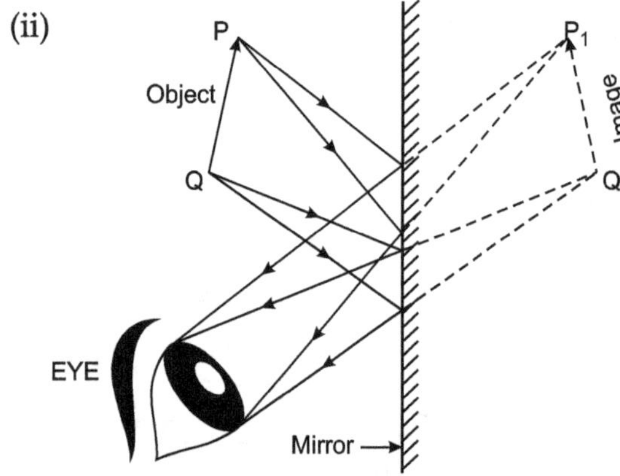

Q. 6. What will be the image of the word 'PIE' if you see it in a plane mirror kept vertical on the line AB. [No ray diagram is required.

[November, 2019]

Ans. bIE will be the image of the word PIE as seen in the plane mirror in the given situation.

Q.7. Complete the ray diagram shown in the figure below to show image formation on a concave mirror for parallel incident ray. State location, nature and image size established.

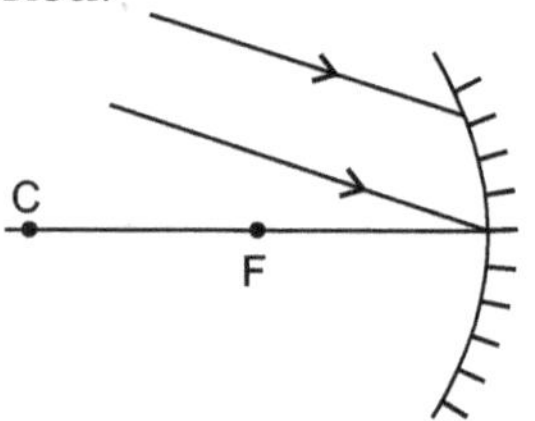

Ans. The diagram related with all the rays is shown below:

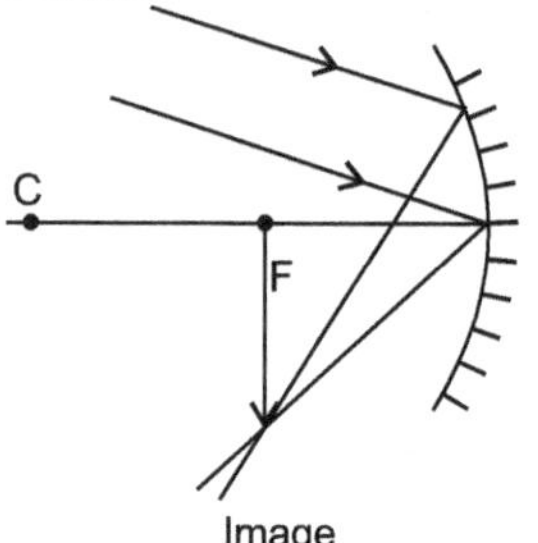

The image is formed at the focus F. It is real, inverted and diminished.

Q. 8. Draw the ray diagram for following in case of concave mirror:

(i)   The object is at the infinity.

(ii) The object is just at the Centre of curvature.

Ans. (i)   The diagram for object at infinity for a concave mirror:

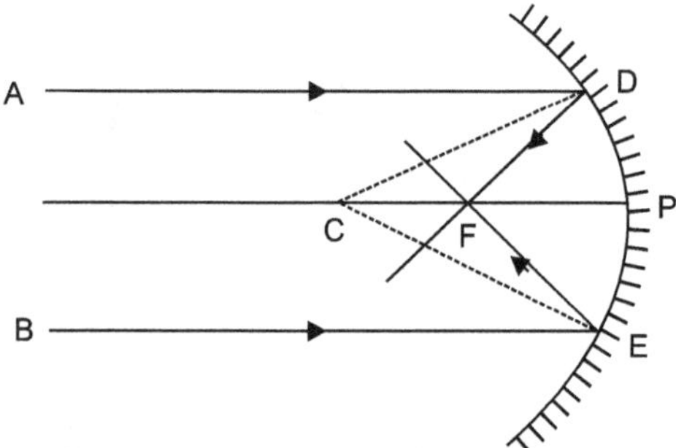

(ii) The diagram for object just at the centre of the curvature:

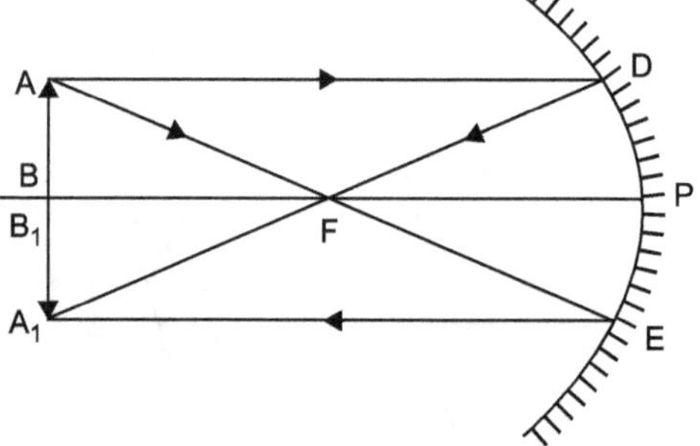

Q. 9. Draw the ray diagram of concave mirror when the object is between the Centre of curvature C and focus F.

Ans. The ray diagram of a concave mirror when the object is between the Centre of curvature C and focus F is

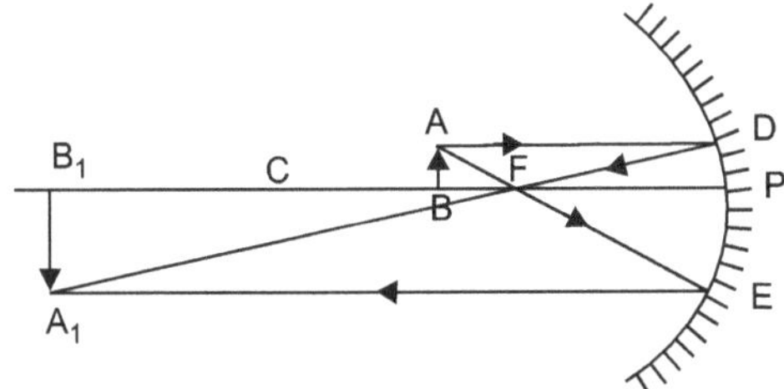

Q. 10. Draw a ray diagram if an object is between focus F and pole P of a concave mirror.

Ans.

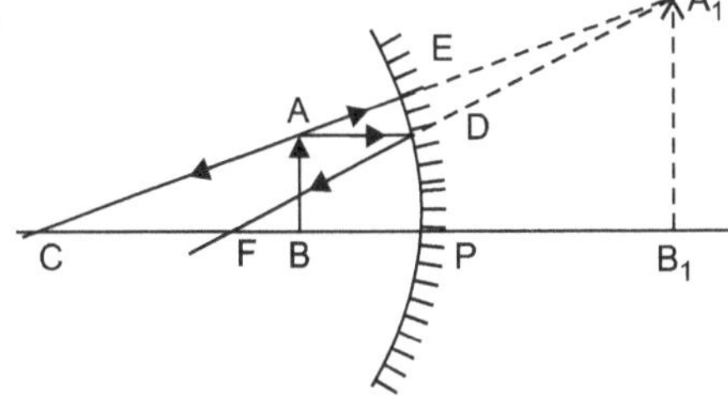

Q. 11. Draw a neat and clean diagram showing displacement of images in a plane mirror when the object moves.

Ans.

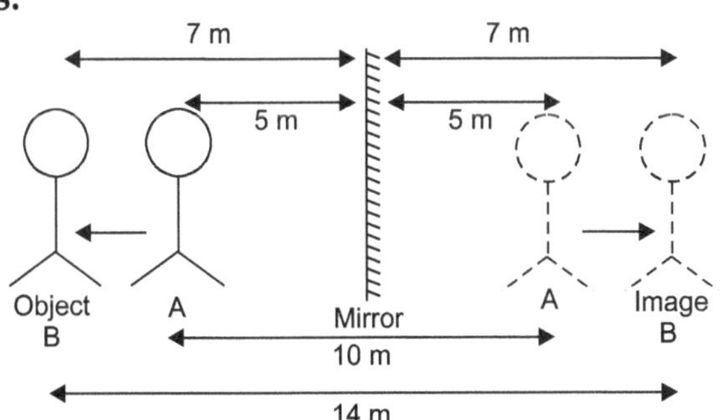

Q. 12. Draw neat and clean sign convention for spherical mirror (concave mirror).

Ans. Sign convention for spherical mirror (concave mirror) are drawn below

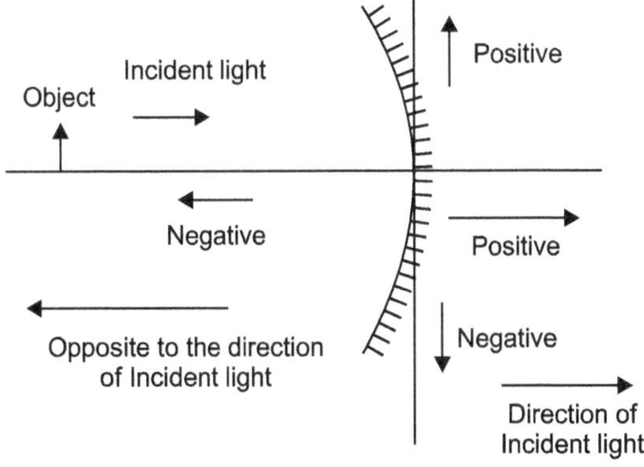

Q. 13. Draw diagrams of plane mirror and convex mirror used as a rear-view mirror.

Ans.

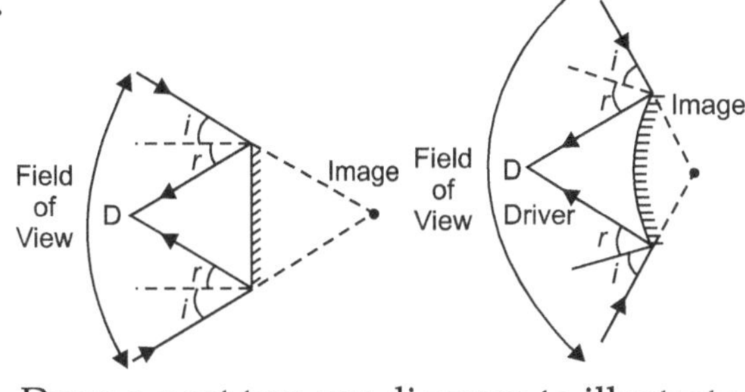

Q. 14. Draw a neat two ray diagram to illustrate, how a concave mirror is used as a shaving mirror.

Ans.

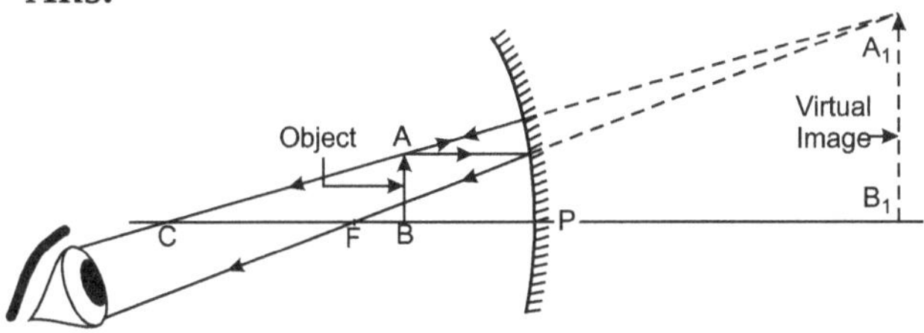

Q. 15. Draw diagrams to show difference between regular and irregular reflection.

Ans.

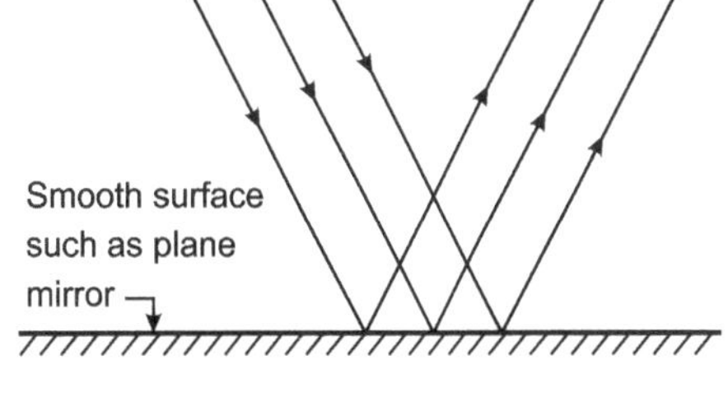

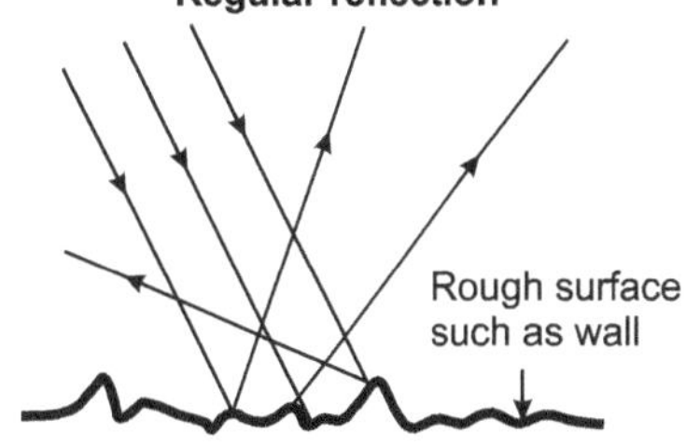

Q. 16. Draw a labelled diagram to show the formation of an image on a plane mirror.

Ans.

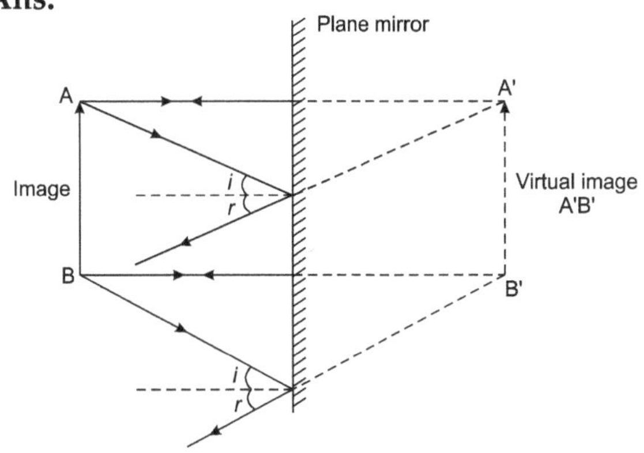

Q. 17. Draw a ray diagram to show reflection of an incident ray parallel to principal axis by a convex mirror.

Ans.

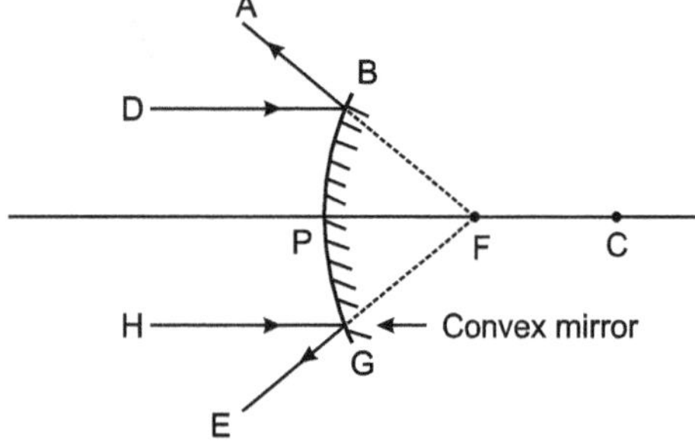

Q. 18. Draw ray diagrams to show the formation of images when the object is placed in front of concave mirror:
(i) between its pole and focus point.
(ii) between the centre of curvature and focus point.

Ans. (i) Between its pole and focus point:

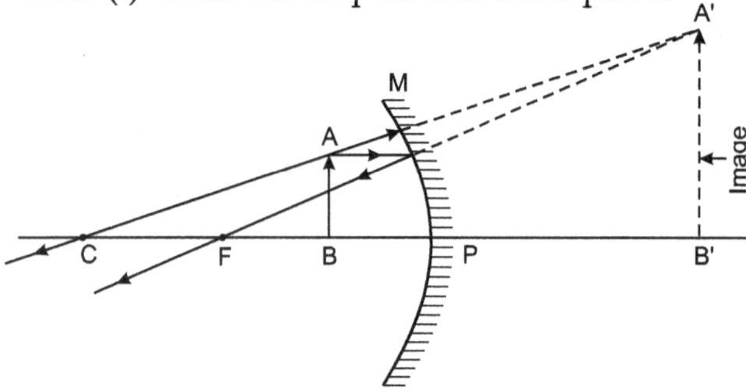

Position of image: Behind the concave mirror.
Nature of image: Virtual, erect and magnified.

(ii) Between the centre of curvature and focus point:

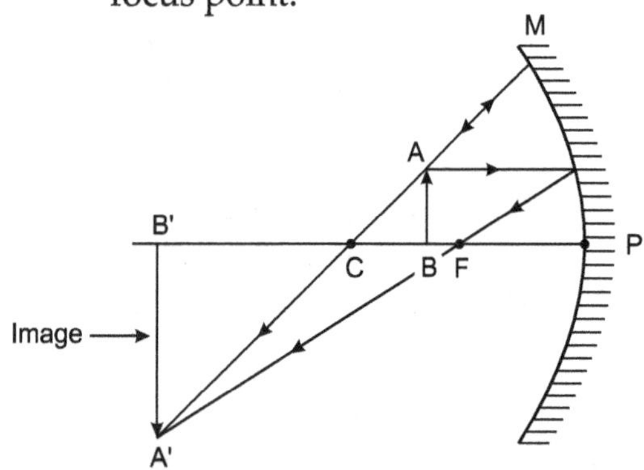

Position of image: Beyond the centre of curvature (C) of the concave mirror.
Nature of image: Real, inverted and magnified.

Q. 19. Draw a neat two ray diagram for the formation of images in two plane mirrors, when mirrors are
(i) at right angles to each other
(ii) facing each other.

Ans. (i)

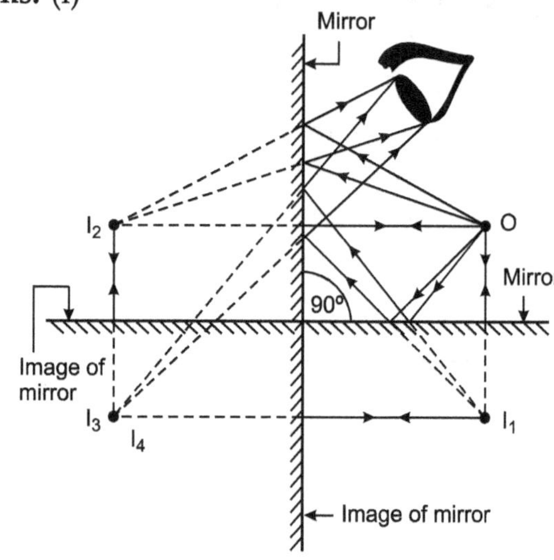

(ii)

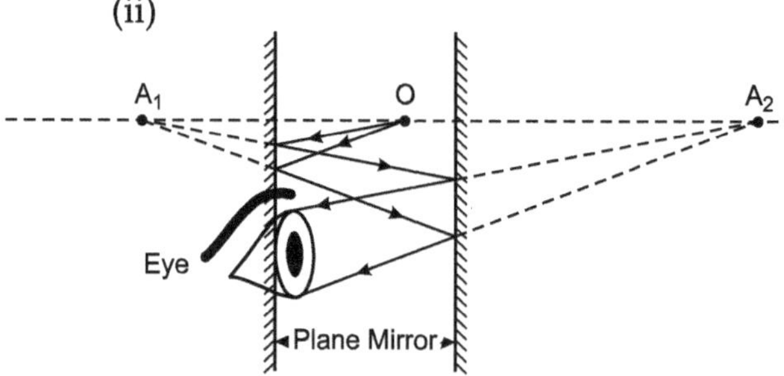

Q. 20. (i) Draw a ray diagram and get the image formed by a concave mirror when an object is kept beyond the centre of curvature at a finite distance.
(ii) State any one characteristics of the image formed in (i).

[November, 2019]

Ans. (i)

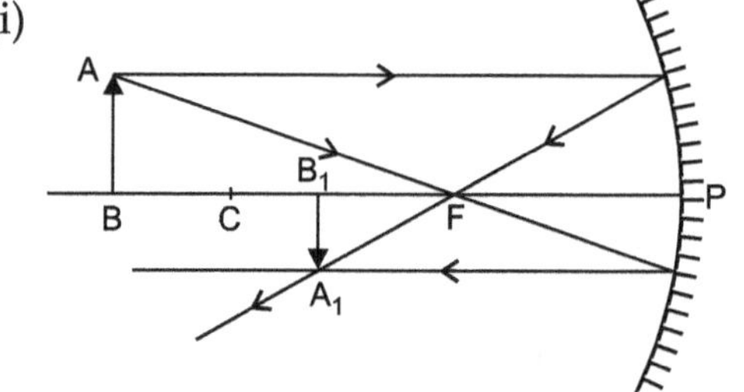

(ii) Image formed is real, inverted and diminished.

Q. 21. Complete the path of the ray AB over plane mirrors M_1 and M_2 and label all the angles of incidences.

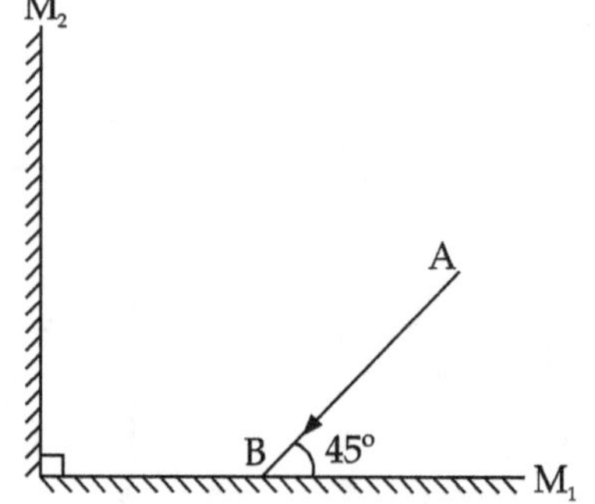

Ans. The complete ray diagram is as follow:

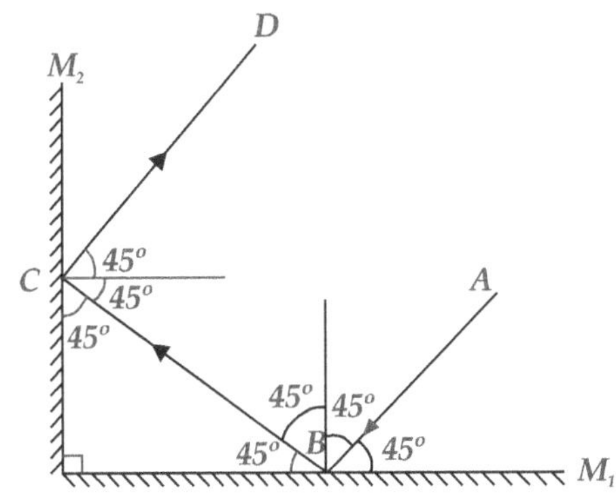

Q. 22. Redraw the following diagram. Complete it by drawing two rays to show the formation of the image of an object AB. What is the size, position and nature of the image formed?

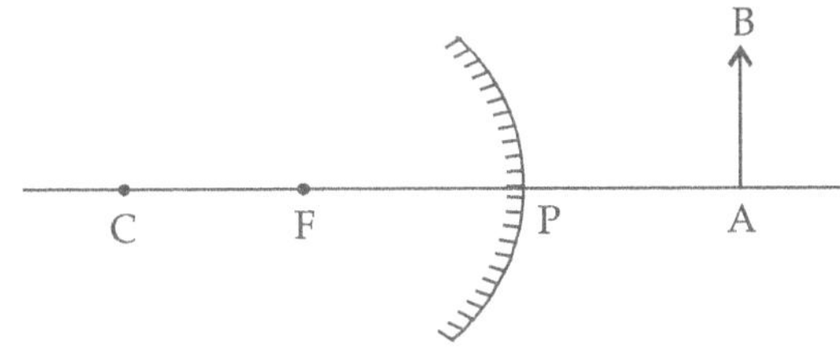

Ans. The required rays are as shown.

The image formed is:

(i)   Smaller in size than the object,

(ii) Formed between P and F, *i.e.*, the pole and the focus of the mirror.

(iii) Virtual in nature.

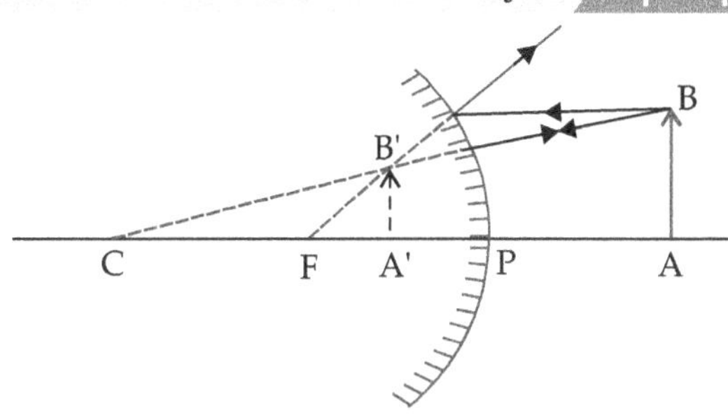

Q. 23. In the given figure, name the kind of mirror shown in the diagram. Complete the ray diagram and find the position of centre of curvature and focus of the mirror if A_1B_1 is the image of object AB.

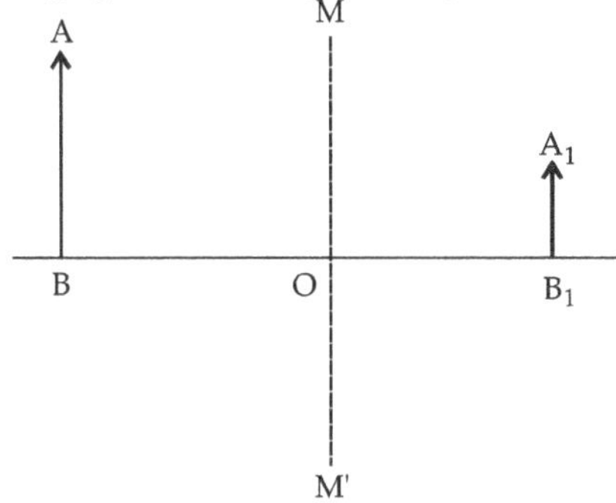

Ans. The complete ray diagram is shown below and the mirror used is a convex mirror.

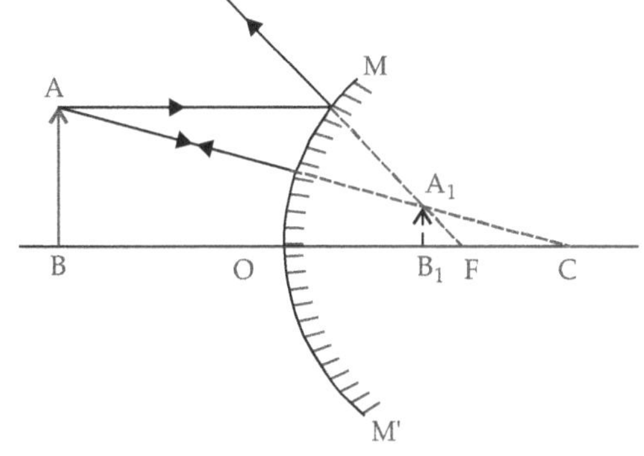

Chapter 8. Propagation of Sound Waves

Q. 1. Draw a diagram representing a wave of amplitude 4 cm and wavelength 2 m. If the frequency of wave is 150 Hz, calculate its velocity.

Ans.

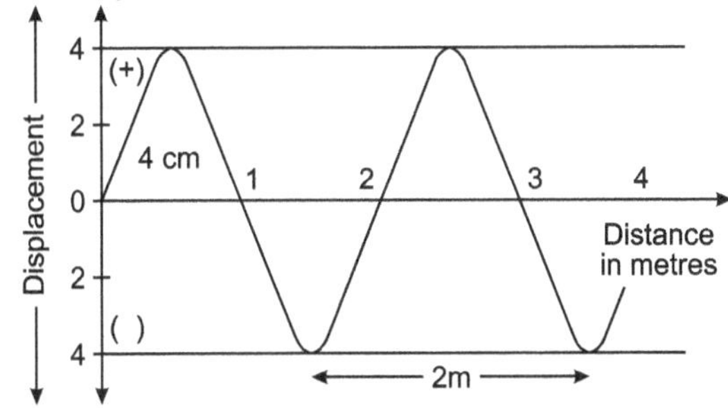

Given, $f = 150$ Hz; $\lambda = 2$ m

$\therefore$ $v = f\lambda = 150 \times 2 = 300$ ms^{-1}.

Q. 2. The diagram shows a vibrating metal blade clamped at one end. P and R are the extreme positions occupied by the blade during its course of vibration, Q, being its position of rest. The vibrating blade produces a note of 480 Hz.

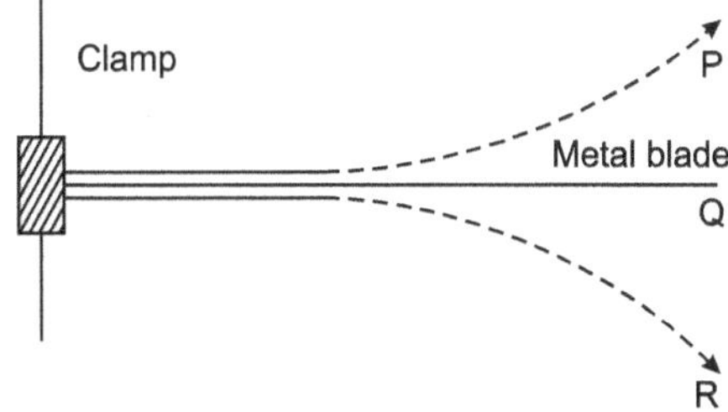

(i)   Mark on the diagram amplitude of vibration.

(ii) If the velocity of sound in air is 320 ms–1, what is the wavelength of sound produced?

Ans. (i)

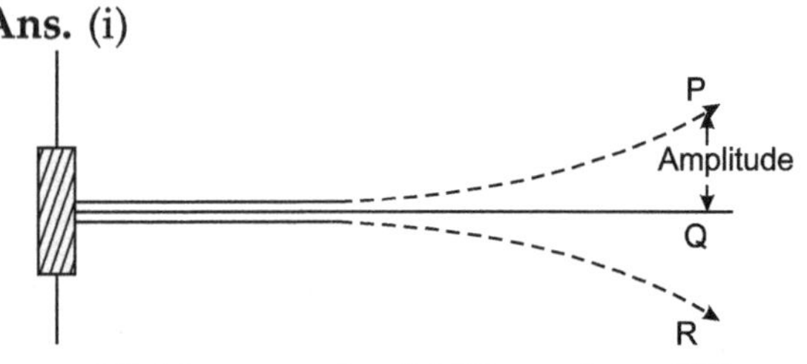

(ii) Given: $f = 480$ Hz and $v = 320$ ms^{-1}

$$\therefore \quad \lambda = \frac{v}{f} = \frac{320}{480} = 0.66 \text{ m}$$

Q. 3. Draw the displacement-time graph of a wave particle.

Ans. The displacement-time graph of a wave particle is

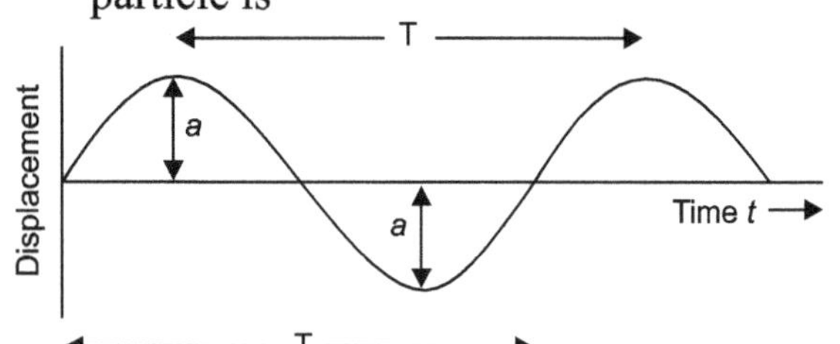

Q. 4. Draw a displacement-distance graph of a wave and mark on it, the amplitude of wave by the letter '*a*' and wavelength of wave by the letter λ.

Ans.

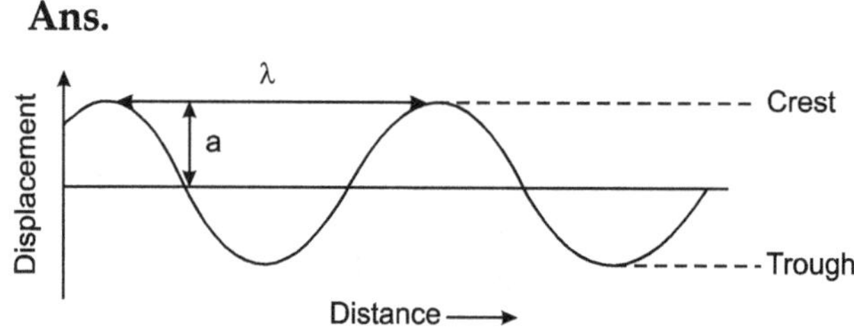

Q. 5. Draw displacement-time graph of a wave and show on it the amplitude and time period of wave.

Ans.

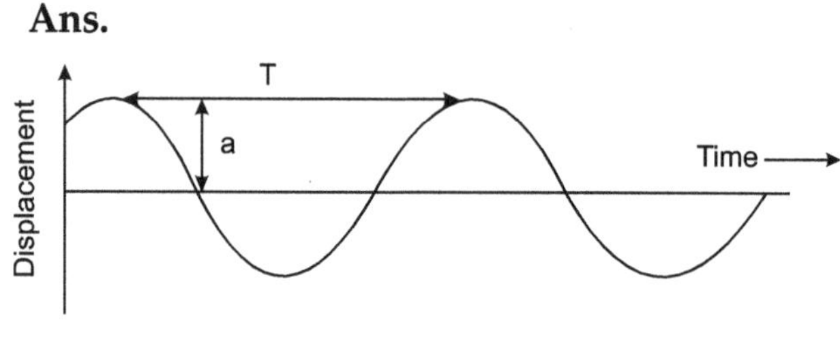

Chapter 9. Current Electricity

Q. 1. Using a cell, key, rheostat, bulb, voltmeter and ammeter,

  (i) Draw an electric circuit

  (ii) Explain the setup.

Ans. (i) The required diagram is,

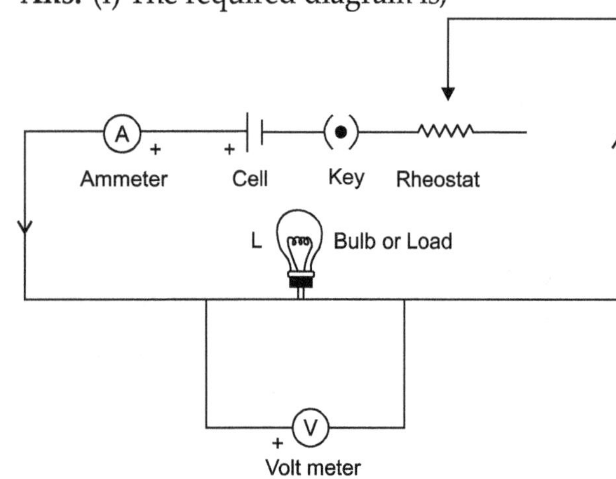

(ii) In the setup of a circuit using a cell, key, rheostat, bulb, voltmeter and ammeter, the bulb act as a load. The ammeter, cell, key and the rheostat are in series with the bulb. And the voltmeter is in parallel connection with the bulb.

Q. 2. How can you make one galvanometer into ammeter? Draw neat and clean diagram.

Ans. Galvanometer can be made an ammeter by adding one resistance parallel to it as shown below:

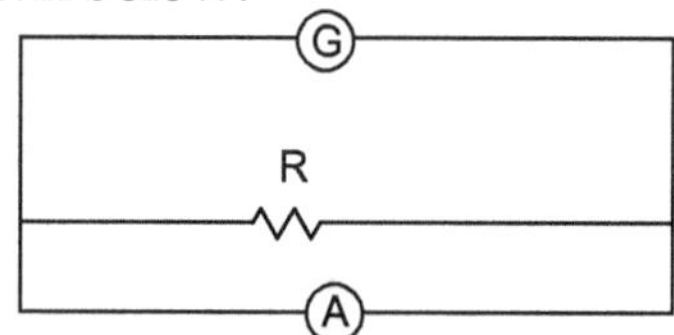

Q. 3. Draw a graph of alternating current.

Ans. The graph of alternating current is a sine curve.

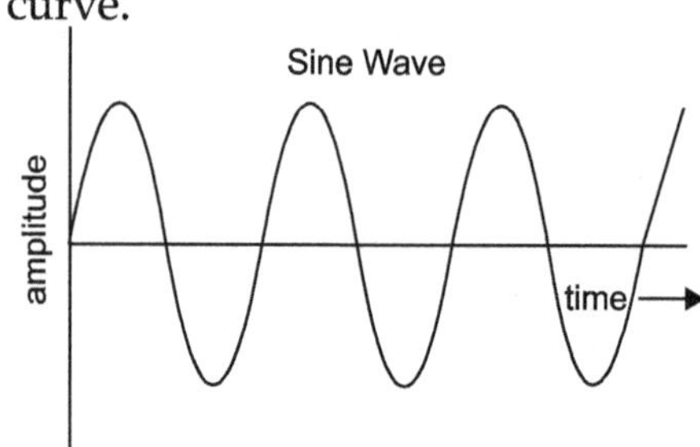

Q. 4. What is Rheostat? Draw the internal structure of Rheostat?

Ans. Rheostat is a device by which resistance in circuit can be varied continuously. It is used to control the magnitude of current in circuit by changing the length of the resistance wire included in the circuit. Circuits of Rheostat is shown below:

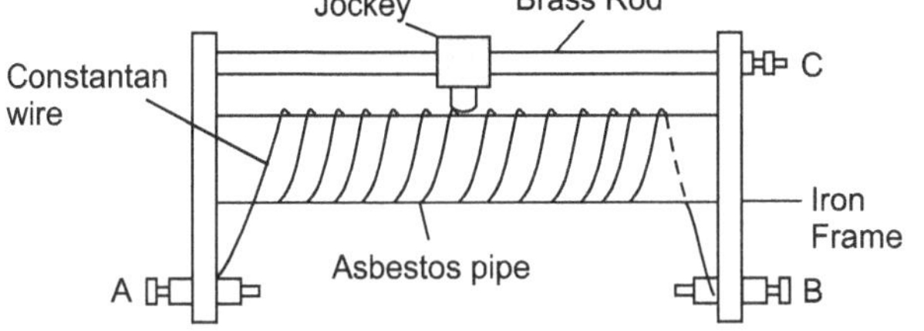

Q. 5. Draw a systematic representation of sources of current.

Ans. All the current sources are shown below:

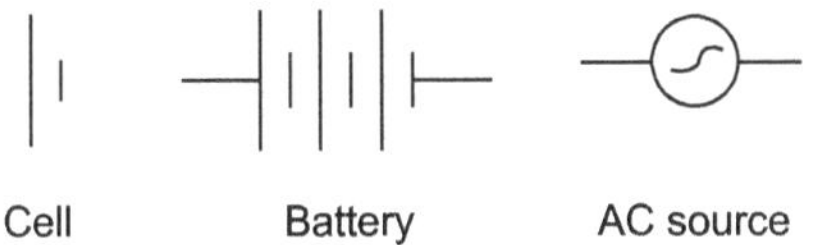

Q. 6. Draw a simple electric circuit.

Ans. A simple circuit diagram is,

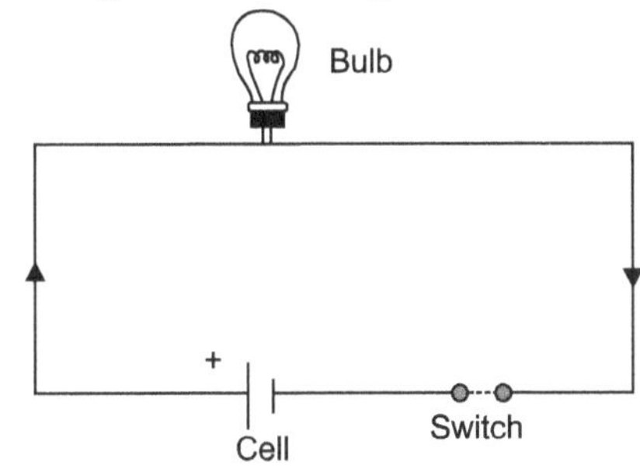

Q. 7. Draw a neat diagram showing

(i) Closed Circuit

(ii) Open circuit

Ans. (i)

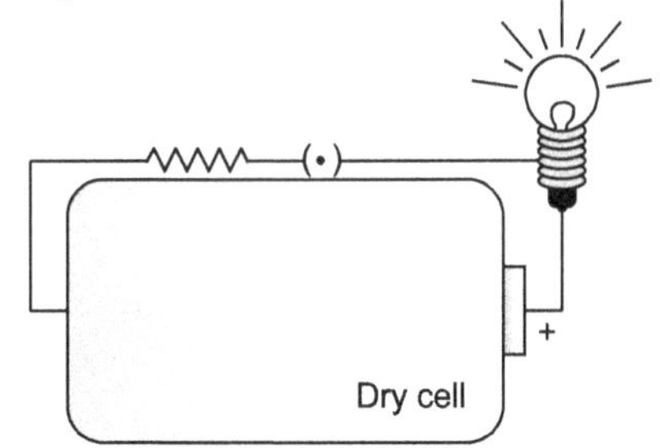

(ii)

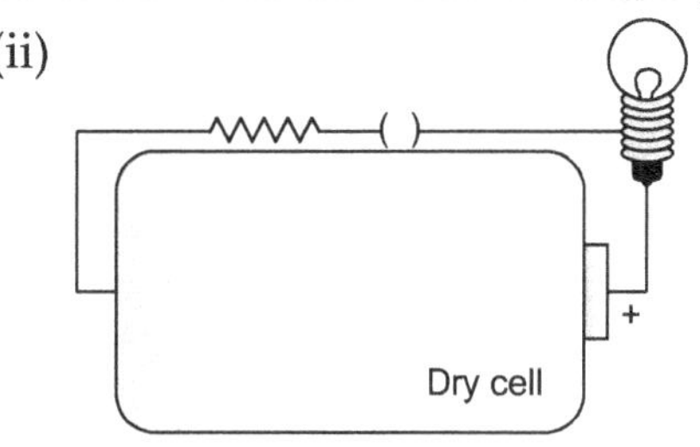

Q. 8. Draw the diagram for collision of electrons with the positive ions due to which the wire offers resistance.

Ans.

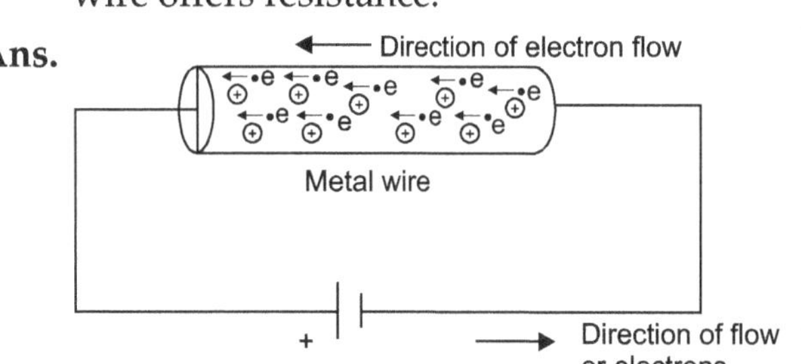

Q. 9. You are given a resistance wire AB connected with a cell and a key. You are required to measure the current in wire AB and the potential difference across it.

(i) Name the instrument that you would use.

(ii) Draw a circuit diagram to show how they are connected.

Ans. (i) To measure current – Ammeter

To measure potential difference – Voltmeter

(ii)

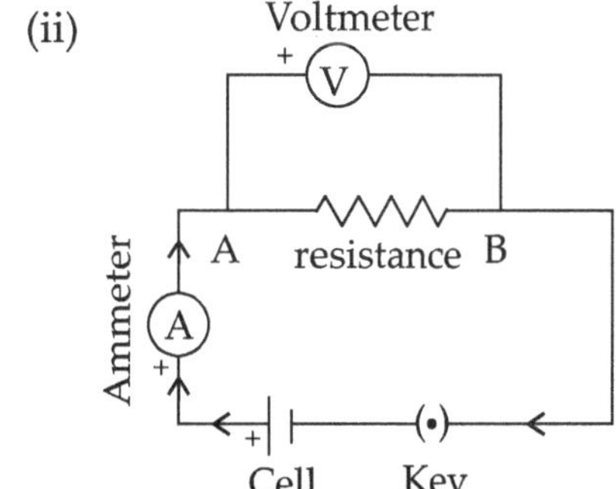

Chapter 10. Magnetism

Q. 1. How does current flow through I-shape electromagnet? Draw a neat and clean diagram of it.

Ans. I shape electromagnet is shown below:

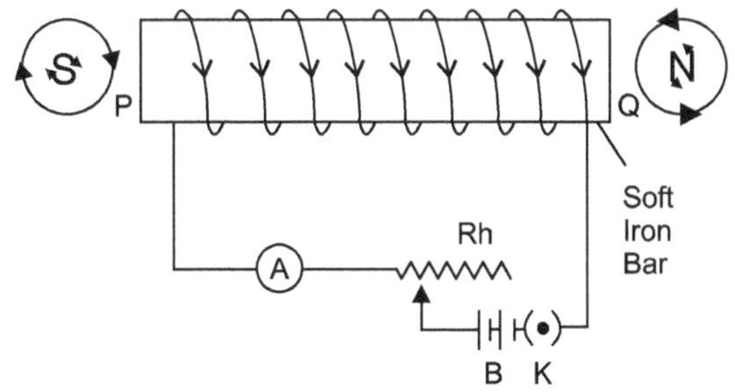

Q. 2. In the following figure, draw at least two magnetic field lines between the two magnets.

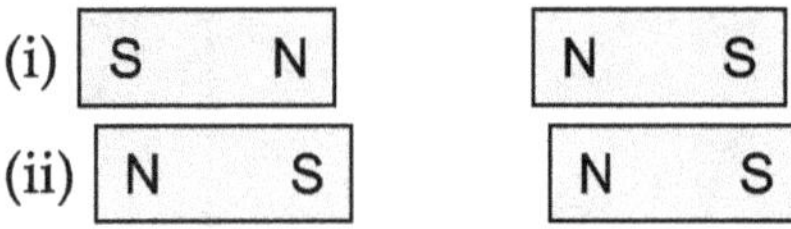

Ans. (i)

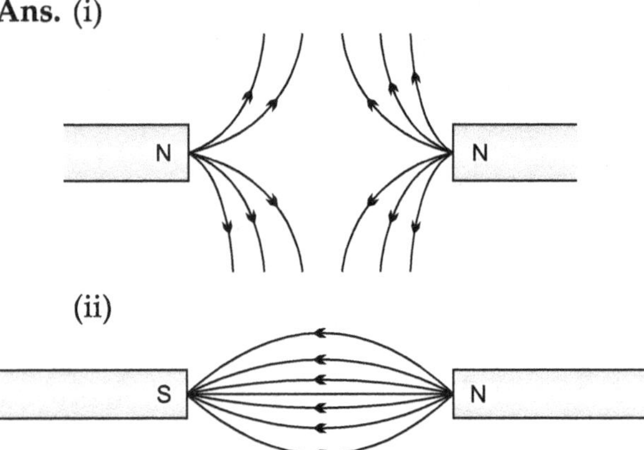

Q. 3. When one bar magnet is broken into two pieces then fill the blank below:

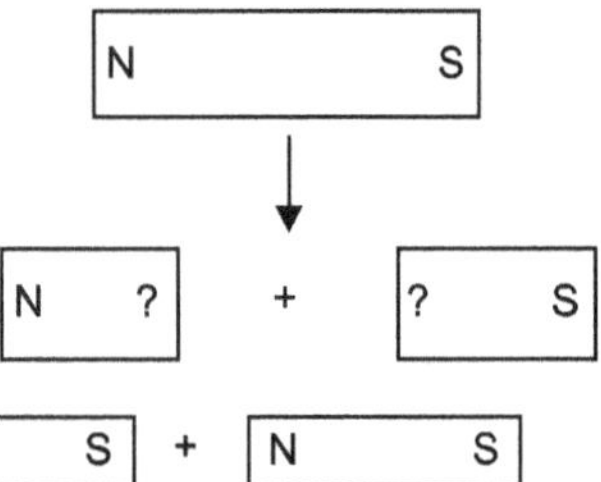

Ans. N   S + N   S

Q. 4. What type of magnetic field does a bar magnet shows? Draw a diagram of it.

Ans. A bar magnet shows non-uniform magnetic field.

The required diagram is

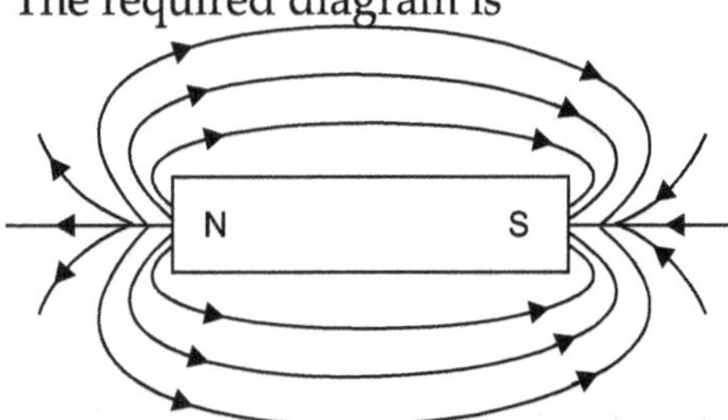

Q. 5. Draw the magnetic field of a horse shoe magnet.

Ans. The magnetic field of horse shoe magnet is

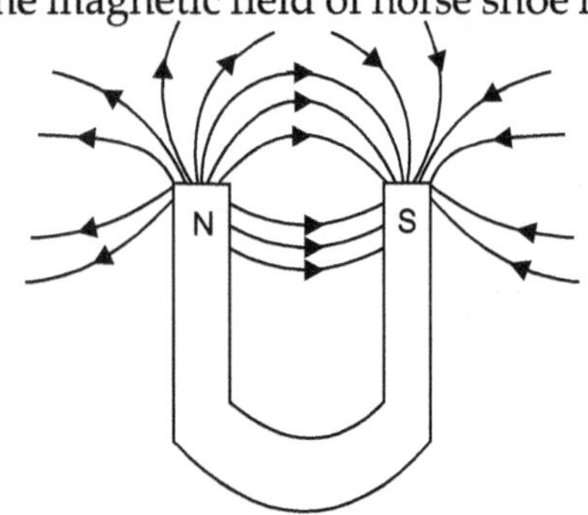

Draw magnetic needle at different place on earth.

Ans. Diagram of magnetic needle at different place on earth is shown below:

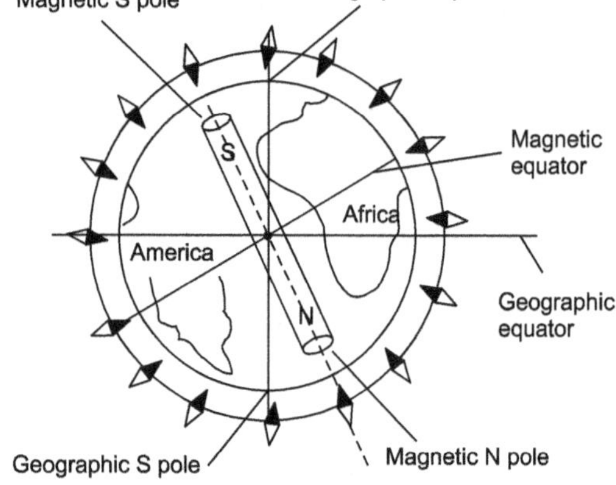

Q. 7. Fig. shows a bar magnet placed on the table top with its north pole pointing towards south. The arrow shows the north-south direction. There are no other magnets or magnetic materials nearby.

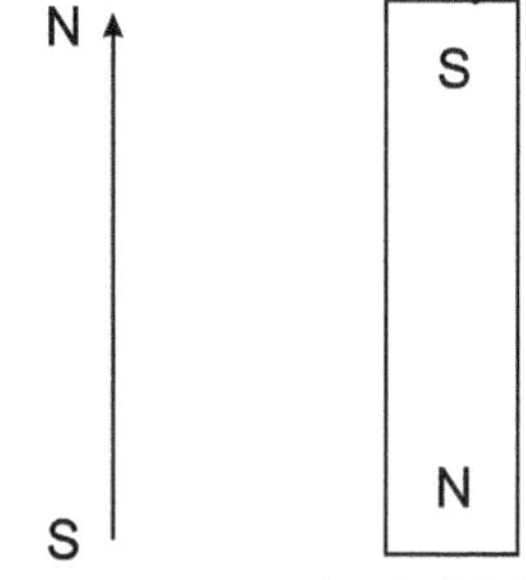

(i) Insert two magnetic field lines on either side of the magnet using arrow head to show the direction of each field line.

(ii) Indicate by crosses, the likely positions of the neutral points.

(iii) What is the magnitude of the magnetic field at each neutral point?
Give a reason for your answer.

Ans. (i)

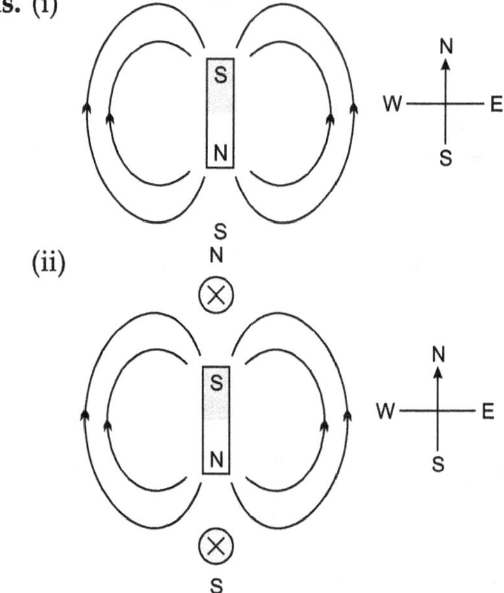

(iii) Magnitude of magnetic field at neutral points is zero. It is so because at these points, the magnetic field of the magnet is equal in magnitude to the earth's horizontal magnetic field, but it is in opposite direction. Hence, they cancel each other.

Q. 8. You are required to make an electromagnet from a soft iron bar by using a cell, an insulated coil of copper wire and a switch.

(i) Draw a circuit diagram to represent the process and label the poles of the electromagnet.

(ii) Name two factors on which the strength of magnetic field of the electromagnet depends.

Ans. (i)

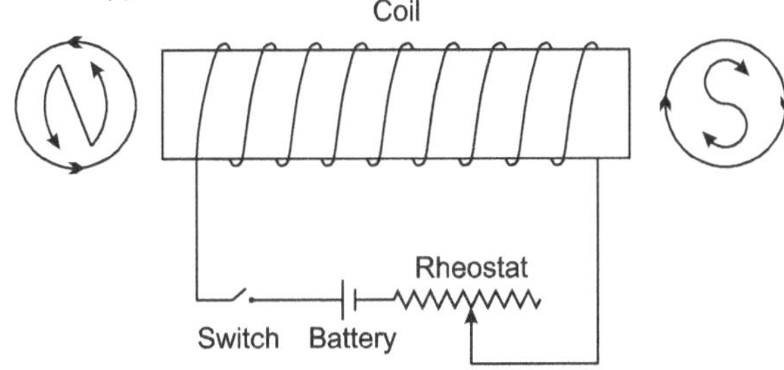

(ii) The strength of magnetic field of an electromagnet depends on:

(a) The number of turns of wire wound around the coil, and

(b) The amount of current flowing through the wire.

Q. 9. (i) Draw the pattern of magnetic field lines near a bar magnet placed with its North Pole pointing towards the geographic North. Indicate the position of neutral points by marking X.

(ii) State whether the magnetic field lines in part (i) represent a uniform magnetic field or non-uniform magnetic field?

Ans. (i)

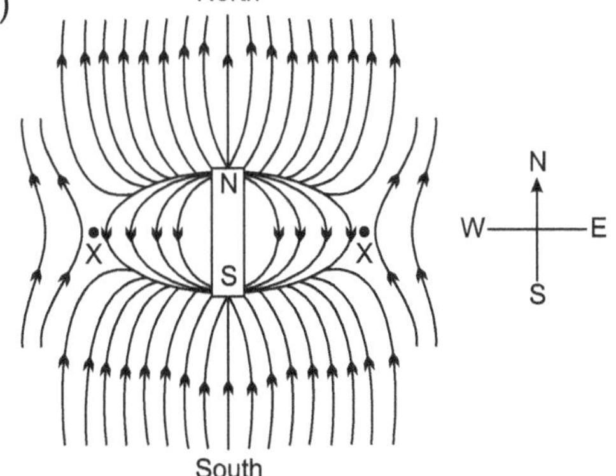

(ii) The magnetic field lines are non-uniform in nature.

Q. 10. Draw diagrams showing the arrangements of the lines of force for:

(i) a single magnet.

(ii) two magnets in line, with unlike poles facing one another.

Ans. (i) Arrangement of the lines of force for a single magnet:

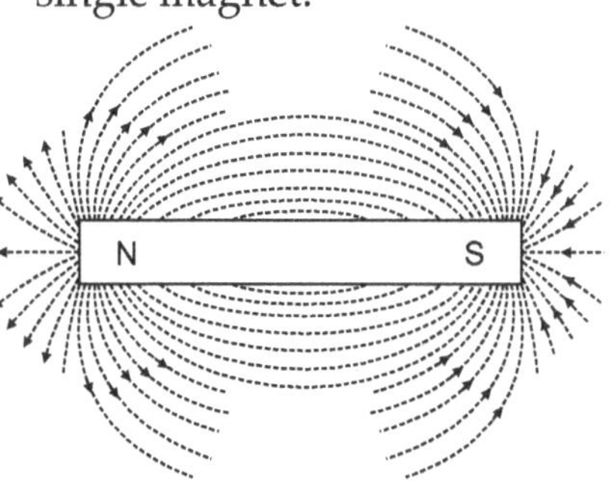

(ii) Arrangement of lines of force for two magnets in line, with unlike poles facing one another:

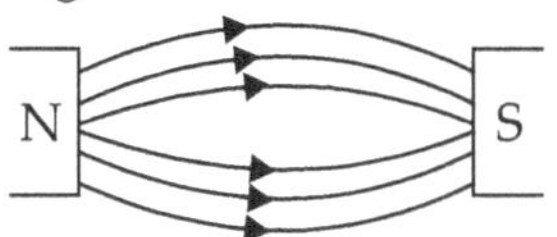

Q. 11. Draw the magnetic flux pattern near a bar magnet placed with its axis in the magnetic meridian and the south pole pointing towards geographic north.

Ans.

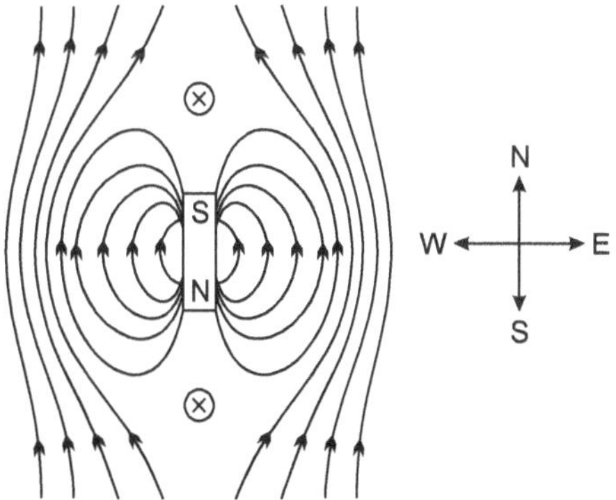

Q. 12. Draw diagrams showing the arrangements of the lines of force for a piece of soft iron laid in line with magnetic field.

Ans. Arrangement of lines of force for a piece of soft iron laid in line with the magnetic is placed in a line with magnetic field.

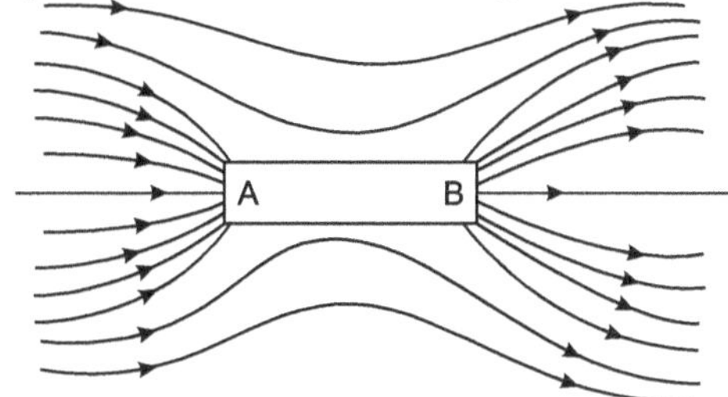

AB is a soft iron rod whose end A behaves as south and end B behaves as north pole when soft iron rod is placed in a line with magnetic field.

Q. 13. Draw lines of force surrounding a bar magnet when it is placed in the magnetic meridian with its

(i) north pole pointing geographic north

(ii) north pole pointing geographic south.

Ans. (i) Bar magnet placed in magnetic meridian with its north pole pointing geographic north.

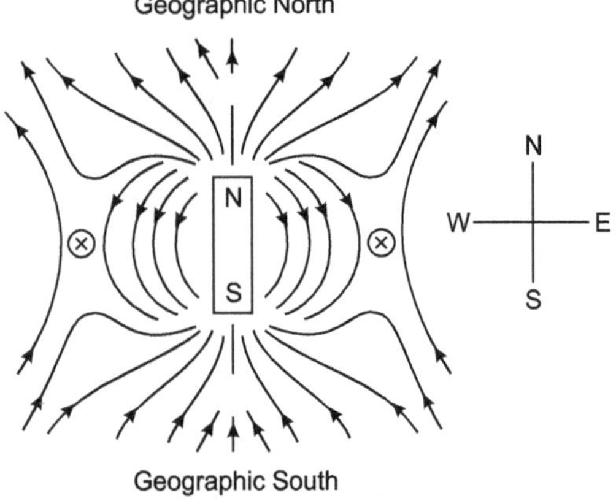

(ii) Bar magnet placed in magnetic meridian with its north pole pointing geographic south.

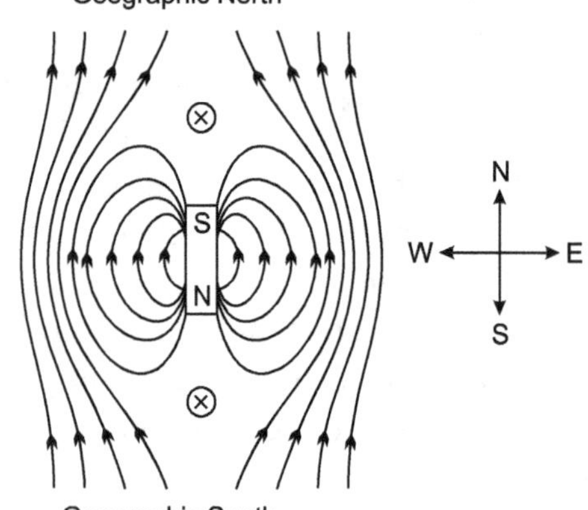

Q. 14. The given figure shows the magnetic field between two magnets.

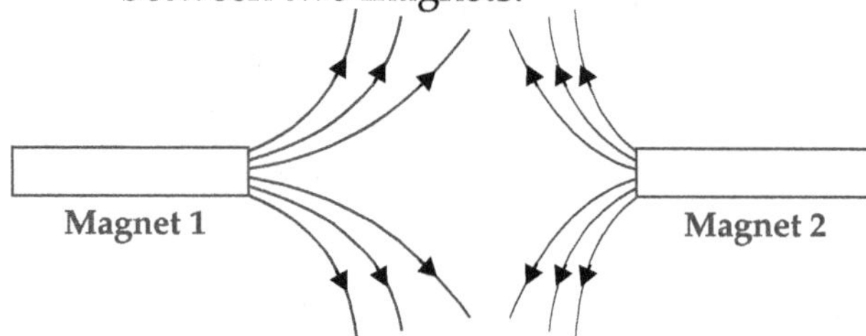

(i) Copy the diagram and label the poles of the magnet.

(ii) Which is the weaker magnet?

Ans. (i) The completed diagram is as follows:

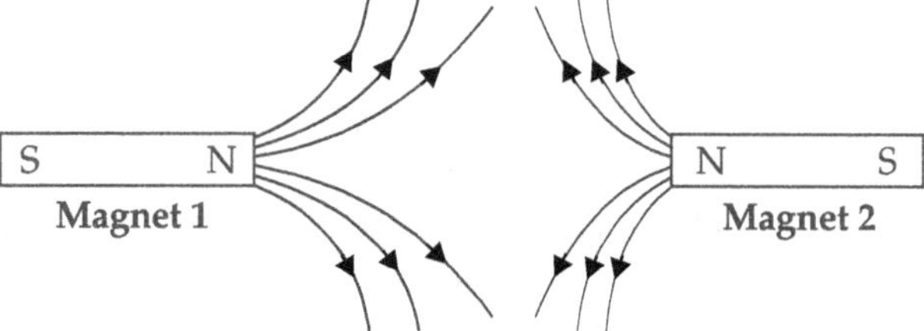

(ii) Magnet 2 is the weaker magnet.

❑

Numericals | Set 8 |

Chapter 1. Measurements and Experimentation

Q. 1. Calculate the time period of a pendulum of length 0.84 m, when $g = 9.8$ ms^{-2}.

Ans. Time period $= 2\pi\sqrt{\dfrac{l}{g}}$

$$= 2\pi\sqrt{\dfrac{0.84}{9.8}}$$

$$= 2 \times 3.14 \times \sqrt{0.0857}$$

$$= 1.84$$

The time period of the pendulum is 1.84 seconds.

Q. 2. Calculate the time period of a simple pendulum of length 1.44 m on the surface of moon where acceleration due to gravity is $\dfrac{1}{6}^{th}$ that of the earth.

Ans. Acceleration due to gravity on earth is 9.8 ms^{-2}

Hence its value on surface of moon is $\left[\dfrac{9.8}{6}\right]$ ms^{-2}

$$\text{Time period} = 2\pi\sqrt{\dfrac{l}{g}}$$

$$= 2 \times 3.14 \times \sqrt{1.44 \times \dfrac{6}{9.8}}$$

$$= 5.90$$

The time period of the pendulum on surface of moon is 5.90 sec.

Q. 3. A simple pendulum completes 60 oscillations in one minute. Find (i) its frequency (ii) its time period.

Ans (i) Number of oscillations in 1 minute (60 seconds) = 60

∴ Number of oscillations in 1 second

$$= \dfrac{60}{60} = 1$$

∴ Frequency = 1 Hz

(ii) Time period $= \dfrac{1}{\text{Frequency}}$

$$= \dfrac{1}{1} = 1 \text{ second}$$

Q. 4. Compare the time periods of a simple pendulum at places where acceleration due to gravity is 2.45 ms^{-2} and 9.8 ms^{-2}.

Ans. Given : $g_1 = 2.45$ ms^{-2} and $g_2 = 9.8$ ms^{-2}

We know, $T \propto \dfrac{1}{\sqrt{g}}$

∴ $\dfrac{T_1}{T_2} = \sqrt{\dfrac{g_2}{g_1}}$

$$\sqrt{\dfrac{9.8}{2.45}} = \sqrt{\dfrac{4}{1}} = \dfrac{2}{1}$$

The ratio of their time periods is 2 : 1.

Q. 5. Length of second's pendulum is 100 cm. Find the length of pendulum whose time period is 2.4 sec.

Ans. Case 1: Time period = 2 sec

Length = 100 cm

Case 2: Time period = 2.4 sec

Length =?

Using the relation,

$$\dfrac{T_1}{T_2} = \sqrt{\dfrac{l_1}{l_2}}$$

$$\dfrac{2}{2.4} = \sqrt{\dfrac{100}{l_2}}$$

$$l_2 = 144 \text{ cm}$$

$$= 1.44 \text{ m}$$

The length of the pendulum is 1.44 m

Q. 6. Compare the time periods of two pendulums at a given place when their lengths are 110 cm and 27.5 cm respectively.

Ans. Using the relation,

$$\frac{T_1}{T_2} = \sqrt{\frac{l_1}{l_2}}$$

$$= \sqrt{\frac{110}{27.5}}$$

$$= \sqrt{\frac{4}{1}}$$

The ratio of their time periods is 2 : 1.

Q. 7. The time periods of two pendulums are 1.44 s and 0.36 s respectively. Calculate the ratio of their lengths.

Ans. Using the relation,

$$\frac{T_1}{T_2} = \sqrt{\frac{l_1}{l_2}}$$

$$\frac{1.44}{0.36} = \sqrt{\frac{l_1}{l_2}}$$

$$\frac{4}{1} = \sqrt{\frac{l_1}{l_2}}$$

The ratio of their lengths is 16 : 1.

Q. 8. An instrument has 20 divisions on Vernier scale which coincides with 19th division of the main scale. If one cm of the main scale is divided into 20 parts, find its least count.

Ans. Value of one division on main scale

$$= \frac{1}{20} = 0.05 \text{ cm}$$

Total number of divisions on vernier scale

$$= 20$$

Least count of vernier caliper

$$= \frac{\text{Value of smallest division on main scale}}{\text{Total number of divisions on vernier scale}}$$

$$= \frac{0.05}{20} = 0.0025 \text{ cm}$$

Q. 9. A vernier scale has 50 divisions which coincide with 49th division of the main scale. The main scale is graduated in ½ mm steps. What is the least count of vernier?

Ans. Least count of vernier caliper

$$= \frac{\text{Value of smallest division on main scale}}{\text{Total number of divisions on vernier scale}}$$

$$= \frac{0.5}{50} = 0.01 \text{mm} = 0.001 \text{cm}$$

Q. 10. The pitch of micrometer screw gauge is 0.1 cm. Find its least count if number of divisions on circular scale is 50.

Ans. Least count of screw gauge is

$$= \frac{\text{Pitch of main scale}}{\text{Total number of divisions on circular scale}}$$

$$= \frac{0.1}{50} = 0.002 \text{ cm}$$

Q. 11. The thimble of a screw gauge has 50 divisions for one revolution. The spindle advances 1 mm when the screw is turned through two revolutions. What is the pitch of the screw? What is the least count of the screw gauge?

OR

If the screw gauge's circular head is divided into 50 division, and the screw travels 1 mm forward in two circular head revolutions. Calculate its

(i) Pitch and

(ii) Least count.

Ans. Pitch of screw = Distance advanced by spindle in one complete revolution

$$= ½ \text{ mm}$$

$$= 0.5 \text{ mm}$$

Least count of screw gauge

$$= \frac{\text{Pitch of main scale}}{\text{Total number of divisions on circular scale}}$$

$$= \frac{0.5}{50} = 0.01 \text{ mm} = 0.001 \text{ cm}$$

Q. 12. Calculate the length of a second's pendulum at a place where acceleration due to gravity is 9.8 m/s².

Ans.

$$l = \frac{gt^2}{4\pi^2}$$

$$= 9.8 \times \frac{2^2}{4 \times \pi^2}$$

$$= 0.992 \text{ m}$$

Q. 13. In an instrument, there are 25 divisions on the Vernier scale which have length of 24 divisions of the main scale. 1 cm on main scale is divided into 20 uniform parts. Find the least count.

Ans. The value of one main scale division (x)

$$= \frac{1}{20} \text{ cm}$$

The number of divisions on Vernier scale(n)

$= 25$

L.C. of vernier

$$= \frac{\text{Value of one main scale division } (x)}{\text{Number of divisions on vernier scale } (n)}$$

$$= \frac{\frac{1}{20}}{25} \text{ cm}$$

$$= \frac{1}{500} \text{ cm}$$

$$= 0.002 \text{ cm}$$

Q. 14. A boy measures the length of a piece of pencil by meter rule, Vernier calipers and screw gauge to be 1.2 cm, 1.24 cm and 1.243 cm respectively. State (i) the least count of each measuring instrument (ii) the accuracy in each measurement.

Ans. (i) Least count of meter scale = 0.1 cm
Least count of Vernier calipers = 0.01 cm
Least count of screw gauge = 0.001 cm
(ii) Accuracy in 1.2 cm = 0.1 cm
Accuracy in 1.24 cm = 0.01 cm
Accuracy in 1.243 cm = 0.001 cm

Q. 15. The pitch of the screw is 0.1cm. Find the reading observed on the screw gauge.

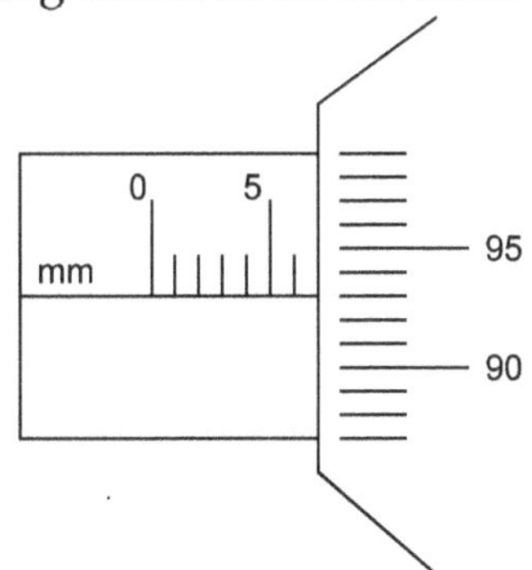

Ans. Least count

$$= \frac{\text{Pitch}}{\text{Number of divisions on circular scale}}$$

$$= \frac{0.1}{100} = 0.001$$

Now, observed reading = main scale reading + (circular scale division × least count)
$= 0.6 \text{ cm} + (92 \times 0.001)$
$= 0.6 + 0.092$
$= 0.692 \text{ cm}$

Q. 16. Find the observed reading and corrected reading in case of vernier calliper shown below if the zero error is + 0.02cm?

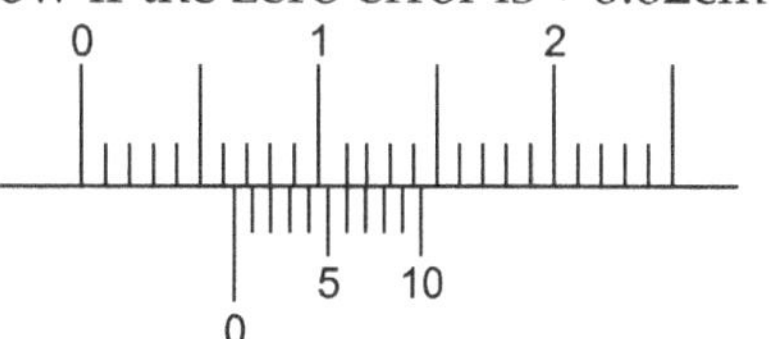

Ans. Least count =

$$\frac{\text{Value of one main scale division } (x)}{\text{Number of divisions on vernier scale } (p)}$$

$$= \frac{0.1}{10} = 0.01$$

Now, observed reading = main scale reading + vernier scale reading
$= 0.6 \text{ cm} + (3 \times 0.01)$
$= 0.6 + 0.03$
$= 0.63 \text{ cm}$

Corrected reading = observed reading – zero error
$= 0.63 – (+ 0.02)$
$= 0.61 \text{ cm}$

Q. 17. Study the following figure carefully and hence calculate (i) pitch (ii) L.C. (iii) reading shown by vernier calliper.

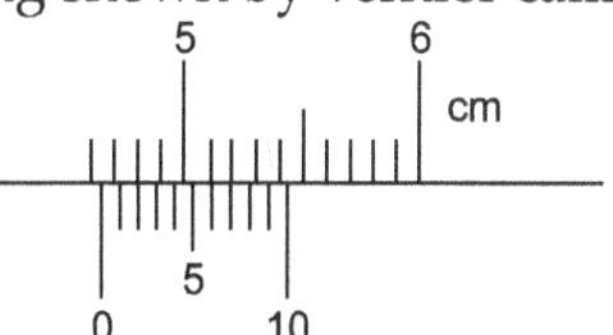

Ans. (i) Pitch $= \dfrac{\text{Unit of main scale}}{\text{Number of divisions in the unit}}$

$$= \frac{1 \text{cm}}{10} = 0.1 \text{ cm}$$

(ii) Least count

$$= \frac{\text{Pitch}}{\text{Number of divisions on vernier scale}}$$

$$= \frac{0.1}{10} = 0.01 \text{ cm}$$

(iii) Observed reading = main scale reading + Vernier scale reading

$= 4.6 + (3 \times 0.01)$

$= 4.6 + 0.03$

$= 4.63$ cm

Q. 18. Figure below shows a screw gauge in which the thimble has 100 divisions. The spindle moves 1 mm ahead in one complete rotation. Calculate the (i) Least count (ii) Diameter of wire.

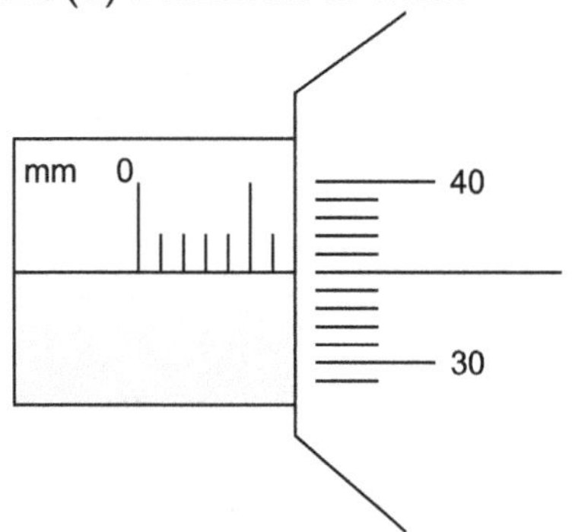

Ans. (i) Pitch = Distance move ahead in one rotation

$= 1$ mm

∴ Least count

$$= \frac{\text{Pitch}}{\text{Number of divisions on circular head}}$$

$$= \frac{1 \text{ mm}}{100} = 0.01 \text{ mm or } 0.001 \text{ cm}$$

(ii) Diameter of wire = Main scale reading + Circular scale reading

$= 0.6$ cm $+ (35 \times 0.001$ cm$)$

$= 0.6 + 0.035$

$= 0.635$ cm.

Chapter 2. Motion in One Dimension

Q. 1. Find the distance covered by a train in 2½ minutes if it travels with uniform speed of 72 km/hr.

Ans. Given : Initial velocity, $u = 72$ kmh^{-1}

$$= 72 \times \frac{5}{18} \text{ ms}^{-1}$$

$$= 20 \text{ ms}^{-1}$$

time, $t = 2½$ min.

$$= \frac{5}{2} \times 60 \text{ s}$$

$$= 150 \text{ s}$$

Distance = Speed × time

$$= 20 \text{ ms}^{-1} \times 150 \text{ s}$$

$$= 3000 \text{ m.}$$

$$= 3 \text{ km}$$

Q. 2. A car starting from rest acquires a velocity 180 ms^{-1} in 0.05 h. Find the acceleration.

Ans. Given : $u = 0$, $v = 180$ ms^{-1} and $t = 0.05\, h$

$0.05\, h = 0.05 \times 60 \times 60$ sec.

$$= 180 \text{ sec.}$$

$$\text{Acceleration} = \frac{v - u}{t}$$

$$= \frac{180 - 0}{180}$$

$$= 1 \text{ ms}^{-2}$$

Q. 3. The displacement of a car with time is given. Draw displacements-time graph and find the average velocity of car. Find its displacements at 1.5 sec and 3.5 sec.

Time (s)	0	1	2	3	4
Displacement (m)	0	5	10	15	20

Ans.

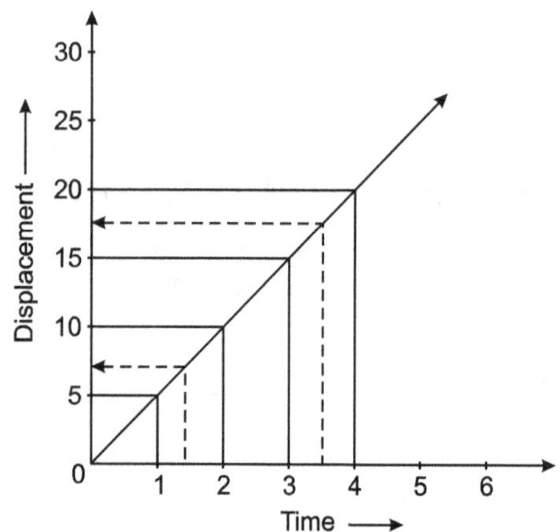

$$\text{Average velocity} = \frac{20}{4}$$

$$= 5 \text{ ms}^{-1}$$

Displacement at 1½ sec. = 7.5 m

At 3½ sec = 17.5 m

Q. 4. Diagram below shows a velocity-time graph of two cars A and B, which start from the same place and move along a straight road in the same direction.

(i) Calculate the acceleration of car A.

(ii) What is the acceleration of car B between 2 s to 4 s?

(iii) At what time intervals both cars have same velocity?

(iv) Which of the two cars is ahead after 8 seconds and by how much?

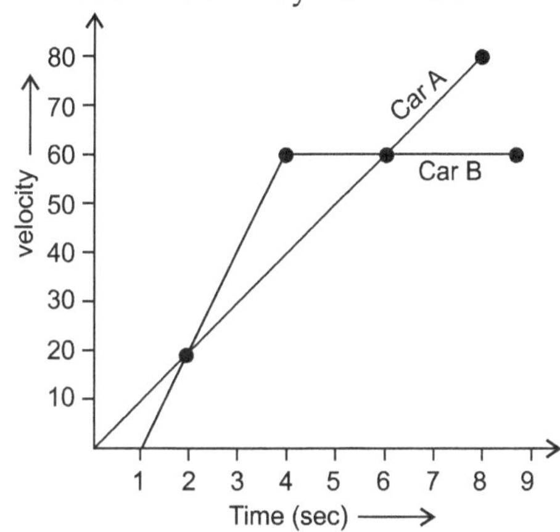

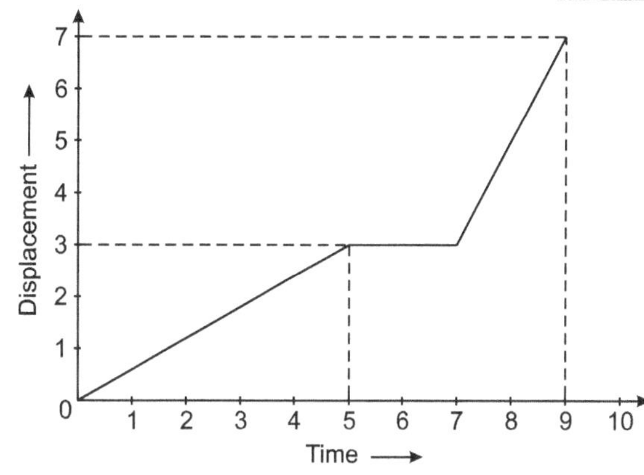

Ans. (i) Acceleration of car A $= \dfrac{80}{8}$

$$= 10 \text{ ms}^{-2}$$

(ii) Acceleration of car B $= \dfrac{60-20}{4-2}$

$$= 13.33 \text{ ms}^{-2}$$

(iii) Both the cars have the same velocity at 2 s and 6 s time interval.

(iv) Distance travelled by car A in 8 s

$$= \dfrac{1}{2} \times 80 \times 8$$

$$= 40 \times 8$$

$$= 320 \text{ m}$$

Distance travelled by car B in 8 s

$$= \dfrac{1}{2} \times (7+4) \times 60$$

$$= \dfrac{1}{2} \times 11 \times 60$$

$$= 330 \text{ m}$$

Hence, car B is ahead of car A by 10 m.

Q. 5. Express 15 ms^{-1} in kmh^{-1}

Ans. $15 \text{ ms}^{-1} = 15 \times \dfrac{1}{1000} \times 3600 \text{ kmh}^{-1}$

$$= 54 \text{ kmh}^{-1}$$

Q. 6. In the figure given below, the displacement of a body is shown at different times.

(i) Calculate the velocity of the body as it moves for :

(a) 0 to 5 s

(b) 5s to 7 s

(c) 7s to 9 s

(ii) Find the average velocity during the time interval 5 s to 9 s.

Ans. (i) (a) Velocity $= \dfrac{\text{Displacement}}{\text{Time}}$

$$V_1 = \left[\dfrac{3-0}{5-0}\right]$$

$$= 0.6 \text{ ms}^{-1}$$

(b) $V_2 = \dfrac{0}{7-5}$

$$= 0 \text{ ms}^{-1}$$

(c) $V_3 = \dfrac{7-3}{9-7}$

$$= \dfrac{4}{2}$$

$$= 2 \text{ ms}^{-1}.$$

(ii) Average velocity

$$= \dfrac{\text{Total displacement}}{\text{Total time taken}}$$

$$= \dfrac{7-3}{9-5}$$

$$= \dfrac{4}{4}$$

$$= 1 \text{ ms}^{-1}.$$

Q. 7. The figure given below, shows the velocity-time graph of a particle moving in a straight line.

(i) Is the motion uniform?

(ii) Is the motion uniformly accelerated?

(iii) Does the particle change its direction of motion?

(iv) Is the distance travelled by the particle from 0 to 4 s same as from 4s to 6 s? If no, compare them.

(v) Find the acceleration from 0 to 4 s and retardation from 4 to 6 s.

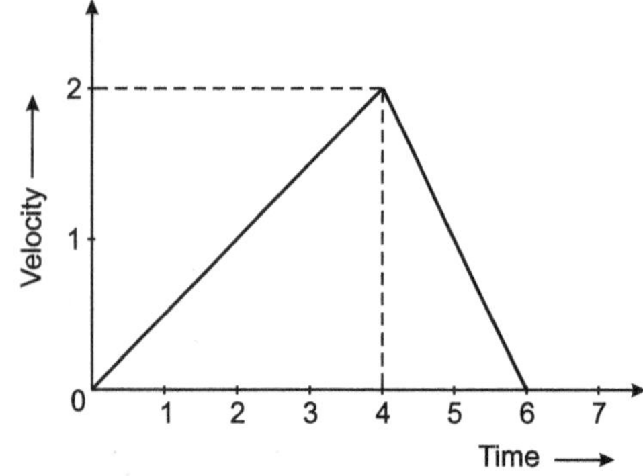

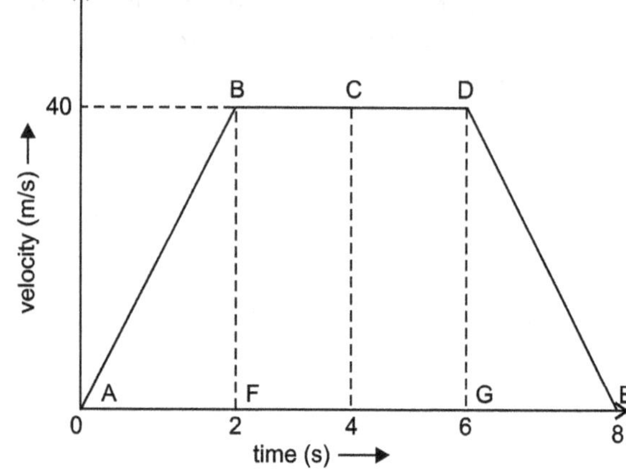

Ans. (i) Particle accelerates from 0 to 4 s and retards from 4 s to 6 s, hence the motion is not uniform.

(ii) No, the motion is not uniform acceleration.

(iii) Since no part of the graph is below the time axis, therefore, there is no displacement in the negative direction and hence no change in the   direction of motion.

(iv) No

Distance travelled from 0 to 4 s
$$= \text{Area of triangle}$$
$$= \frac{1}{2} \times 4 \times 2$$
$$= 4 \text{ m.}$$

Distance travelled from 4s to 6 s
$$= \text{Area of triangle}$$
$$= \frac{1}{2} \times 2 \times 2$$
$$= 2 \text{ m.}$$
$$\text{Ratio} = \frac{4}{2}$$
$$= 2 : 1$$

(v) Acceleration from 0 to 4 s
$$= \text{Slope}$$
$$= \frac{2}{4}$$
$$= 0.5 \text{ ms}^{-2}$$

Retardation from 4 s to 6 s
$$= \frac{-2}{2}$$
$$= -1 \text{ ms}^{-2}$$

Q. 8. From the velocity–time graph given below, calculate :

(i) Acceleration along AB.

(ii) Acceleration along BD

(iii) Total distance travelled.

[November, 2019]

Ans. (i)   A = (0, 0)

B = (2, 40)

$$\text{Acceleration along AB} = \frac{40 - 0}{2 - 0} \text{ ms}^{-2}$$
$$= 20 \text{ ms}^{-2}$$

(ii) B = (2, 40)

D = (6, 40)

$$\text{Acceleration along BD} = \frac{40 - 40}{6 - 2} \text{ ms}^{-2}$$
$$= \frac{0}{4} = 0 \text{ ms}^{-2}$$

(iii) Total distance = Area of trapezium ABDE.

$$= \frac{1}{2} (BD + AE) \times BF$$
$$= \frac{1}{2} (4 + 8) \, 40$$
$$= \frac{1}{2} \times 12 \times 40$$
$$= 240 \text{ m.}$$

Q. 9. Consider the following velocity-time graph of the body in motion as shown and find displacement of the body and distance travelled by the body.

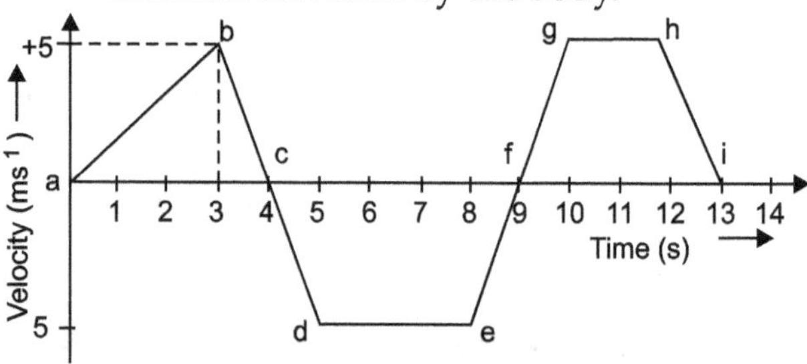

Ans. As shown in figure, area of $\triangle abc$
$$= \frac{1}{2} \times \text{base} \times \text{height}$$

$$= \frac{1}{2} \times 4 \times 5$$

$$= 10 \text{ m}$$

Area of trapezium *cdef*

$$= \frac{1}{2} \times (\text{sum of parallel sides}) \times \text{height}$$

$$= \frac{1}{2} \times (5 + 3) \times 5$$

$$= 20 \text{ m}$$

Area of trapezium *fghi*

$$= \frac{1}{2} \times (4 + 2) \times 5 = 15 \text{ m}$$

Then the displacement of the body = area of Δabc – area of trapezium *cdef* + area of trapezium *fghi*

$= (10 - 20 + 15) \text{ m} = 5 \text{ m}.$

But the total distance travelled by body = area of Δabc + area of trapezium *cdef* + area of trapezium *fghi* = 10 m + 20 m + 15 m = 45 m

Q. 10. From the following displacement-time graph of a cyclist, find :

(i) the average velocity in first 4 s,

(ii) the displacement from the initial position at the end of 10 s,

(iii) the time after which he will reach the starting point.

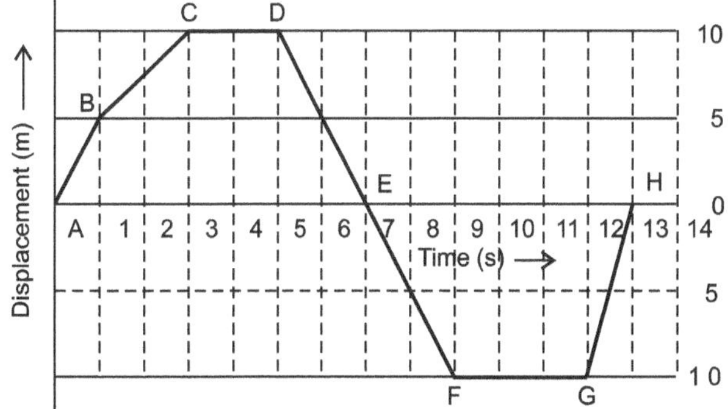

Ans. (i) Average velocity in first 4 s

$$= \frac{\text{Displacement in 4 s}}{\text{Time interval}}$$

$$= \frac{10 \text{ m}}{4 \text{ s}} = 2.5 \text{ m/s}$$

(ii) Displacement from the initial position to the end of 10 s = – 10 m

(iii) At 7 s and 13 s, the displacement is 0, so after 7 s and 13 s, the cyclist will reach at the starting point.

Q. 11. From the given velocity-time graph, find

(i) the acceleration in parts AB, BC and CD.

(ii) displacement in each pair, and

(iii) total displacement.

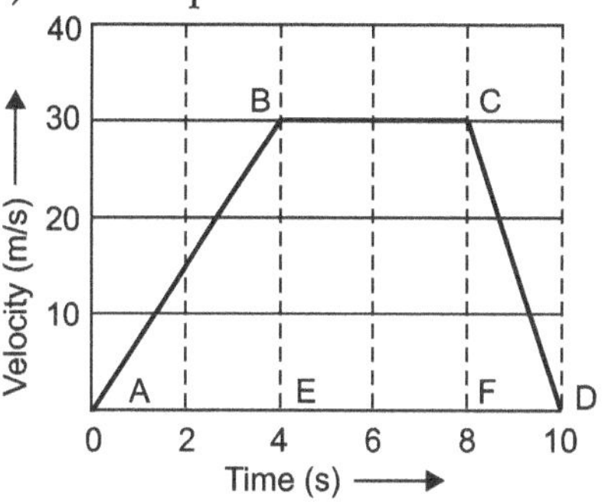

Ans. Acceleration in part AB

$$= \frac{(30 - 0) \text{ m/s}}{(4 - 0) \text{ s}} = 7.5 \text{ m/s}^2$$

Acceleration in part BC

$$= \frac{(30 - 30) \text{ m/s}}{(8 - 4) \text{ s}} = 0$$

Acceleration in part CD

$$= \frac{(0 - 30) \text{ m/s}}{(10 - 8) \text{ s}} = -15 \text{ m/s}^2$$

(ii) Displacement in part AB = Area of

$$\Delta\text{ABE} = \frac{1}{2} \times \text{BE} \times \text{AE}$$

$$= \frac{1}{2} \times 30 \times 4 = 60 \text{ m}$$

Displacement in part BC = Area of $\square$ BCFE = BC × CF = 4 × 30 = 120 m

Displacement in part CD = Area of ΔCFD

$$= \frac{1}{2} \times \text{CF} \times \text{FD} = \frac{1}{2} \times 30 \times 2 = 30 \text{ m}$$

(iii) Total displacement = 60 m + 120 m + 30 m = 210 m.

Q. 12. The given figure represents the displacement-time sketch of motion of two cars X and Y. Find :

(i) The distance by which the car Y was initially ahead of car X.

(ii) Velocities of cars X and Y.

(iii) The time in which the car X will catch the car Y.

(iv) The distance from start when the car X will catch car Y.

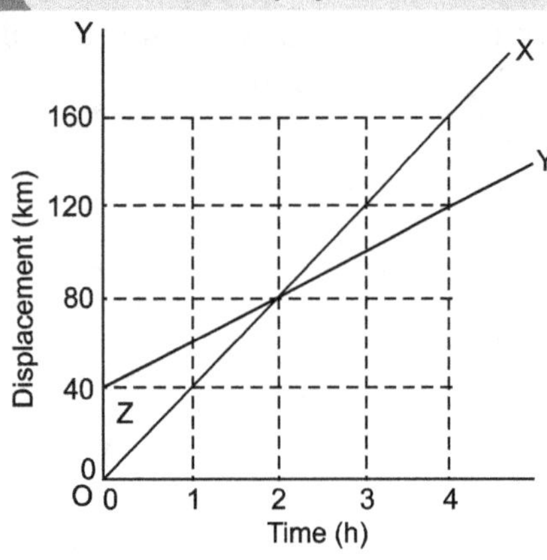

Ans. (i) Initially the car Y was ahead of car X by 40 km.

(ii) Velocity of car X = slope of OX

$$= \frac{(160-0)\,\text{km}}{(4-0)\,\text{h}} = 40 \text{ km/h}$$

Velocity of car Y = slope of line ZY

$$= \frac{(120-40)\,\text{km}}{(4-0)\,\text{h}} = \frac{80\,\text{km}}{4\,\text{h}} = 20 \text{ km/h}$$

(iii) The car X will catch the car Y after 2 h.

(iv) From start, the car X will catch the car Y at a distance of 80 km.

Q. 13. The figure below shows the velocity-time graph of a body moving in a straight line.

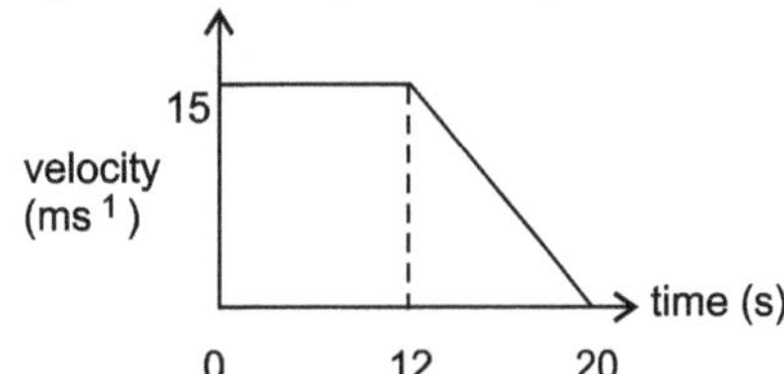

Find :

(i) The time interval in which the body is moving with zero acceleration.

(ii) The total displacement of the body.

[February, 2020]

Ans. (i) The body has zero acceleration from time interval 0 s to 12 s.

(ii) Total displacement = Area of trapezium ABCO

$$= \frac{1}{2}\,(AB + CO) \times OA$$

$$= \frac{1}{2}\,(12 + 20) \times 15 \text{ m}$$

$$= \frac{1}{2} \times 32 \times 15 \text{ m}$$

$$= 240 \text{ m.}$$

Q. 14. An athlete runs around a circular path of circumference 360 m in 1 minute and reaches the starting point. Calculate:
(i) distance covered by the athlete
(ii) displacement
(iii) average speed
(iv) average velocity.

Ans. (i) Distance covered = Length of path travelled along circumference

= 360 m

(ii) Displacement = Zero. It is because the athlete reaches back at the initial point.

(iii) Average speed = $\dfrac{\text{Distance covered}}{\text{time taken}}$

$$= \frac{360\,\text{m}}{60\,\text{s}}$$

$$= 6 \text{ ms}^{-1}$$

(iv) Average velocity = $\dfrac{\text{displacement}}{\text{time}}$

$$= \frac{0}{60}$$

$$= 0 \text{ ms}^{-1}$$

Q. 15. A train takes 80 minutes to travel from station P to Q and 40 minutes to return from Q to P. If the distance between P to Q is 60 km, calculate
(i) average speed
(ii) average velocity of train.

Ans. (i) Total distance between P and Q on both ways journey = 2 × 60

= 120 km.

Total time for journey

= 40 + 80

= 120 min

= 2 hr.

(i) Average speed = $\dfrac{\text{Total Distance}}{\text{Total Time}}$

$$= \frac{120}{2}$$

$$= 60 \text{ kmh}^{-1}$$

(ii) Average velocity = $\dfrac{\text{Displacement}}{\text{Time}}$

$$= \frac{0}{2}$$

$$= 0 \text{ kmh}^{-1}$$

Q. 16. A car travels first 30 km with a uniform speed of 60 kmh^{-1} and the next 30 km with a uniform speed of 40 kmh^{-1}. Calculate :
(i) The total time of journey
(ii) The average speed of the car

Ans. (i) Time taken for the first journey

$$= \frac{\text{Distance covered}}{\text{Speed}}$$

$$= \frac{30}{60}$$

$$= \frac{1}{2} \text{ hr.}$$

Time taken for the second journey

$$= \frac{30}{40}$$

$$= \frac{3}{4} \text{ hr}$$

Total time of journey $t = t_1 + t_2$

$$\therefore \quad = \frac{1}{2} + \frac{3}{4}$$

$$= \frac{5}{4} \text{ hr}$$

$$= 1.25 \text{ hr.}$$

(ii) Average speed

$$= \frac{\text{Total distance covered}}{\text{Total time taken}}$$

$$= \frac{30 + 30}{5/4}$$

$$= 60 \times \frac{4}{5}$$

$$= 48 \text{ kmh}^{-1}$$

Q. 17. The Shatabadi Express covers a distance of 450 km in 5 hr between Amritsar and Delhi. What is average speed of train in (i) kmh^{-1} (ii)ms^{-1}.

Ans. Distance between Amritsar and Delhi

$$= 450 \text{ km.}$$

Time for journey $= 5$ hr.

(i) Speed of train $= \dfrac{\text{distance covered}}{\text{time taken}}$

$$= \frac{450}{5}$$

$$= 90 \text{ kmh}^{-1}.$$

(ii) Speed of train in ms^{-1}

$$= 90 \times \frac{5}{18} \text{ ms}^{-1}$$

$$= 25 \text{ ms}^{-1}$$

Q. 18. A car at rest attains a velocity of 25 ms^{-1} in 10 s. Then brakes are applied and car is brought to rest in 5 sec. Find:-
(i) acceleration of car (ii) retardation of car.

Ans. (i) By Newton's 1st equation of motion,

$$v = u + at$$

$$\therefore \quad a = \frac{v - u}{t}$$

$$= \frac{25 - 0}{10}$$

$$= 2.5 \text{ ms}^{-2}$$

$\therefore$ acceleration of the car is 2.5 ms^{-2}

(ii) For retardation,

$$r = \frac{v - u}{t}$$

$$= \frac{0 - 25}{5}$$

$$= -5 \text{ ms}^{-2}$$

$\therefore$ retardation of the car is $- 5$ ms^{-2}

Q. 19. A motorboat starting from rest on a lake accelerates in a straight line at a constant rate of 3 ms^{-2} for 8.0 s. How far does the boat travel during this time?

Ans. By Newton's 2nd equation of motion,

$$S = ut + \frac{1}{2} at^2$$

we have,

$$S = 0 \times 8 + \frac{1}{2} \times 3 \times 8^2$$

$$= 96 \text{ m.}$$

Q. 20. As one blinks, the eyelids move to close the eyes for a moment and again move back to open them. If the radius of the eyeball is about 1 cm and the lids move about double of the radius of the eyeball. estimate the speed with which we blink our eyes, if the time for 50 blinks is 16.67 s.

Ans. For one blink, the time required

$$= 16.67 \times \frac{1}{50}$$

$$= \frac{1}{3} \text{ s}$$

Numericals

Speed with which we blink our eyes

$$= \frac{\text{distance}}{\text{time}}$$

$$= 2 \times 3 \text{ cms}^{-1}$$
$$= 6 \text{ cms}^{-1}$$

Q. 21. A spacecraft travelling in space at 300 kms^{-1} fires the engine for 15 second such that its final velocity is 600 kms^{-1}. Calculate the total distance travelled by the ship in one minute starting from the time of firing.

Ans. Case (i) When the space ship is accelerating, applying the Newton's 1st equation of motion,

$$v = u + at$$
$$600 = 300 + a \times 15$$
$$a = 20 \text{ kms}^{-2}$$

Applying Newton's 2nd equation,

$$S = ut + \frac{1}{2} at^2$$

$$= 300 \times 15 + \frac{1}{2} \times 20 \times 15^2$$

$$= 6750 \text{ km}$$

Case (ii) When space ship is moving with uniform velocity of 600 kms^{-1} for next 45 s

Distance covered

$$= \text{Uniform velocity} \times \text{time}$$
$$= 600 \times 45$$
$$= 27000 \text{ km}$$

$\therefore$ Total distance travelled by spaceship in one minute

$$= 6750 + 27000$$
$$= 33,750 \text{ km.}$$

Q. 22. A scooter moving at a velocity of 5 m/s picks up a velocity of 35 m/s in 5 seconds. Calculate the average acceleration.

[November, 2019]

Ans. $u = 5 \text{ ms}^{-1}$, $v = 35 \text{ ms}^{-1}$, $t = 5$ s.

$\therefore$ Average acceleration

$$= \frac{\text{Change in velocity}}{\text{time}}$$

$$= \frac{(35 - 5)}{5} \text{ ms}^{-2}$$

$$= \frac{30}{5} \text{ ms}^{-2} = 6 \text{ ms}^{-2}$$

Q. 23. A train moving with uniform speed covers approximately 120 m in 2 s. calculate(i) the speed of the train, (ii) the time it will take to cover 240 m.

Ans. Given, S = 120 m, t = 2 s

(i) Speed of the train $= \dfrac{\text{distance travelled}}{\text{time taken}}$

$$= \frac{120 \text{ m}}{2 \text{s}}$$

$$= 60 \text{ ms}^{-1}$$

(ii) Time taken to cover 240 m distance

$$= \frac{\text{distance}}{\text{speed}}$$

$$= \frac{240 \text{ m}}{60 \text{ ms}^{-1}}$$

$$= 4 \text{ s}$$

Q. 24. A car initially at rest starts moving with a constant acceleration of 0.5 ms^{-2} and travels a distance of 25 m. Find :
(i) the final velocity, and
(ii) the time taken.

Ans. Given,
Initial velocity $u = 0$,
Acceleration $a = 0.5 \text{ ms}^{-2}$
Distance travelled S = 25 m
(i) From the 3rd equation of motion
$$v^2 = u^2 + 2aS$$
$$v^2 = 0 + 2 \times 0.5 \times 25$$
$$v = 5$$
Hence, final velocity is $v = 5 \text{ ms}^{-1}$.
(ii) From the 1st equation of motion,
$$v = u + at$$
$$5 = 0 + 0.5 \times t$$
$$t = \frac{5}{0.5} = 10$$

Therefore, time taken is 10 s.

Q. 25. A particle begins to move in a straight line from a point with velocity 20 ms^{-1} and acceleration of $- 2.0 \text{ ms}^{-2}$. Find out position and velocity of the particle at $t = 10$ s.

Ans. Given, $u = 20 \text{ ms}^{-1}$, $a = - 2.0 \text{ ms}^{-2}$, $t = 10$ s

Displacement, $S = ut + \dfrac{1}{2} at^2$

Substituting all values in above equation, we have

$$S = 20 \times 10 + \frac{1}{2}(-2.0) \times 100$$

$$S = 100 \text{ m}$$

After 10s, particle will be at distance 100 m.

Velocity at $t = 10$ is,

$$v = u + at$$
$$= 20 + (-2.0)10$$
$$= 0$$

Particle is momentarily at rest at $t = 10$ s.

Q. 26. A pebble thrown vertically upward with an initial velocity 50 ms^{-1} comes to a stop in 5 second. Find the retardation

Ans. Given, $u = 50$ ms^{-1}, $v = 0$ ms^{-1}, $t = 5$ s

Acceleration would be

$$a = \frac{v - u}{t} = \frac{(0 - 50)\text{ms}^{-1}}{5\text{s}} = -10 \text{ ms}^{-2}$$

Hence, retardation = 10 ms^{-2}

Q. 27. A body having an initial velocity of 20 kmh^{-1} accelerates uniformly at the rate of 9 cm.s^{-2} to cover a distance of 200 m. Find the final velocity of the body.

Ans. Given,

$$a = 9 \text{ cm s}^{-2}$$
$$= \frac{9}{100} \text{ ms}^{-2}$$
$$= 0.09 \text{ ms}^{-2}$$

Also, $\quad u = 20 \text{ kmh}^{-1}$

$$= \frac{20 \times 1000}{60 \times 60} \text{ ms}^{-1}$$
$$= \frac{200}{36} \text{ ms}^{-1}$$
$$= 5.56 \text{ ms}^{-1}$$

And, the distance $S = 200$ m

From 3rd equation of motion, we have

$$v^2 = u^2 + 2aS$$
$$v^2 = (5.56)^2 + 2 \times 0.09 \times 200$$
$$= 30.91 + 36$$
$$= 66.91$$
$$v = \sqrt{66.91}$$
$$= 8.1799$$
$$\approx 8.18 \text{ ms}^{-1}$$

Hence, final velocity is $v = 8.189$ ms^{-1}.

Q. 28. A ball is initially moving with a velocity 0.5 ms^{-1}. Its velocity decreases at a rate of 0.05 ms^{-2}.

(i) How long will it take to stop?

(ii) How far the ball can travel before it stops?

Ans. Given,

$$u = 0.5 \text{ ms}^{-1}$$
$$v = 0$$
$$a = -0.05 \text{ ms}^{-2}$$

(i) From the 1st equation of motion,

$$v = u + at$$
$$0 = 0.5 - 0.05 \times t$$
$$0.05t = 0.5$$
$$t = 10 \text{ s}$$

(ii) From the 3rd equation of motion,

$$v^2 = u^2 + 2aS$$
$$0 = 0.5^2 - 2 \times 0.05 \times S$$
$$0.1S = 0.25$$
$$S = \frac{0.25}{0.1}$$
$$S = 2.5 \text{ m}$$

Q. 29. A bicycle initially is moving in a straight line with velocity 5.0 ms^{-1} which afterwards accelerates for 5 s at a rate of 2 ms^{-2}. What will be its final velocity?

Ans. Given,

$$v = 5.0 \text{ ms}^{-1}, t = 5s, a = 2 \text{ ms}^{-2}$$

From 1st equation of motion,

$$v = u + at$$
$$v = 5 + 2 \times 5$$
$$v = 5 + 10$$
$$v = 15 \text{ ms}^{-1}$$

Q. 30. After applying brakes, a car travels a distance of 0.25 km for a 5 s. Calculate the instantaneous speed of the car during the retardation period.

Ans. Given,

$$S = 0.25 \text{ km}$$
$$t = 5 \text{ s}$$

$$\text{Instantaneous speed} = \frac{\text{distance}}{\text{time}}$$
$$= \frac{0.25}{5}$$
$$= 0.05 \text{ kms}^{-1}$$

Q. 31. A car is moving with a velocity 20 ms^{-1}. When the brakes are used it is retarded at a rate of 2 ms^{-2}. What will the velocity after 5 s of applying the brakes?

Ans. Given,

$$u = 20 \text{ ms}^{-1}$$
$$a = -2 \text{ ms}^{-2}$$
$$t = 5 \text{ s}$$

Acceleration is given by,

$$a = \frac{v - u}{t}$$

$$-2 = \frac{v - 20}{5}$$

$$-10 + 20 = v$$
$$v = 10 \text{ ms}^{-1}$$

After 5 s, the velocity of the car will be 10 ms^{-1}.

Q. 32. A body initially at rest travels a distance 100 m in 5 s with a constant acceleration. Calculate: (i) the acceleration, (ii) the final velocity.

Ans. Given,

$$u = 0$$
$$S = 100 \text{ m}$$
$$t = 5 \text{ s}$$

(i) The 2nd equation of motion is

$$S = ut + \frac{1}{2} at^2$$

$$100 = 0 \times 5 + \frac{1}{2} \times a \times 5^2$$

$$100 = \frac{1}{2} \times 25a$$

$$a = 8 \text{ ms}^{-2}$$

(ii) The 1st equation of motion is,

$$v = u + at$$
$$v = 0 + 8 \times 5$$
$$v = 40 \text{ ms}^{-1}$$

Q. 33. A car starting from rest acquires a velocity of 54 kmh^{-1} in 20 s.

Calculate the acceleration of the car in S.I. unit. **[February 2020]**

Ans. Given : $u = 0$, $v = 54$ kmh^{-1}, $t = 20$ s

$$v = 54 \text{ km h}^{-1}$$

$$= \frac{54 \times 1000}{60 \times 60} \text{ ms}^{-1}$$

$$= 15 \text{ ms}^{-1}$$

$$\text{Acceleration, } a = \frac{v - u}{t} = \frac{15 - 0}{20}$$

$$= 0.75 \text{ ms}^{-2}.$$

Chapter 3. Laws of Motion

Q. 1. The mass of a body is 12 kg. What is the force acting on it if $g = 10$ ms^{-2}?

Ans. Force acting on the body is the weight of the body exerted due to the force of gravity.

$$\therefore \text{ Weight} = \text{mass} \times \text{acceleration due to gravity}$$
$$= 12 \times 10$$
$$= 120 \text{ N}$$

Q. 2. The mass of an object is 20 kg. What will be the weight on earth and mass on moon? Assume acceleration due to gravity on earth is 9.8 ms^{-2}.

Ans. Weight of the object on earth

$$= \text{mass} \times \text{acceleration due to gravity}$$
$$= 20 \times 9.8$$
$$= 196 \text{ N}$$

Mass of an object remains constant from place to place as it is the matter contained in a body.

So, mass of the object on moon will be 20 kg.

Q. 3. How much force should be applied to a body of mass 250 g to produce and acceleration of 12 ms^{-2} in it?

Ans. According to Newton's second law,

$$\text{Force} = \text{mass} \times \text{acceleration}$$

$$= \left(\frac{250}{1000} \right) \times 12$$

$$= 3\text{N}$$

Hence, a force of 3N must be applied.

Q. 4. A body has a linear momentum of 5Ns. If the velocity of the body is 200 ms^{-1}, find the mass of the body.

Ans. Linear momentum

$$= \text{mass} \times \text{linear velocity}$$
$$5 = \text{mass} \times 200$$

$$\text{Mass} = \frac{5}{200}$$

$$= 0.025 \text{ kg.}$$

Q. 5. A body of mass 200 g is moving with a velocity of 5 ms^{-1}. If the velocity of

body changes to 17 ms^{-1} in time 2 sec find :
(i) change in momentum (ii) rate of change of momentum.

Ans. Given the mass of the body
$$= 200 \text{ g}$$
$$= 0.2 \text{ kg}$$
Initial momentum
$$= \text{mass} \times \text{initial velocity}$$
$$= 0.2 \times 5$$
$$= 1 \text{ kgms}^{-1}$$
Final momentum
$$= \text{mass} \times \text{final velocity}$$
$$= 0.2 \times 17$$
$$= 3.4 \text{ kgms}^{-1}$$
(i) Change in momentum
$$= \text{Final momentum} - \text{initial momentum}$$
$$= 3.4 - 1$$
$$= 2.4 \text{ kgms}^{-1}$$
(ii) Rate of change of momentum
$$= \frac{\text{Change in momentum}}{\text{time}}$$
$$= \frac{2.4}{2}$$
$$= 1.2 \text{ kgms}^{-2}$$

Q. 6. A motor bike of mass 100 kg is running at 10 ms^{-1}. If the engine develops an extra linear momentum of 3000 N.s, calculate the final velocity of the motorbike.

Ans. Given, mass of a motorbike
$$= 100 \text{ kg}$$
Initial velocity of bike $= 10 \text{ ms}^{-1}$
Initial momentum $= \text{mass} \times \text{initial}$
$$\text{velocity}$$
$$= 100 \times 10$$
$$= 1000 \text{ N.s}$$
The engine develops and extra linear momentum of 3000 N.s
Final momentum $= (1000 + 3000) \text{ N.s}$
$$= 4000 \text{ N.s}$$
Now, Final momentum
$$= \text{mass} \times \text{final}$$
$$\text{velocity}$$
$$4000 = 100 \times \text{final velocity}$$
$$\text{Final velocity} = \left(\frac{4000}{100}\right)$$
$$= 40 \text{ ms}^{-1}$$
Hence the final velocity of the motorbike is 40 ms^{-1}.

Q. 7. A force of 60 N acts on a body of mass 10 kg initially at rest such that it gains a velocity 24 ms^{-1}. Find :

(i) Initial momentum
(ii) Final momentum
(iii) Change in momentum
(iv) Time required to gain the velocity.

Ans. (i) Initial momentum
$$= \text{mass} \times \text{initial velocity}$$
$$= (10 \times 0)$$
$$[\because u = 0, \text{ as the body initially is at rest}]$$
$$= 0 \text{ N.s}$$
(ii) Final momentum
$$= \text{mass} \times \text{final velocity}$$
$$= (10 \times 24)$$
$$= 240 \text{ N.s}$$
(iii) Change in momentum
$$= \text{final momentum} - \text{initial momentum}$$
$$= (240 - 0)$$
$$= 240 \text{ N.s}$$
(iv) According to the Newton's second law,
$$\text{Force} = \frac{\text{Change in momentum}}{\text{Time}}$$
$$\text{or} \quad \text{Time} = \frac{\text{Change in momentum}}{\text{Force}}$$
$$= \frac{240}{60}$$
$$= 4 \text{ sec.}$$

Q. 8. A car initially at rest picks up a velocity of 72 kmh^{-1} in 20 second. If the mass of the car is 1 ton. Find :
(i) Force developed by the car engine.
(ii) Distance covered by the car.

Ans. Initial velocity of car
$$= 0 \text{ ms}^{-1}$$
$$[\text{as the car initially is at rest.}]$$
Final velocity of car
$$= 72 \text{ km h}^{-1}$$
$$= \frac{72 \times 5}{18} \text{ ms}^{-1}$$
$$= 20 \text{ ms}^{-1}$$
$$\text{Time} = 20 \text{ sec}$$
$$\text{Acceleration} = \frac{\text{Change in velocity}}{\text{Time}}$$
$$= \frac{20 - 0}{20}$$
$$= 1 \text{ ms}^{-2}$$
(i) Now, according to Newton's second law,
$$\text{Force} = \text{mass} \times \text{acceleration}$$
$$= 1000 \text{ kg} \times 1 \text{ ms}^{-2}$$
$$= 1000 \text{ N}$$

(ii) Using the Newton's second equation of motion,

$$S = ut + \frac{1}{2}at^2$$

$$= 0 + \frac{1}{2} \times 1 \times (20)^2$$

$$= 200 \text{ m}$$

Distance covered by the car is 200 m.

Q. 9. A force of 4 kg wt acts on a body of mass 9.8 kg. Calculate its acceleration.

Ans. Using the relation,

$$\text{Force} = \text{mass} \times \text{acceleration}$$

$$\Rightarrow \quad 4 \times 9.8 \text{ N} = 9.8 \times a$$

$$\Rightarrow \quad \text{Acceleration} = \frac{4 \times 9.8}{9.8}$$

$$\Rightarrow \quad \text{Acceleration} = 4 \text{ ms}^{-2}$$

Q. 10. A force of 4 N accelerates a body of mass m_1 with an acceleration of 4 ms^{-2} and another body of mass m_2 with acceleration of 12 ms^{-2}. If both the masses are tied together what would be the total acceleration of the combined system?

Ans. Case 1 : Force = mass$_1$ × acceleration$_1$

$$\text{Mass}_1 = \frac{\text{Force}}{\text{acceleration}_1}$$

$$= \frac{4}{4}$$

$$= 1 \text{ kg.}$$

Case 2 :

$$\text{Force} = \text{mass}_2 \times \text{acceleration}_2$$

$$\text{Mass}_2 = \frac{\text{Force}}{\text{acceleration}_2}$$

$$= \left(\frac{4}{12}\right)$$

$$= \frac{1}{3} \text{ kg.}$$

Total mass of the two bodies tied together

$$= m_1 + m_2$$

$$= 1 + \frac{1}{3}$$

$$= \frac{4}{3} \text{ kg}$$

Now, the acceleration of the combined system of two bodies can be calculated as,

$$\text{Force} = \text{Total mass} \times \text{acceleration}$$

$$\text{Acceleration} = \frac{\text{Force}}{\text{Total mass}}$$

$$= \frac{4}{(4/3)}$$

$$= 3 \text{ ms}^{-2}$$

Q. 11. A constant retarding force of 40 N is applied on a body of mass 20 kg moving with initial speed of 14 ms^{-1}. Find the time required by the body to come to halt.

Ans. According to Newton's second law,

$$\text{Retarding force} = \text{mass} \times \text{retardation}$$

$$\text{Retardation} = \frac{\text{Retarding force}}{\text{mass}}$$

$$= \frac{40}{20}$$

$$= 2 \text{ ms}^{-2}$$

$$\text{Acceleration} = -2 \text{ ms}^{-2}$$

[acceleration is negative i.e., retardation]

Now, by Newton's first equation of motion,

$$v = u + at$$

$$\Rightarrow \quad \text{Time} = \frac{v - u}{a}$$

$$\Rightarrow \quad = \frac{0 - 14}{-2}$$

$$= 7 \text{ seconds.}$$

Q. 12. A football player kicks a soccer ball initially at rest. The ball has a mass of 10 kg and attains a speed of 74 ms^{-1} in 20 microsecond.

(i) Find the change in momentum of the ball.

(ii) What is the average force against the force during the impact?

Ans. (i) Change in momentum

$$= \text{final momentum} - \text{initial momentum}$$

$$= mv - mu$$

$$= m \,(v - u)$$

$$= 10 \,(74 - 0) \text{ (ball initially at rest)}$$

$$= 740 \text{ N.s}$$

(ii) Average force

$$= \text{Rate of change of momentum}$$

$$= \frac{\text{Change in momentum}}{\text{Time}}$$

$$= \frac{740}{20 \times 10^{-6}}$$

$$= 37 \times 10^{6} \text{ N}$$

Q. 13. Calculate the magnitude of force required to accelerate a body of mass 20 kg from 1.5 ms^{-1} to 9 ms^{-1} in one-third of a minute.

Ans. According to Newton's second law,

$$\text{Force} = \text{mass} \times \text{acceleration}$$
$$= m \times a$$
$$= m \times \frac{v-u}{t}$$
$$= 20 \left(\frac{9-1.5}{20} \right)$$

$$\left[\begin{array}{l} \because 1\,\text{min} = 60\,\text{sec} \\ \therefore \frac{1}{3}\text{min} = \frac{1}{3} \times 60 = 20\,\text{sec} \end{array} \right]$$

$$= 7.5\,\text{N}$$

Q. 14. The speed-time graph of a moving car is shown below.

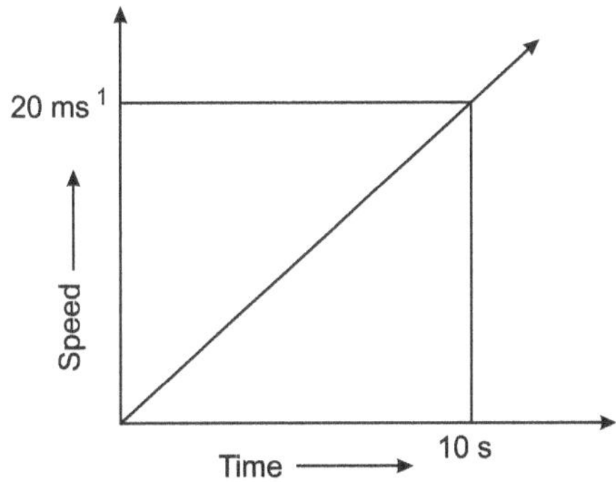

Calculate the : (i) distance covered by the car in 10 seconds.

(ii) Acceleration of the car.

Ans. (i) The distance covered by the car

$$= \frac{1}{2} \text{ area under the curve}$$
$$= \frac{1}{2} \times 10 \times 20$$
$$= 100\,\text{m}$$

(ii) Acceleration of the car $= \dfrac{v-u}{t}$

$$= \frac{20-0}{10}$$
$$= 2\,\text{ms}^{-2}$$

Q. 15. A truck weighing 400 kg moves with a velocity of 36 kmh^{-1}. It is stopped 25 m beyond the point at which brakes are applied. Find the braking force.

Ans. Given : Initial velocity $= 36\,\text{kmh}^{-1}$

$$= \frac{36 \times 5}{18}\,\text{ms}^{-1}$$
$$= 10\,\text{ms}^{-1}$$

Final velocity $= 0\,\text{ms}^{-1}$

[comes to rest]

Distance covered $= 25\,\text{m}$

Using Newton's third equation of motion,

$$v^2 = u^2 + 2aS$$
$$0 = 10^2 + 2 \times a \times 25$$
$$a = -2\,\text{ms}^{-2}$$

So retardation $= 2\,\text{ms}^{-2}$

Now, by Newton's second law,

$$\text{Braking force} = \text{mass} \times \text{retardation}$$
$$= 400 \times 2$$
$$= 800\,\text{N}$$

Q. 16. From the given graph describing the motion of a car whose mass is 5 ton, calculate :

(i) Acceleration of the car

(ii) Retardation of the car

(iii) Retarding force applied for it to come to rest.

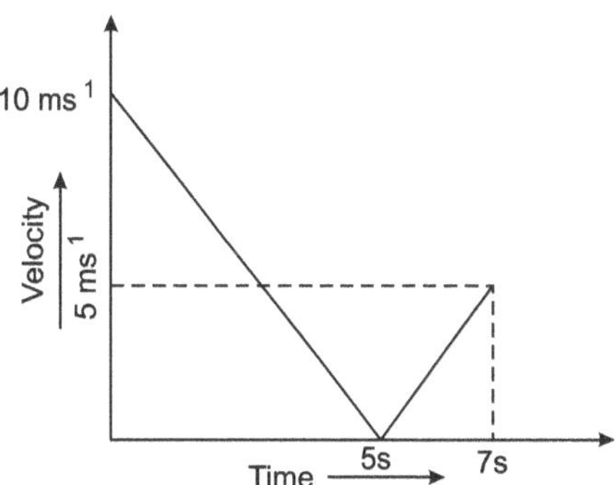

Ans. (i) Acceleration $= \dfrac{\text{Increase in velocity}}{\text{time}}$

$$= \frac{5-0}{7-5}$$
$$= \frac{5}{2}$$
$$= 2.5\,\text{ms}^{-2}$$

(ii) Retardation $= \dfrac{\text{Decrease in velocity}}{\text{time}}$

$$= \frac{0-10}{5}$$
$$= \frac{-10}{5}$$
$$= -2\,\text{ms}^{-2}$$

(iii) Retarding force = Mass × retardation

$$= 5000 \times (-2)$$

$$= -10{,}000 \text{ N}$$

Q. 17. Calculate the gravitational force of attraction between the two bodies of mass 50 kg and mass 90 kg separated by a distance 15 m.

Take $G = 6.7 \times 10^{-11} \text{ Nm}^2/\text{kg}^2$

Ans. Given :

$$m_1 = 50\text{kg}, m_2 = 90 \text{ kg}, r = 15 \text{ m}$$

Gravitational force of attraction

$$F = G \frac{m_1 m_2}{r^2}$$

$$= 6.67 \times 10^{-11} \times \frac{50 \times 90}{15^2}$$

$$= 1.34 \times 10^{-9} \text{ N}$$

Q. 18. A body is dropped freely under gravity from the top of a tower of height 98.6 m. Calculate :

(i) The time at which it strikes the ground.

(ii) The velocity with which it strikes the ground

Ans. Given : $u = 0$, $h = 98.6$ m, $a = g = 9.8 \text{ ms}^{-2}$

(i) From 2nd equation of motion,

$$h = ut + \frac{1}{2} at^2$$

$$98.6 = 0 \times t + \frac{1}{2} \, 9.8 \, t^2$$

$$t = 4.5 \text{ s}$$

(ii) From 1st equation of motion,

$$v = u + at$$

$$v = 0 + 9.8 \times 4.5 = 44.1 \text{ ms}^{-1}$$

Q. 19. A man weighs 800 N on earth. What would be his approximate weight on the moon?

Ans. The value of g on moon $= \frac{1}{6}^{\text{th}}$ of value of g on earth

So approximate weight of man on moon will be 133.3 N.

Q. 20. Two balls a and b of masses m and $2m$ are in motion with velocities $2v$ and v respectively. Compare their (i) inertia (ii) momentum (iii) the force needed to stop them in the same time.

Ans. Given : $m_a = m$, $v_a = 2v$, $m_b = 2m$, $v_b = v$.

(i) $\because$ Inertia $\propto$ mass

$$\therefore \quad \frac{I_a}{I_b} = \frac{m_a}{m_b}$$

$$= \frac{m}{2m} = \frac{1}{2}$$

(ii) Momentum of ball a, $p_a = m_a v_a$

$$= m \times 2v$$

$$= 2mv$$

Momentum of ball b, $p_b = m_b v_b$

$$= 2m \times v$$

$$= 2mv$$

$$\therefore \quad p_a : p_b = 2mv : 2mv$$

$$= 1 : 1$$

(iii) According to Newton's second law of motion, rate of change of momentum is directly proportional to the force applied on it.

$$\therefore \quad F_a : F_b = p_a : p_b = 1 : 1$$

Q. 21. A man weighs 880 N at the equator.

(i) Calculate his mass. (g = 10 m/s2)

(ii) How will his weight change if taken to the poles? **[November, 2019]**

Ans. (i) Weight (W) = 880 N

$$g = 10 \text{ ms}^{-2}$$

We know, W = mg

$$\Rightarrow \quad m = \frac{W}{g} = \frac{880}{10}$$

$$= 88 \text{ kg}$$

(ii) Weight of the body will increase if it is taken to the poles.

Q. 22. A force of 0.4 N acts on a mass of 4 kg at rest. Calculate its velocity and momentum at the end of 10 s. **[November 2019]**

Ans. Given : F = 0.4 N, $m = 4$ kg, $u = 0$, $t = 10$ s

$$\text{Acceleration, } a = \frac{F}{m} = \frac{0.4}{4} \text{ ms}^{-2}$$

$$= 0.1 \text{ ms}^{-2}$$

Velocity after 10 s,

$$v = u + at$$

$$= 0 + 0.1 \times (10)$$

$$= \frac{1}{10} \times 10 = 1 \text{ ms}^{-1}$$

Momentum at the end of 10 s,

$$p = mv$$

$$= 4 \times 1 \text{ kg ms}^{-1}$$

$$= 4 \text{ kg ms}^{-1}$$

Q. 23. Calculate the force that is needed to produce an acceleration of 2 m/s^2 in a body of mass 0.8 kg.

Ans. Given, $m = 0.8$ kg, $a = 2$ ms^{-2}

$\therefore \qquad \text{F} = ma$

$\Rightarrow \qquad \text{F} = 0.8 \text{ kg} \times 2 \text{ ms}^{-2}$

$\Rightarrow \qquad \text{F} = 1.6$ N

Q. 24. A body of mass 10 kg is taken from earth to moon. If the value of g on earth is 9.8 ms^{-2} and on moon is 1.6 ms^{-2}, find :

(i) the weight of the body on earth.

(ii) the mass and weight of the body on moon.

Ans. Given,

Mass of body, $m = 10$ kg

$g_{\text{earth}} = 9.8$ ms^{-2}

$g_{\text{moon}} = 1.6$ ms^{-2}

(i) Weight of the body on earth

$\qquad = \text{mass of body} \times g_{\text{earth}}$

$\qquad = 10 \times 9.8$

$\qquad = 98$ N

(ii) Mass of the body on moon = Mass of body on earth = 10 kg

$\therefore$ Weight of the body on moon

$\qquad = \text{mass of body} \times g_{\text{moon}}$

$\qquad = 10 \times 1.6$

$\qquad = 16$ N

Q. 25. A car is moving with a uniform velocity of 30 ms^{-1}. It is stopped in 2 s by applying a force of 1500 N through its break. Calculate the change in momentum of the car and retardation produced in the car.

Ans. Given,

$v = 30$ ms^{-1}, $t = 2$ s, F = 1500 N

Form Newton's second law of motion,

$$\text{F} = \frac{\Delta \text{P}}{\Delta t}$$

$\Rightarrow \qquad \text{F} \times \Delta t = \Delta \text{P}$

$\Rightarrow \qquad \Delta \text{P} = 1500 \times 2 = 3000$ kg. m.s^{-1}

$\therefore \qquad \Delta \text{P} = 3000$ kg. ms^{-1}

From 1st equation of motion,

$$v = u + at$$

$\Rightarrow \qquad a = \dfrac{v - u}{t}$

$\Rightarrow \qquad a = \dfrac{0 - 30}{2}$

$\Rightarrow \qquad a = 15$ ms^{-2}.

Q. 26. Find the force exerted on a mass of 20 g if the acceleration produced in it is 8 m s^{-2}.

[February 2020]

Ans. Given : $\qquad m = 20\, g = \dfrac{20}{1000}$ kg

and $\qquad a = 8$ ms^{-2}

$\therefore$ Force exerted, F= ma

$\qquad = \dfrac{20}{1000} \times 8$

$\qquad = 0.16$ N.

Q. 27. The gravitational force of attraction between two bodies at a distance X is 20 N. What will be the force of attraction between them if the distance between them is made 2X?

Ans. Since, gravitational force of attraction is inversely proportional to the square of the distance between them.

i.e., $\qquad \text{F} \propto \dfrac{1}{r^2}$

Here, distance of separation has increased two times hence, the gravitational force of attraction will decrease four times.

$\therefore \qquad \text{F} = \dfrac{20}{4} = 5$ N.

Q. 28. A ball is projected up with certain velocity. It reaches a height of 19.6 m and then returns to ground. Find:

(i) initial velocity

(ii) total time of flight

(iii) final velocity with which ball reaches the ground. [Take g = 9.8 ms^{-2}]

Ans. (i) By newton's 3rd equation of motion,

$$v^2 = u^2 + 2gh$$

$\qquad 0 = u^2 - [2 \times 9.8 \times 19.6]$

$\therefore \qquad u^2 = [2 \times 9.8]^2$

$\therefore \qquad u = 19.6$ ms^{-1}

Initial velocity = 19.6 ms^{-1}

(ii) Let t be time taken to reach the highest point.

By newton's 1st equation of motion,

$$v = u - gt$$

$\qquad 0 = 19.6 - 9.8 \times t$

$\therefore \qquad t = \dfrac{19.6}{9.8}$

$\qquad = 2$ sec

It will take same time to reach ground.

$\therefore$ Total time of flight $= 2 \times 2$

$$= 4 \text{ sec}$$

(iii) The final velocity with which the ball strikes the ground = initial velocity with which it was thrown upwards

$\therefore$ Final velocity $= 19.6 \text{ ms}^{-1}$

Q. 29. A body is fall from the top of a building and reaches the ground 2.5 s later. How high is the building?

Ans. By Newton's 2nd equation of motion,

$$\text{height } h = ut + \frac{1}{2} gt^2$$

$$h = \frac{1}{2} \times 9.8 \times (2.5)^2 \qquad [\because u = 0]$$

$$= 30.6 \text{ m}$$

Q. 30. A body rises vertically up to a height of 125 m in 5 s and then comes back at the point of projection. Find:
(i) the total distance travelled,
(ii) the displacement,
(iii) the average speed.

Ans. Given, $S = 125$ m, $t = 5$ s

(i) Total distance travelled

$$= S + S$$
$$= 2S$$
$$= 2 \times 125 \text{ m}$$
$$= 250 \text{ m}$$

(ii) Displacement $= 0$

(iii) Average speed

$$= \frac{\text{total distance travelled}}{\text{total time of journey}}$$

$$= \frac{2S}{2t}$$

$$= \frac{2 \times 125}{2 \times 5}$$

$$= \frac{250}{10} = 25 \text{ ms–1}.$$

Q. 31. A body is dropped freely under gravity from the top of a tower of height 78.4 m. Calculate:
(i) the time to reach the ground
(ii) the velocity with which it will strike the ground. Take $g = 9.8 \text{ ms}^{-2}$.

Ans. Given,

$$u = 0$$
$$h = 78.4 \text{ m}$$
$$a = g = 9.8 \text{ ms}^{-2}$$

The 2nd equation of motion is

$$h = ut + \frac{1}{2} at^2$$

$$78.4 = 0 \times t + \frac{1}{2} \times 9.8 \times t^2$$

$$78.4 = 4.9 \, t^2$$

$$t^2 = \frac{78.4}{4.9} = 16$$

Time to reach the ground $t = 4$ s

The 1st equation of motion is

$$v = u + at$$
$$v = 0 + 9.8 \times 4$$
$$v = 39.2 \text{ ms}^{-1}$$

The body strikes the ground with velocity 39.2 ms^{-1}.

Q. 32. A ball is thrown vertically upwards from the top of a building of height 24.5 m with initial velocity 19.6 ms^{-1}. Taking $g = 9.8 \text{ ms}^{-2}$, Calculate :
(i) The height to which it will rise before returning to the ground.
(ii) The velocity with which it will strike the ground.

Ans. Given,

$u = 19.6 \text{ ms}^{-1}$ (upwards), height of building $x = 24.5$ m,

At the highest point, $v = 0$

(i) For upward journey, from the relation,

$$v^2 = u^2 - 2gh$$
$$0 = u^2 - 2gh$$
$$h = \frac{u^2}{2g}$$

$$h = \frac{(19.6)^2}{2 \times 9.8} = 19.6 \text{ m}$$

Hence, the height to which it will rise is 19.6 m.

(ii) While returning from highest point, $u = 0$, total height travelled $= 19.6 + 24.5 = 44.1$ m. Let v be the velocity with which it strikes the ground. Then from relation

$$v^2 = u^2 + 2gh$$
$$v^2 = 0 + 2 \times 9.8 \times 44.1$$
$$v = \sqrt{2 \times 9.8 \times 44.1}$$
$$v = 29.4 \text{ ms}^{-1}$$

Hence, the velocity with which it will strike the ground is 29.4 ms^{-1}.

Chapter 4. Pressure in fluids and Atmospheric Pressure

Numericals

Q. 1. Calculate the pressure exerted by 0.8 m vertical length of alcohol of density 0.8 g cm^{-3} in Pascal.

Ans.
$$\text{Height} = 0.8 \text{ m}$$
$$\text{Density} = 0.8 \text{ g cm}^{-3}$$
$$= 800 \text{ kg m}^{-3}$$
$$\text{Acceleration due to gravity} = 9.8 \text{ ms}^{-2}$$
$$\text{Pressure exerted} = h\rho g$$
$$= 0.8 \times 800 \times 9.8$$
$$= 6272 \text{ pascal.}$$

Q. 2. The base of cylindrical vessel measures 300 cm^2. Water is poured into it to a depth of 6 cm. Calculate the pressure on base of vessel.

Ans.
$$\text{Height} = 6 \text{ cm}$$
$$= 0.6 \text{ m}$$
$$\rho_{water} = 1000 \text{ kgm}^{-3}$$
$$\text{Acceleration due to gravity } g$$
$$= 9.8 \text{ ms}^{-2}$$
$$\therefore \quad \text{Pressure in base} = hdg$$
$$= 0.06 \times 1000 \times 9.8$$
$$= 588 \text{ Pa.}$$

Q. 3. Normal pressure of air is 76 cm of mercury. Calculate its pressure in SI units. $\rho_{Hg} = 13600 \text{ kgm}^{-3}, g = 10 \text{ ms}^{-2}$]

Ans.
$$\text{Height} = 76 \text{ cm}$$
$$= 0.76 \text{ m}$$
$$\rho_{Hg} = 13600 \text{ kgm}^{-3}$$
$$\text{Acceleration due to gravity}$$
$$= 10 \text{ ms}^{-2}$$
$$\therefore \text{ Pressure exerted} = h\rho g$$
$$= 0.76 \times 13600 \times 10$$
$$= 1,03,360 \text{ Pa.}$$

Q. 4. The pressure of water on ground floor is 1,60,000 Pa. Calculate pressure on 5th floor at a height of 15 m.

Ans. Pressure on ground floor
$$= 1,60,000 \text{ Pa}$$
$$\text{Height of fifth floor} = 15 \text{ m}$$
$$\text{Density of water, } \rho = 1000 \text{ kgm}^{-3}$$
$$\therefore \text{ Pressure due to 15m} = h\rho g$$
$$= 15 \times 1000 \times 10$$
$$= 1,50,000 \text{ Pa.}$$
$$\therefore \text{ Pressure on fifth floor}$$
$$= [1,60,000 - 1,50,000]$$
$$= 10,000 \text{ Pa.}$$

Q. 5. The atmospheric pressure at a place is 650 mm of mercury. Express the pressure in lascal and millibar. Given that density of mercury is 13600 kgm^{-3}.

Ans.
$$\text{Height } h = 650 \text{ mm}$$
$$= 0.65 \text{ m}$$
$$\text{Density of mercury } \rho$$
$$= 13,600 \text{ kg m}^{-3}$$
$$\text{Acceleration due to gravity } g$$
$$= 9.8 \text{ ms}^{-2}$$
$$\text{Pressure} = h\rho g$$
$$= 0.65 \times 13,600 \times 9.8$$
$$= 86632 \text{ Pa}$$
$$\because \quad 1 \text{ Pa} = 0.01 \text{ millibar}$$
$$\therefore \quad 86632 \text{ Pa} = 86632 \times 0.01$$
$$= 866.32 \text{ mb}$$

Q. 6. A cube of each side 5 cm is placed inside a liquid. The pressure at the centre of one face of cube is 10 Pa. Calculate the thrust exerted by the liquid on this face.

Ans. Given, pressure = 10 Pa
$$\text{Area of face of cube A} = 5 \text{ cm} \times 5 \text{ cm}$$
$$= 0.05 \text{ m} \times 0.05 \text{ m}$$
$$= 25 \times 10^{-4} \text{ m}^2$$
Thrust exerted by the liquid on the face of cube
$$= \text{Pressure} \times \text{Area}$$
$$= 10 \text{ Pa} \times 25 \times 10^{-4} \text{ m}^2$$
$$= 2.5 \times 10^{-2} \text{ N}$$

Q. 7. Pressure at the bottom of sea is 8,968,960 Pa. If density of sea water is 1040 kg m^{-3}, Calculate the depth of sea.

Ans. Pressure at bottom of sea = 8,968,960 Pa
$$\text{Density of sea water} = 1040 \text{ kg m}^{-3}$$
$$\text{Acceleration due to gravity} = 9.8 \text{ ms}^{-2}$$
$$\because \quad \text{Pressure exerted} = h\rho g$$
$$\therefore \quad \text{Depth } (h) = \frac{P}{\rho g}$$
$$= \frac{8,968,960}{1040 \times 9.8}$$
$$\therefore \quad \text{Depth of the sea} = 880 \text{ m.}$$

Q. 8. The atmospheric pressure is 10^5 Nm^{-2} and density of water is 10^3 kgm^{-3}, calculate the depth of water at which pressure is double the atmospheric pressure.

Ans. Let atmospheric pressure = P

$$\therefore \quad 2P = P + h_{water} \cdot \rho_{water} \cdot g$$

$$\therefore \quad P = h_{water} \cdot \rho_{water} \cdot g$$

$$\therefore \quad h_{water} = \frac{\rho}{\rho_{water} g}$$

$$= \frac{10^5}{10^3 \times 9.8} = 10.2$$

Hence, the depth of water at which pressure is double the atmospheric pressure is 10.2 m.

Q. 9. Atmospheric pressure at sea level is 76 cm of Hg. Calculate the vertical height of air column exerting the above pressure. Assume the density of air = 1.29 kgm^{-3} and that of Hg = 13600 kgm^{-3}. Why is the height calculated by you far less than actual height of atmosphere?

Ans.

$$h_{Hg} = 0.76 \text{ m}$$
$$h_{air} = ?$$
$$d_{Hg} = 13,600 \text{ kgm}^{-3}$$
$$d_{air} = 1.29 \text{ kgm}^{-3}$$
$$\because \quad h_{Hg} \times d_{Hg} = h_{air} \times d_{air}$$
$$\therefore \quad h_{air} = \frac{h_{Hg} \times d_{Hg}}{d_{air}}$$

$$= \frac{0.76 \times 13600}{1.29}$$

$$= 8012.40 \text{ m}$$

Here it is assumed that density of air is constant. However, in actual practice, density of air decreases rapidly with gain in height. Thus actual height of atmosphere is greater than calculated height.

Q. 10. The pressure of water on ground floor in a water pipe is 1,50,000 Pa whereas pressure on fourth floor is 30,000 Pa. Calculate the height of fourth floor.

Ans. Pressure of water on ground floor

$$= 1,50,000 \text{ Pa}$$

Pressure of water on fourth floor

$$= 30,000 \text{ Pa}$$

$$\therefore \text{ Difference of pressure}$$

$$= 1,20,000 \text{ Pa}$$

$$= h_{water} \times d_{water} \times g$$

$$\therefore \quad 1,20,000 = h_{water} \times 1000 \times 9.8$$

$$\therefore \quad h = 12.245$$

$$\therefore \text{ Height of 4th floor} = 12.245 \text{ m}$$

Q. 11. What vertical height of water will exert a pressure of 3,33,200 Pa? Density of water is 1000 kgm^{-3} and $g = 9.8$ ms^{-2}.

Ans.

$$\text{Pressure} = 333200 \text{ Pa}$$
$$\text{Density of water} = 1000 \text{ kgm}^{-3}$$

Acceleration due to gravity g

$$= 9.8 \text{ ms}^{-2}$$

$$\because \quad P = h\rho g$$

$$\therefore \quad \text{Height} = \frac{P}{\rho g}$$

$$= \frac{333200}{1000 \times 9.8}$$

$$\therefore \text{ Height of water column} = 34 \text{ m}$$

Q. 12. A metal plate of length 1.5 m and width 0.2 m is placed 40 cm below alcohol of density 800 kgm^{-3}. If the atmospheric pressure is 80 cm of Hg. Calculate force experienced by the plate. (Density of mercury = 13600 kg m^{-3})

Ans. Surface area of plate = (1.5×0.2) m^2

$$= 0.3 \text{ m}^2$$

Pressure due to air alone

$$= h_{Hg} \times d_{Hg} \times g$$
$$= 0.8 \times 13600 \times 10$$
$$= 108,800 \text{ Pa}$$

Pressure due to alcohol only

$$= h_{Alco} \times d_{Alco} \times g$$
$$= 0.4 \times 800 \times 10$$
$$= 3200 \text{ Pa}$$

$$\therefore \quad \text{Total pressure} = P_{Air} + P_{Alc}$$
$$= 108,800 + 3200$$
$$= 1,12,000 \text{ Pa}$$

$$\therefore \text{ Force acting on plate} = P \times \text{Area}$$
$$= 1,12,000 \times 0.3$$
$$= 33600 \text{ N}$$

Q. 13. In a hydraulic machine, two pistons are of cross section in the ratio 2 : 10. What force is needed on the narrow piston to overcome a force of magnitude 200 N on wider piston?

Ans. Given,

$$A_1 : A_2 = 2 : 10$$

By the principle of hydraulic machine,

Pressure on narrow piston = Pressure on wider piston

$$\text{or} \quad \frac{F_1}{A_1} = \frac{F_2}{A_2}$$

$$\Rightarrow \qquad F_1 = \frac{A_1}{A_2} \times F_2$$

$$\Rightarrow \qquad F_1 = \frac{2}{10} \times 200 = 40$$

Hence, the required force is 40 N.

Q. 14. A barometer with mercury reads 75 cm. when 3cm^3 of atmospheric air is introduced into the tube, the mercury suddenly falls to a height of 65 cm and the air column length above the mercury is obtained to be 15 cm. What is the cross-sectional area of the barometer tube?

Ans. Given,

Initial volume of air $V_1 = 3 \text{ cm}^3$ at pressure P_1 = atmospheric pressure = 75 cm of mercury. The level of mercury falls to 65 cm because the air in the tube exerts pressure on it. Therefore, pressure of air inside the tube is $P_2 = 75 - 65 = 10$ cm of Hg.

Given, length of air column = 15 cm. If A is the cross-sectional area of the tube, then volume of the trapped air $V_2 = 15 \times A \text{ cm}^3$.

By Boyle's law,

$$P_1 V_1 = P_2 V_2$$
$$75 \times 3 = 10 \times (15 \times A)$$
$$A = \frac{75 \times 3}{10 \times 15}$$
$$A = 1.5 \text{ cm}^2.$$

Hence, required cross-sectional area is A = 1.5 cm^2.

Q. 15. A cube of each side 15 cm immersed in a tube containing water of density 10^3 such that its top surface is 20 cm below the free surface of water.

Calculate :

(i)   The pressure at the top of cube.

(ii) The pressure at the bottom of the cube.

(Atmospheric pressure = 10^5 Pa and g = 9.8 ms^{-2})

Ans. Given,

atmospheric pressure $P_0 = 10^5$, $g = 9.8$ ms^{-2}.

Depth of top of the cube from the free surface water $h_1 = 20$ cm = 0.2 m

Depth of bottom of cube from the free surface of water

$$h_2 = (20 + 15) \text{ cm}$$
$$= 35 \text{ cm}$$
$$= 0.35 \text{ cm}$$

(i) Pressure at the top of cube
$$P_1 = P_0 + h_1 \rho g$$
$$= 10^5 + (0.20 \times 10^3 \times 9.8)$$
$$= 1.02 \times 10^5 \text{ Pa}$$

(ii) Pressure at the bottom surface of cube
$$P_1 = P_0 + h_1 \rho g$$
$$= 10^5 + (0.35 \times 10^3 \times 9.8)$$
$$= 1.03 \times 10^5 \text{ Pa.}$$

Q. 16. An air bubble rises from the bottom of a lake of depth 10.34 m to its surface. Compare the pressure on bubble at the bottom to that on surface. (atmospheric pressure = 0.76m of Hg, density of Hg = 13.6×10^3 kgm^{-3}, density of water = 10^3 kgm^{-3}.)

Ans. Given,

$$P_0 = 0.76 \text{ of Hg}$$
$$= 0.76 \times (13.6 \times 10^3) \times 9.8$$
$$= 1.013 \times 10^5 \text{ Nm}^{-2}$$
$$h = 10.34 \text{ m}$$
$$\rho = 10^3 \text{kgm}^{-3}$$
$$g = 9.8 \text{ ms}^{-2}$$

Pressure on bubble on the bottom of lake,

P_1 = Atmospheric pressure + Pressure due to water column

$$= P_0 + h \rho g$$
$$= (1.013 \times 10^5) + (10.34 \times 10^3 \times 9.8)$$
$$= 2.026 \times 10^5 \text{ Nm}^{-2}$$

Pressure on bubble at the surface of lake,

$$P_2 = \text{Atmospheric presure}$$
$$= P_0$$
$$= 1.013 \times 10^5 \text{ Nm}^{-2}$$

Now,

$$\frac{P_1}{P_2} = \frac{2.026 \times 10^5 \, \text{Nm}^{-2}}{1.013 \times 10^5 \, \text{Nm}^{-2}}$$
$$= \frac{2}{1}.$$

Q. 17. What is the depth below the surface of water with pressure being equal to twice the atmospheric pressure? Here, the atmospheric pressure is 20 Ncm^{-2}, density of water is 10^3 kgm^{-3} and $g = 9.8$ ms^{-2}.

Ans. Atmospheric pressure $P_0 = 20$ Ncm^{-2}

$$= \frac{20}{10^{-2}} = 2 \times 10^3 \text{ Nm}^{-2}$$

$\rho = 10^3$ kgm^{-3} and $g = 9.8$ ms^{-2}

Here, Pressure at a depth h below the surface of water = Atmospheric pressure + Pressure due to water column of height h

$$\Rightarrow \quad 2P_0 = P_0 + h\rho g$$

$$\Rightarrow \quad h = \frac{P_0}{\rho g}$$

$$= \frac{2 \times 10^5}{10^3 \times 9.8}$$

$$\Rightarrow \quad h = 20.40 \text{ m.}$$

Q. 18. A U tube is first partly filled with mercury. Then water is being added in one arm and an oil in the other arm. Find the ratio of water and oil columns so that mercury level is same in both the arms of U tube. Given : density of water = 10^3 kgm^{-3}, density of oil = 900 kgm^{-3}.

Ans. Given,

h_1 = height of water column

ρ_1 = density of water = 10^3 kgm^{-3}

h_2 = height of oil column

ρ_2 = density of oil = 900 kgm^{-3}

Since mercury level is same in both the arms of the U tube,

∴ Pressure of water column on the surface of mercury in one arm = Pressure of oil column on the surface of mercury in the other arm

$$\Rightarrow \quad h_1 \rho_1 g = h_2 \rho_2 g$$

$$\Rightarrow \quad \frac{h_1}{h_2} = \frac{\rho_2}{\rho_1} = \frac{900}{10^3} = \frac{9}{10}$$

Q. 19. The area of cross-section of press plunger of a hydraulic press is 8 m^2. A resistive load of 400 kgf must be surmounted on it. Evaluate the required force on a pump plunger if the cross sectional area of it is 0.05 m^2.

Ans. Let F be the force required on the pump plunger.

So, for pump plunger, $F_1 = F$, $A_1 = 0.05$ m^2,

For press plunger, $F_2 = 400$ kgf, $A_2 = 8$ m^2.

By Pascal's law,

Pressure on pump plunger = Pressure on press plunger

$$\text{or} \quad \frac{F_1}{A_1} = \frac{F_2}{A_2}$$

$$\Rightarrow \quad \frac{F}{0.05} = \frac{400}{8}$$

$$\Rightarrow \quad F = \frac{400 \times 0.05}{8} = 2.5 \text{ kgf.}$$

Q. 20. A vessel of base area 100 cm × 60 cm and height 200 cm is totally filled with a liquid of density 1.1×10^3 kgm^{-3}. Ignoring the atmospheric pressure, calculate (i) the thrust of the vessel at the bottom, (ii) the pressure at the bottom, (iii) the pressure at the depth of 5 cm from the surface, (iv) the net force experience by a metal foil of area 10 cm^2 which is placed at a depth of 5 cm from the free suface.

Ans. Given,

Area of base of vessel = 100cm × 60 cm

$$= \frac{100}{100} \text{ m} \times \frac{60}{100} \text{ m} = 0.6 \text{ m}^2$$

Height, $h = 200$ cm

$\rho = 1.1 \times 10^3$ kgm^{-3}

$g = 9.8$ ms^{-2}

Volume of vessel, V

$$= 100 \times 60 \times 200 \text{ cm}^3 = 1.2 \text{ m}^2$$

(i) Thrust at the bottom of the vessel = weight of the liquid in the vessel

$$= V\rho g$$

$$= 1.2 \times 1.1 \times 10^3 \times 9.8$$

$$= 1.294 \times 10^4 \text{ Nm}^{-2}$$

(ii) Pressure at the bottom of the vessel

$$= \frac{\text{Thrust}}{\text{Area}}$$

$$= \frac{1.294 \times 10^4 \text{ N}}{0.6 \text{ m}^2}$$

$$= 2.16 \times 10^4 \text{ Nm}^{-2}$$

(iii) Pressure at the depth of 5 cm from the free surface = $h\rho g$

$$= 0.05 \times 1.1 \times 10^3 \times 9.8$$

$$= 539 \text{ N}$$

(iv) Net force will be zero, because the force experienced by the liquid on each of the two faces of foil will be equal and opposite.

Q. 21. A tube with length of 200 cm which is filled with a liquid of density 0.90×10^3 kgm^{-3} is placed inclined vertically such that the level A of liquid in the tube is at vertical height 100 cm from its lowest point C. There is another point B in the tube below the point A at a vertical depth 60 cm. What is the pressure at points A and B?

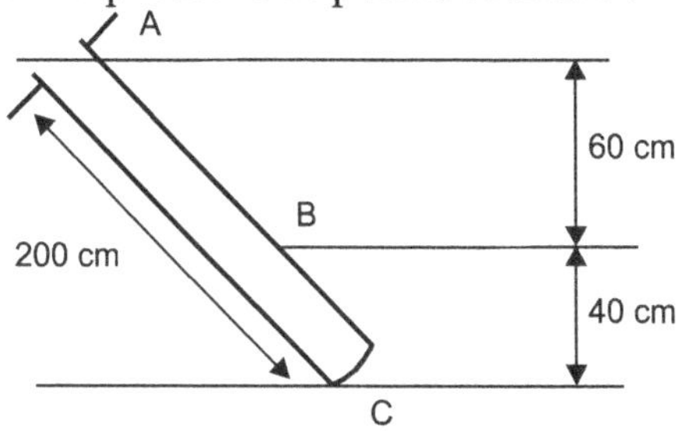

Ans. Given,

$\rho = 0.9 \times 10^3$ kgm^{-3}, P$_0$ = 1.013×10^5 Nm^{-2},

$g = 9.8$ ms^{-2}

At point A,

Pressure = Atmospheric pressure P$_0$

$= 1.013 \times 10^5$ Nm^{-2}

At point B,

Pressure = Atmospheric pressure + Pressure due to liquid column of vertical height 60 cm

$= $ P$_0 + h\rho g$

$= (1.013 \times 10^5) + [(0.6 \times (0.9 \times 10^3) \times 9.8)]$

$= 1.066 \times 10^5$ Nm^{-2}.

Chapter 5. Upthrust in Fluids, Archimedes' Principle and Floatation

Q. 1. A metal cube of 5 cm side and relative density 9 is suspended by thread so as to be completely immersed in a liquid of relative density 1.2. Find the tension in the thread.

Ans. In CGS system,

Density = Relative density

$\therefore$ Density of cube = 9 gcm^{-3}

Density of liquid = 1.2 gcm^{-3}

Volume of cube = 5^3 = 125 cm^3

$\therefore$ Weight of cube = Volume × density

$= (125 \times 9)$

$= 1125$ gf.

Now, Upthrust = weight of liquid displaced

$= $ volume of liquid × density of liquid

$= (125 \times 1.2)$

$= 150$ gf.

$\therefore$ Tension in the string

$= $ Net downward force

$= $ Weight – Upthrust

$= (1125 - 150)$

$= 975$ gf.

$\therefore$ Tension in the string = 975 gf.

Q. 2. A body of mass 3.5 kg displace 1000 cm^3 of water when fully immersed inside it. Density of water is 1 g/cm^3.

Calculate :

(i) The volume of the body

(ii) The upthrust on the body

(iii) The weight of the body inside water.

[November, 2019]

Ans. Given : $m = 3.5$ kg = 3500 g, $\rho = 1$ g cm^{-3}

Volume of water displaced when body is completely immersed in it (V) = 1000 cm^3

(i) Volume of body = Volume of water displaced by it when it is completely immersed

$= 1000$ cm^3.

(ii) Upthrust on the body

$= $ Volume of submerged part of body × Density of water × g

$= 1000 \times 1 \times g$

$= 1000$

(iii) Weight of the body inside water = Weight of the body in air – upthrust

$= (3.5$ kg × $g) - 1000$ gf

$= 3.5\ kgf - 1$ kgf

$= 2.5$ kgf.

Q. 3. A balloon of volume 800 cm^3 is filled with hydrogen gas of density 0.09 gm/lit. If empty balloon weighs 0.3 g and density of air is 1.3 g/lit, find the lifting power of the balloon.

Ans. Lifting power of balloon

$= $ Net upward thrust.

$\therefore$ Upthrust = Wt. of displaced air

$= $ Volume × density × g

$$= 800 \times \frac{1.3}{1000} \times g$$

$$= 1.04 \text{ gf}$$

Downthrust = wt. of enclosed hydrogen + wt. of empty balloon

$$= 800 \times \frac{0.9}{1000} + 0.3$$

$$= 0.372 \text{ gf.}$$

$\therefore$ Lifting power $= 1.04 - 0.372$

$$= 0.668 \text{ gf}$$

Q. 4. A block of mask 7 kg and volume 0.07 m^3 floats in a liquid of density 140 kg/m^3. Calculate :

(i) Density of block.

(ii) Volume of block above surface of liquid.

Ans. (i)   Mass of block = 7 kg

$\therefore$ Weight of block = 7 kgf

Volume of block = 0.07 m^3

$$\text{Density of block} = \frac{\text{mass}}{\text{volume}}$$

$$= \frac{7}{0.07}$$

$$= 100 \text{ kg m}^{-3}$$

(ii)   Weight = Upthrust

7 kgf = Volume of liquid displaced×density of liquid × g

$\therefore$ 7 kg = (Volume × 140)

Volume of liquid displaced

$$= 0.05 \text{ m}^3$$

Volume of liquid displaced

= Volume of solid immersed

$$= 0.05 \text{ m}^3$$

$\therefore$ Volume of block above the surface of liquid

$$= (0.07 - 0.05)$$

$$= 0.02 \text{ m}^3$$

Q. 5. A solid weighs 200 gf in air and 160 gf in water. Calculate its density. What is the volume of the solid?

Ans. We know,

Relative density of a solid

$$= \frac{\text{Weight of solid in air}}{\text{Loss in weight of solid in water}}$$

$$= \frac{200}{200 - 160}$$

$$= \frac{200}{40}$$

$$= 5$$

$\because$ Density of water = 1 g cm^{-3}

$\therefore$ Density of solid = 5 g cm^{-3}

Volume of solid

= Apparent loss of weight of solid in water

$$= 200 - 160$$

$$= 40 \text{ cm}^3.$$

Q. 6. A solid body weighs 2.10 N in air, its relative density is 8.4. How much will the body weigh if placed (i) in water, and (ii) in a liquid of relative density 1.2?

Ans.   Weight of solid = 2.10 N

$\Rightarrow$ Mass of solid = 0.21 kg

$$= 210 \text{ g}$$

$\because$ Density in g cm^{-3} = R.D.

Density in solid = 8.4. g cm^{-3}

$$\text{Volume of solid} = \frac{\text{Mass of solid}}{\text{Density of solid}}$$

$$= \frac{210}{8.4}$$

$$= 25 \text{ cm}^3$$

(i) Upthrust in water

= Volume of solid × Density of liquid

$$= 25 \times 1$$

$$= 25 \text{ gf}$$

$$= 0.25 \text{ N}$$

Apparent weight in water

= Weight of soild in air – Upthrust due to water

$$= (2.1 - 0.25)$$

$$= 1.85 \text{ N}$$

(ii) Upthrust in liquid

= Volume of solid × Density of liquid

$$= 25 \times 1.2$$

$$= 30 \text{ gf}$$

$$= 0.30 \text{ N}$$

Apparent weight in liquid

= Weight of solid in air – Upthrust due to liquid

$$= (2.1 - 0.30)$$

$$= 1.80 \text{ N}$$

Q. 7. A solid of density 5000 kgm^{-3} weighs 0.5 kg in air. It is completely immersed in a liquid of density 800 kgm^{-3}. Calculate the apparent weight of solid in the liquid.

Ans.   Density of solid = 5000 kgm^{-3}

Mass of solid = 0.5 kg

$\therefore$ Volume of solid = $\dfrac{\text{Mass}}{\text{Density}}$

$$= \dfrac{0.5}{5000}$$

$$= 10^{-4} \text{ m}^3$$

$\therefore$ Upthrust = V × ρ_L × g

$$= 10^{-4} \times 800 \times g$$

$$= 0.08 \text{ kgf}$$

$\therefore$ Loss of weight = Upthrust

$$= 0.08 \text{ kgf}$$

$\therefore$ Apparent weight of solid in the liquid

$$= (0.5 - 0.08)$$

$$= 0.42 \text{ kg.}$$

Q. 8. A block of wood is floating in water. The portion of the block inside water measures 50 cm × 50 cm × 50 cm. What is the magnitude of buoyancy force acting on the block?

Ans. Volume of block immersed in water

$$= (50 \times 50 \times 50)$$

$$= 125 \times 10^3 \text{ cm}^3$$

According to law of floatation,

Force of buoyancy acting on a body

$$= \text{Upthrust}$$

$$= \text{V} \times \rho \times g$$

$$= (125 \times 10^3) \times (1) \times (980)$$

$$= (1225 \times 10^5) \text{ dyne}$$

$$= 1225 \text{ N}$$

$\therefore$ The buoyancy force acting on the block

$$= 1225 \text{ N}$$

Q. 9. A solid of relative density 5.5 is found to weigh 70 gf in a liquid of relative density 0.7. Find its weight in air and apparent weight in water.

Ans. Relative density of solid

$$= \dfrac{\text{weight. of solid in air}}{\text{loss in weight. of solid in water}}$$

Also, Relative density of liquid

$$= \dfrac{\text{Loss of weight of solid in liquid}}{\text{Loss of weight of solid in water}}$$

Let weight of solid in air = x gf

and weight of solid in water = y gf

$\therefore$ Loss in weight solid in water = $(x - y)$gf

$\therefore$ $5.5 = \dfrac{x}{x-y}$

$\therefore$ $4.5\,x = 5.5\,y$

$\therefore$ $y = 0.82\,x$

Loss in weight of solid in liquid

$$= (x - 70) \text{ gf.}$$

$\therefore$ $0.7 = \dfrac{x-70}{x-y}$

$\therefore$ $0.7x - 0.7y = x - 70$

$\therefore$ $0.7x - 0.7\,(0.82\,x) = x - 70$

$\therefore$ $0.874\,x = 70.$

$\therefore$ $x = 80.1 \text{ gf}$

and $y = 65.67 \text{ gf}$

$\therefore$ Weight of solid in air = 80.1 gf, and

Weight of solid in water = 65.7 gf

Q. 10. A solid weighs 75 gf in air, 56.7 gf in water and 59.2 gf in liquid. If the solid is tied to a cork of 4 gf, the combination weighs 40.5 gf in water. Find relative density of :

(i) solid

(ii) liquid

(iii) cork

Ans. (i) Relative density of solid

$$= \dfrac{\text{Weight of solid in air}}{\substack{\text{Apparent loss of weight} \\ \text{of solid in water}}}$$

$$= \dfrac{75}{75 - 56.7}$$

$$= 4.09$$

(ii) Relative density of liquid

$$= \dfrac{\substack{\text{Apparent loss in weight} \\ \text{of solid in liquid}}}{\substack{\text{Apparent loss in weight} \\ \text{of solid in water}}}$$

$$= \dfrac{75 - 59.2}{75 - 56.7}$$

$$= 0.86$$

(iii) Now, weight of cork in water

$$= 40.5 - 56.7$$
$$= -16.2 \text{ gf}$$

Weight of cork in air $= 4 \text{ gf}$

Loss in weight of cork in water

$$= 4 - (-16.2)$$
$$= 20.2 \text{ gf}$$

$$\therefore \quad \text{Relative density of cork} = \frac{4}{20.2}$$
$$= 0.198$$

Q. 11. A solid weighs 20 g in air, 18.2 g in liquid and 18 g in water. Calculate the relative density of the solid and the relative density of the liquid

Ans. Relative density of solid

$$= \frac{\text{Weight of solid in air}}{\text{Loss in weight of solid in water}}$$

$$= \frac{20}{20 - 18}$$

$$= \frac{20}{2}$$

$$= 10.$$

Relative density of liquid

$$= \frac{\text{Apparent loss in weight of solid in liquid}}{\text{Apparent loss in weight of solid in water}}$$

$$= \frac{20 - 18.2}{20 - 18}$$

$$= 0.9$$

Q. 12. A test tube loaded with lead shots floats to the mark X in the water. The test tube along with lead shots weighs 25 g in water. When test tube is floated in brine, 5 g of lead shots are added to make it float upto level X again. Find the relative density of brine.

Ans. Weight of floating test tube in water

$$= 25 \text{ gf}$$

Weight of floating test tube in brine

$$= (25 + 5)$$
$$= 30 \text{ gf}$$

Relative density of brine

$$= \frac{\text{Weight of liquid}}{\text{Weight of equal volume of water}}$$

$$= \frac{30}{25}$$

$$= 1.2$$

Q. 13. Relative density of silver is 10.8. What is the density of silver in SI units?

Ans. Since relative density is ratio of density of substance to the density of water at 4°C.

$$\therefore \text{Density of silver} = \text{RD} \times \text{Density of water}$$
$$= 10.8 \times 1000$$
$$= 10,800 \text{ kg m}^{-3}$$

Q. 14. An iceberg floats in fresh water with a part of it outside the water surface. Calculate the fraction of volume of iceberg which is below the water surface. [Given density of ice $= 917 \text{ kgm}^{-3}$]

Ans. Let 'V' be the volume of iceberg and 'v' be the volume of ice below the water sarface. For equilibrium of the iceberg,

Weight of the iceberg

$$= \text{Weight of water displaced by the immersed part of the iceberg.}$$

$$\Rightarrow V \times 917 \times g = v \times 1000 \times g$$

$$\Rightarrow \quad \frac{v}{V} = \frac{917}{1000}$$

$$= 0.917$$

$\therefore$ 0.917 fraction of volume of the iceberg will be below the water surface.

Q. 15. A cube of ice whose side is 4 cm is allowed to melt. The volume of water so formed is 58.24 cm^3. Find the density of ice.

Ans. Actual volume of solid ice $= (4 \times 4 \times 4)$
$$= 64 \text{ cm}^3$$

Volume of water so formed $= 58.24 \text{ cm}^3$

Density of water in CGS unit $= 1\text{g cm}^{-3}$

Using the relation,

$$(V.\rho.g)_{\text{ice}} = (V.\rho.g)_{\text{Water}}$$
$$64 \times \rho_{\text{ice}} \times g = 58.24 \times 1 \times g$$

$$\rho_{\text{ice}} = \frac{58.24}{60}$$

$$= 0.9 \text{ gcm}^{-3}$$

Density of ice in CGS unit $= 0.9 \text{ gcm}^{-3}$

Q. 16. A jeweller claims that he makes ornaments of pure gold that has relative density 19.3. He sells bangles weighing 25.5 g to a person. The clever customer weighs the bangle when immersed in water and finds the weight to be 23.075 g in water. With the help of suitable calculations find out whether the jeweller was authentic or not.

Numericals

Ans. Relative density of pure gold = 19.3

Weight of bangle in air = 25.5 g

Weight of bangle in water = 23.075 g

If the gold used by the jeweller is pure then,

Relative density of gold

$$= \frac{\text{weight of gold in air}}{\text{weight of gold in air} - \text{weight of gold in water}}$$

$$\Rightarrow \text{Relative density} = \frac{25.5}{25.5 - 23.075}$$

$$= \frac{25.5}{2.425}$$

$$= 10.51$$

Since the value of relative density in the above case differs with that for pure gold, the clever customer concludes that the gold used is not pure and that the jeweller is not authentic.

Q. 17. Calculate the presure exerted by 6 cm of water on its base in SI unit. Density of water is 1000 $\frac{\text{kg}}{\text{m}^3}$. ($g = 10$ ms^{-2})

[November 2019]

Ans.

$$h = 6 \text{ cm} = \frac{6}{100} \text{ m}$$

$$\rho = 1000 \text{ kg m}^{-3}$$

$$g = 10 \text{ ms}^{-2}$$

$\therefore$ Pressure on its base (P) $= h\rho g$

$$= \frac{6}{100} \times 1000 \times 10$$

$$P = 600 \text{ Pa}$$

Q. 18. A square plate of side 10 m is placed horizontally 1 m below the surface of water. The atmospheric pressure is 1.013 × 10^5 Nm^{-2}. Calculate the total thrust on the plate.

Ans. Given,

$$h = 1 \text{ m}$$

$$\rho = 10^3 \text{ kg m}^{-3}$$

$$g = 9.8 \text{ ms}^{-2}$$

Atmospheric pressure, $P_0 = 1.013 \times 10^5$ Nm^{-2}

Area of plate = 10 m × 10 m = 100 m^2

Total pressure at a point below the water surface = Atmospheric pressure + Pressure due to column of water

$$= P_0 + h\rho g$$

$$= (1.013 \times 10^5) + (1 \times 10^3 \times 9.8)$$

$$= 1.111 \times 10^5 \text{ Nm}^{-2}$$

Total thrust on the plate = pressure × area of the plate

$$= (1.11 \times 10^5) \times 10^2$$

$$= 1.111 \times 10^7 \text{ N.}$$

Q.19. The volume of a balloon is 1000 m^3. It is filled with helium of density 0.18 kg m^{-3}. What is the maximum load that it can lift? Density of air is 1.29 kg m^{-3}.

Ans. Given,

Volume of the balloon V = 1000 m^3

Density of helium $\rho = 0.18$ kg m^{-3}

Density of air = 1.29 kg m^{-3}

Weight of helium filled balloon

$$= V \times \rho \times g$$

$$= 1000 \times 0.18 \times g$$

$$= 180g \text{ N}$$

$$= 180 \text{ kgf}$$

Weight of air displaced upthrust

$$= V \times (\text{density of air}) \times g$$

$$= 1000 \times 1.29 \times g$$

$$= 1290g \text{ N}$$

$$= 1290 \text{ kgf}$$

Resultant upward force on balloon = upthrust – weight of balloon

$$= (1290 - 180) \text{ kgf}$$

$$= 1110 \text{ kgf}$$

So, it can lift a maximum load of 1110 kgf.

Q. 20. A block of iron floats on mercury. Find the fraction of volume which remains immersed in mercury. (density of iron and mercury are 7.8 g cm^{-3} and 13.6 gcm^{-3} respectively).

Ans. Let V be the volume of iron block and v be its volume immersed in mercury. For floatation, weight of block = weight of mercury displaced by the immersed portion of block.

$$V \times 7.8 \times g = v \times 13.6 \times g$$

$$\frac{v}{V} = \frac{7.8}{13.6}$$

$$v = 0.574V$$

Thus, 0.574 of total volume of iron block will remain immersed in mercury.

Q. 21. A piece of iron of density 7.8 × 10^3 kgm^{-3} and volume 100 cm^3 is completely immersed in water ($\rho = 1000\ \text{kgm}^{-3}$). Calculate : (i) the weight of iron piece in air (ii) the upthrust (iii) its apparent weight in water. (Take $g = 10\ \text{ms}^{-2}$)

Ans. Given,

Volume of iron piece,

$$= 100\ \text{cm}^3$$
$$= 10^{-4}\ \text{m}^3$$

(i) Weight of iron piece in air,

$$= \text{volume} \times \text{density of iron} \times g$$
$$= 10^{-4} \times (7.8 \times 10^3) \times 10$$
$$= 7.8\ \text{N}$$

(ii) Upthrust = volume of water displaced $\times$ density of water $\times g$

Volume of water displaced = volume of iron piece when it is completely immersed

$$\therefore \text{Upthrust} = 10^{-4} \times 1000 \times 10 = 1\text{N}$$

(iii) Apparent weight of iron = True weight – Upthrust

$$= 7.8 - 1$$
$$= 6.8\ \text{N}$$

Q. 22. A block of wood floats on water with $\dfrac{2}{5}$ th of its volume above the water surface. Calculate the density of wood.

Ans. Let the volume of block be V and density of wood be ρ.

Volume of block above the surface of water

$$= \dfrac{2}{5}\text{V}$$

Volume of block immersed $v = \text{V} - \dfrac{2}{5}\text{V} = \dfrac{3}{5}\text{V}$

By the principle of floatation,

Weight of the block = weight of water displaced by the immersed part of the block

$$\text{V} \times \rho \times g = \dfrac{3}{5}\text{V} \times 1 \times g$$

$$\rho = \dfrac{3}{5} = 0.6\ \text{gcm}^{-3}.$$

Q. 23. Two identical blocks A and B of different materials floats on water such that 90% of A and 15% of B remains submerged inside water. Compare densities of A and B.

Ans. Given,

For block A, $\quad \dfrac{v}{\text{V}} = 90\% = 0.9$

For block B, $\quad \dfrac{v}{\text{V}} = 15\% = 0.15$

If ρ_A, ρ_B and ρ_w are the densities of A, B and water, respectively, then,

For block A, $\quad \dfrac{v}{\text{V}} = \dfrac{\rho_A}{\rho_w} = 90\% = 0.9$

For block B, $\quad \dfrac{v}{\text{V}} = \dfrac{\rho_B}{\rho_w} = 15\% = 0.15$

$$\therefore \qquad \dfrac{\rho_\bullet}{\rho_\bullet} = \dfrac{0.9}{0.15} = 6:1$$

Q. 24. A body weighs 550 gf in air and 370 gf in water when it is completely immersed in water. Find :

(i) The upthrust on the body.

(ii) The volume of the body. (density of water $= 1\ \text{g cm}^{-3}$) **[February 2020]**

Ans. Weight of body in air $(\text{W}_1) = 550$ gf, weight of body in water $(\text{W}_2) = 370$ gf

(i) Upthrust on the body

$$= \text{W}_1 - \text{W}_2$$
$$= (550 - 370)\ \text{gf}$$
$$= 180\ \text{gf}$$

(ii) $\qquad$ Upthrust $= \text{V}\rho g$

$\Rightarrow \qquad 180\,g = \text{V}\rho g$

$\Rightarrow \qquad 180 = \text{V} \times 1\ \ [\because \rho = 1\ \text{g cm}^{-3}]$

$\Rightarrow \qquad \text{V} = 180\ \text{cm}^3.$

Chapter 6. Heat and Energy

Q. 1. At what temperature, numerical value of Celsius and Fahrenheit thermometers is same?

Ans. Let the common value be x.

Now, $\quad \dfrac{\text{C}}{5} = \dfrac{\text{F} - 32}{9}$

$\therefore \qquad \dfrac{x}{5} = \dfrac{x - 32}{9}$

$\Rightarrow \qquad 9x = 5x - 160$

$\Rightarrow \qquad 4x = -160$

$\therefore \qquad x = -40°$

Thus, – 40 °C and – 40 °F are common values on both scales.

Q. 2. Convert 45°C into Fahrenheit (°F).

Ans. Conversion from degree Celsius to degree Fahrenheit

$$\frac{C}{5} = \frac{F-32}{9}$$

$$\Rightarrow \quad \frac{9C}{5} = F - 32$$

$$\Rightarrow \quad F = \frac{9C}{5} + 32$$

$$\therefore \quad F = \frac{9 \times 45}{5} + 32$$

$$\Rightarrow \quad F = 81 + 32$$

$$\Rightarrow \quad F = 113° \text{ F.}$$

Q. 3. Convert 96°C into Fahrenheit (°F).

Ans. Conversion from degree Celsius to degree Fahrenheit

$$\frac{C}{5} = \frac{F-32}{9}$$

$$\Rightarrow \quad \frac{9C}{5} = F - 32$$

$$\Rightarrow \quad F = \frac{9C}{5} + 32$$

$$\therefore \quad F = \frac{9 \times 96}{5} + 32$$

$$\Rightarrow \quad F = 81 + 32$$

$$\Rightarrow \quad F = 204.8°F$$

Q. 4. Suppose the amount of energy available at fourth trophic level is 2 kJ in a given food chain. What will be the energy at the producer level?

Ans. By ten per cent law, we have

Fourth tropic level (2kJ) $\xleftarrow{\ 10\%\ }$ Third trophic level(20kJ) $\xleftarrow{\ 10\%\ }$ Second trophic level (200 kJ) $\xleftarrow{\ 10\%\ }$ First trophic level (2000 kJ) (Producer)

Hence, the energy at the producer level is 2000 kJ.

Chapter 7. Reflection of Light

Q. 1. A boy stands 4 m away from plane mirror. If the boy moves 0.5 m towards mirror, what is the distance between the boy and his image? Give a reason for your answer.

Ans. Distance of object from plane mirror = Distance of image from plane mirror.

∴ Initial distance between boy and plane mirror = 4 m.

Final distance between boy and plane mirror = 3.5 m.

Distance between boy and his image = 3.5 m × 2 = 7 m.

Q. 2. An object 4.0 cm in size, is placed 25.0 cm in front of a concave mirror of focal length 15.0 cm. At what distance from the mirror should a screen be placed in order to obtain a sharp image? Find the nature and size of the image.

Ans. Given, object size, h_o = + 4.0 cm

Object distance, u = – 25.0 cm

Focal length, f = – 15.0 cm (concave mirror)

Image distance, v =?

Height of image, h_i =?

According to mirror formula

$$\frac{1}{v} + \frac{1}{u} = \frac{1}{f}$$

$$\Rightarrow \quad \frac{1}{v} = \frac{1}{f} - \frac{1}{u}$$

$$= \frac{1}{-15} - \frac{1}{-25}$$

$$= \frac{-10}{375}$$

$$\Rightarrow \quad v = -37.5 \text{ cm}$$

Magnification, $m = \dfrac{h_i}{h_o} = \dfrac{-v}{u}$

$$\Rightarrow \quad h_i = - \frac{v h_o}{u}$$

$$\Rightarrow \quad h_i = \frac{-(-37.5) \times 4}{-25}$$

$$= \frac{-150}{25}$$

$$\Rightarrow \quad h_i = -6.0 \text{ cm.}$$

The image is real, enlarged and inverted.

Q. 3. At what distance should an object be placed in front of concave mirror of focal length 50 cm so that a real image of triple of its size is obtained.

Ans. Given, $f = -50$ cm,

$$\text{Magnification, } m = -\frac{v}{u}$$

$\because$ Magnification, $m = -3$ [Given]

So, $v = 3u$

Now,

$$\frac{1}{f} = \frac{1}{v} + \frac{1}{u}$$

$$\Rightarrow \quad -\frac{1}{50} = \frac{1}{3u} + \frac{1}{u}$$

$$\Rightarrow \quad 3u = -200 \text{ cm}$$

Hence, $u = -66.7$ cm

So the object should be placed at a distance of 66.7 cm from the pole of the concave mirror.

Q. 4. (i) State the mirror formula for the formation of total number of images formed in two plane mirrors, held at an angle θ.

(ii) Calculate the number of images formed in two plane mirrors, when they are held at angle of (a) 72° (b) 36°.

Ans. (i) Number of images formed in two plane mirrors inclined at angle θ is given by

$$n = \frac{360°}{\theta} - 1$$

where n is a number of images and θ is the angle of inclination between mirrors.

(ii) (a) When θ = 72°,

$$\text{Number of images } (n) = \frac{360°}{72°} - 1$$

$$= 5 - 1 = 4.$$

(b) When θ = 36°,

$$\text{Number of images } (n) = \frac{360°}{36°} - 1$$

$$= 10 - 1 = 9.$$

Q. 5. A ray of light strikes a plane mirror, such that angle of incident ray with the mirror surface is 30°. What is the value of angle of reflection? What is the angle between incident ray and reflected ray?

Ans. Angle of reflection = Angle of incidence

[By the laws of reflection]

Angle of incidence = (90 – 30)° = 60°

$\therefore$ Angle of reflection = 60°

Angle between incident ray and reflected ray = $\angle i + \angle r = 60° + 60° = 120°$.

Q. 6. A boy stands 4 m away from a plane mirror. What is the distance between the boy and his image? **[November, 2019]**

Ans. Distance between boy and image

$$= (4 + 4)\text{m}$$

$$= 8 \text{ m}$$

Q. 7. A convex mirror forms the image of an object placed at a distance of 30 cm in front of the mirror, at a distance 10 cm. Find the focal length of the mirror.

[November, 2019]

Ans. Object distance $(u) = -30$ cm

Image distance $(v) = +10$ cm

$$\because \quad \frac{1}{f} = \frac{1}{u} + \frac{1}{v}$$

$$= \frac{-1}{30} + \frac{1}{10} = \frac{2}{30}$$

$\therefore$ focal length $(f) = +15$ cm

Q. 8. What is the focal length of a spherical mirror having radius of curvature 16 cm?

Ans. Given, radius of curvature, R = 16 cm

$$\text{Focal length, } f = \frac{1}{2}R$$

$$= \frac{16}{2}$$

$$= 8 \text{ cm}$$

Q. 9. A convex mirror forms an erect image of an object of size one-third the size of the mentioned object. If radius of curvature of convex mirror is 36 cm, calculate the position of the object.

Ans. Given,

$$\text{magnification, } m = \frac{1}{3}$$

Radius of curvature, R = 36 cm

$$\therefore \quad \text{Focal length, } f = \frac{R}{2}$$

$$= \frac{36}{2}$$

$$= 18 \text{ cm.}$$

$$\because \quad m = \frac{-v}{u}$$

$$\Rightarrow \quad v = -m \times u$$

$$\Rightarrow \quad v = -\frac{1}{3}u$$

The mirror formula is,

$$\frac{1}{u} + \frac{1}{v} = \frac{1}{f}$$

$$\Rightarrow \quad \frac{1}{u} + \frac{1}{-\frac{1}{3}u} = \frac{1}{18}$$

$$\Rightarrow \quad \frac{1}{u} - \frac{3}{u} = \frac{1}{18}$$

$$\Rightarrow \quad \frac{-2}{u} = \frac{1}{18}$$

$$\Rightarrow \quad u = -36 \text{ cm}$$

The object is placed at a distance of 36 cm in front of the mirror.

Q. 10. The focal length of a convex mirror is 40 cm. A point source of light is placed at a distance 60 cm from the mirror. Find the distance of image from the mirror.

Ans. Given,

$$f = 40 \text{ cm}$$
$$u = -60 \text{ cm}$$

From mirror formula, we have

$$\frac{1}{v} + \frac{1}{u} = \frac{1}{f}$$

$$\Rightarrow \quad \frac{1}{-60} + \frac{1}{v} = \frac{1}{24}$$

$$\Rightarrow \quad \frac{1}{v} = \frac{1}{40} + \frac{1}{60}$$

$$\Rightarrow \quad \frac{1}{v} = \frac{5}{120}$$

$$\Rightarrow \quad v = 24 \text{ cm}$$

Hence, the image is formed at a distance of 24 cm behind the mirror.

Q. 11. **At what distance in front of a concave mirror having focal length 10 cm, an object be placed so that its virtual image of size five times that of the object obtained?**

Ans. Given,

$$f = -10 \text{ cm}$$
$$m = 5$$

We know,

$$m = \frac{-v}{u}$$

$$5 = -\frac{v}{u}$$

$$v = -5u$$

From mirror formula, we have

$$\frac{1}{u} + \frac{1}{v} = \frac{1}{f}$$

$$\Rightarrow \quad \frac{1}{u} + \frac{1}{(-5u)} = \frac{1}{-10}$$

$$\Rightarrow \quad \frac{4}{5u} = \frac{-1}{10}$$

$$\Rightarrow \quad u = -8 \text{ cm}$$

Thus, the object should be placed at a distance of 8 cm in front of the mirror.

Q. 12. A convex mirror forms the image of an object placed at a distance of 40 cm in front of mirror, at a distance of 10 cm. Find the focal length of the mirror.

Ans. Given,

$$u = -40 \text{ cm}$$
$$v = 10 \text{ cm}$$

From mirror formula, we have

$$\frac{1}{u} + \frac{1}{v} = \frac{1}{f}$$

$$\Rightarrow \quad \frac{1}{f} = \frac{1}{-40} + \frac{1}{10}$$

$$\frac{1}{f} = \frac{-1+4}{40}$$

$$\frac{1}{f} = \frac{3}{40}$$

$$f = 13.33 \text{ cm}$$

Hence, the focal length of convex mirror is 13.33 cm.

Q. 13. When an object with a height 1 cm is held at a distance of 4 cm from a concave mirror at a point, its erect 1.5 cm height image is formed at a distance of 6 cm behind the mirror. Find the focal length of the mirror.

Ans. Given,

$$u = -4 \text{ cm}$$
$$v = 6 \text{ cm}$$

From the mirror formula, we have

$$\frac{1}{f} = \frac{1}{u} + \frac{1}{v}$$

$$\Rightarrow \quad \frac{1}{f} = \frac{1}{-4} + \frac{1}{6}$$

$$\Rightarrow \quad \frac{1}{f} = \frac{-6+4}{24}$$

$$\Rightarrow \quad \frac{1}{f} = \frac{-2}{24}$$

$$\Rightarrow \quad f = -12$$

Hence, the focal length of the mirror is 12 cm.

Q. 14. An object is placed at 6 cm distance in front of a concave mirror of focal length 4 cm.

(i) Find the position of the image.

(ii) What will be the nature of the image?

[February, 2020]

Ans. (i) For the given concave mirror,

$$u = -6 \text{ cm}; f = -4 \text{ cm}$$

We have,

$$\frac{1}{f} = \frac{1}{u} + \frac{1}{v}$$

$$\Rightarrow \quad \frac{1}{v} = \frac{1}{f} - \frac{1}{u}$$

$$= \frac{1}{-4} + \frac{1}{6}$$

$$= \frac{-3+2}{12} = -\frac{1}{12}$$

$$\Rightarrow \quad v = -12 \text{ cm}$$

The image is at a distance 12 cm in front of the concave mirror.

(ii) The image formed will be real, inverted and magnified.

Chapter 8. Propagation of Sound Waves

Q. 1. A sound wave of frequency 640 Hz travels 800 m in 2.5 s. Calculate :

(i) speed of sound (ii) wavelength of sound wave.

Ans. (i)

$$\text{Speed of sound} = \frac{\text{Distance}}{\text{Time}}$$

$$= \frac{800}{2.5}$$

$$= 320 \text{ ms}^{-1}.$$

(ii) Speed of sound $(v) = f\lambda$.

$$\therefore \quad 320 = 640 \times \lambda$$

$$\therefore \quad \lambda = \frac{320}{640} = 0.5 \text{ m}.$$

Q. 2. A television station broadcasts at a frequency of 4500 MHz. If the speed of television waves is $3 \times 10^8 \text{ms}^{-1}$. Calculate the wavelength of television waves.

Ans. $v = 3 \times 10^8 \text{ ms}^{-1}, f = 4500 \text{ MHz} = 4.5 \times 10^9 \text{ Hz}.$

$$\therefore \text{ Wavelength, } \lambda = \frac{v}{f}$$

$$= \frac{3 \times 10^8}{4.5 \times 10^9}$$

$$= 0.67 \times 10^{-1} \text{ m} = 0.067 \text{m}.$$

Q. 3. A sound wave has a frequency of 2000 Hz and wavelength 17 cm. If the wavelength increases to 51 cm, what is the frequency, the nature of material through which sound is propagating remains same.

Ans. Initial wavelength $(\lambda_1) = 17$ cm.
Initial frequency $(f_1) = 2000$ Hz.
Final wavelength $(\lambda_2) = 51$ cm.
Final frequency $(f_2) = ?$
For a given material, velocity of sound is a constant quantity.

$$\therefore \quad f_2 \lambda_2 = f_1 \lambda_1$$
$$f_2 \times 51 = 2000 \times 17.$$

$$\therefore \quad f_2 = \frac{2000 \times 17}{51} = 666.67 \text{ Hz}.$$

Q. 4. A thin metal plate is placed against the teeth of a cog wheel. If the cog wheel is rotated at a constant speed of 360 rotations per minute and has 80 teeth, calculate :

(i) frequency of note produced

(ii) speed of sound, if the wavelength is 0.7 m

(iii) What will be the effect, if the speed of cog wheel is halved?

Ans. (i) Number of rotations of cog wheel in 1 minute (60 s) = 360

$$\therefore \quad \text{Number of rotations of}$$
$$\text{cog wheel in} \quad 1 \text{ second} = \frac{360}{60} = 6 \text{ s}^{-1}.$$

$\therefore$ Frequency of note produced

= No. of rotations per second × Teeth in cog wheel

$= 6 \text{ s}^{-1} \times 80 = 480 \text{ s}^{-1}$

= 480 Hz.

(ii) Speed of sound = Frequency × Wavelength

$= 480 \text{ s}^{-1} \times 0.7 \text{ m} = 336.0 \text{ ms}^{-1}$.

(iii) The frequency of note produced is halved. Thus, in turn will lower the pitch of sound, *i.e.*, a bass note is produced.

Q. 5. The wavelength of waves produced on the surface of water is 20 cm. If the wave velocity is 24 ms^{-1}, calculate : (i) number of waves produced in one second (ii) time required to produce one wave.

Ans. (i) Wavelength $(\lambda) = 20 \text{ cm} = 0.2 \text{ m}$

Wave velocity $(v) = 24 \text{ ms}^{-1}$

Number of waves produced in one second = Frequency

$$= \frac{v}{\lambda} = \frac{24}{0.2} = 120 \text{ Hz}$$

(ii) Time required to produce one wave

= Time period (T)

$$= \frac{1}{f}$$

$$= \frac{1}{120}$$

$$= 8.33 \times 10^{-3} \text{ s}$$

Q. 6. A disturbance in air has wavelength of 22 m and speed 330 ms^{-1}. Calculate the frequency of disturbance. State whether above disturbance is audible to normal human ear. Give one reason for your answer.

Ans. $v = 330 \text{ ms}^{-1}$, $\lambda = 22 \text{ m}$.

$$\therefore \text{ Frequency}, f = \frac{v}{\lambda} = \frac{330}{22} = 15 \text{ Hz}.$$

Since the frequency does not lie in the range (20 – 20000) Hz, so it is not audible to normal human ear.

Q. 7. How long will sound take to travel in (i) rod and (ii) air, both 3.3 km in length? Take speed of sound in air to be 330 m/s and in iron to be 5280 m/s.

Ans. (i) Length of iron rail (D) = 3.3 km

= 3300 m

Speed of sound in iron (V) = 5280 m/s

Time taken by sound to travel in iron

rod $(t) = \dfrac{D}{V}$

$$\Rightarrow t = \left(\frac{3300}{5280}\right) \text{s} = 0.625 \text{ s}$$

(ii) Length of iron rail (D) = 3.3 km = 3300 m

Speed of sound in air (V) = 330 m/s

Time taken by sound to travel in air

rod $(t) = \dfrac{D}{V}$

$$\Rightarrow t = \left(\frac{3300}{330}\right) \text{s} = 10 \text{ s}$$

Q. 8. Assuming the speed of sound in air equal to 340 m/s and in water equal to 1360 m/s, find the time taken to travel a distance 1700 m by sound in (i) air (ii) water

Ans. (i) Distance travelled (D) = 1700

Speed of sound in air (V) = 340 m/s

$$\text{Time taken } (t) = \frac{D}{V} = \left(\frac{1700}{340}\right) \text{s} = 5 \text{ s}$$

(ii) Distance travelled (D) = 1700

Speed of sound in water (V) = 1360 m/s

$$\text{Time taken } (t) = \frac{D}{V} = \left(\frac{1700}{1360}\right) \text{s} = 1.25 \text{ s}$$

Q. 9. A longitudinal wave of wavelength 0.03 cm travels in air with a speed of 330 ms^{-1}. Calculate the frequency of the wave. Can this wave be heard by normal human ear? Give a reason for your answer.

Ans. $v = 330 \text{ ms}^{-1}$; $\lambda = 0.03 \text{ cm} = 0.0003 \text{ m}$.

$$\therefore \text{ Frequency}, f = \frac{v}{\lambda} = \frac{330}{0.0003}$$

$$= 1{,}100{,}000 \text{ Hz}.$$

The above wave cannot be heard. It is because, the maximum range to which human ear can hear is 20,000 Hz. As the frequency of 1,100,000 Hz is far in excess therefore it will not produce any sound effect in ear.

Q. 10. An ultraviolet radiation has wavelength 150 Å. If the speed of ultraviolet radiation is $3 \times 10^8 \text{ ms}^{-1}$, calculate (i) frequency of radiation in MHz (ii) Time period.

$[1 \text{ Å} = 10^{-10} \text{ m}]$.

Ans. Given : $\lambda = 150$ Å $= 150 \times 10^{-10}$ m $= 15 \times 10^{-9}$ m; $v = 3 \times 10^8$ ms^{-1}

(i) Frequency, $f = \dfrac{v}{\lambda} = \dfrac{3 \times 10^8}{15 \times 10^{-9}}$

$$= 0.2 \times 10^{17} \text{ Hz}$$

$\therefore$ Frequency in MHz $= \dfrac{0.2 \times 10^{17}}{10^6}$

$$= 2 \times 10^{10} \text{ MHz}$$

(ii) Time period, $T = \dfrac{1}{f} = \dfrac{1}{0.2 \times 10^{17}}$

$$= 5 \times 10^{-17} \text{ s}$$

Q. 11. The distance between one crest and one trough produced on the surface of water is 0.04 m. If the waves are produced at a rate of 180 per minute. Calculate :
(i) time period (ii) wave velocity.

Ans. (i) Number of waves produced in 1 minute (60 s) = 180

$\therefore$ Number of waves produced in 1 second $= \dfrac{180}{60} = 3 \text{ s}^{-1}$

$\therefore$ Frequency of waves = 3 s^{-1}.

$\therefore$ Time period (T) $= \dfrac{1}{3} = 0.33$ s

(ii) Distance between one crest and one trough $= \dfrac{\lambda}{2}$

$\Rightarrow \dfrac{\lambda}{2} = 0.04$ m [Given]

$\therefore \lambda = 0.04 \times 2 = 0.08$ m

$\therefore$ Wave velocity $= \dfrac{\lambda}{T} = \dfrac{0.08}{0.33} = 0.24$ ms^{-1}.

Q. 12. A vibrating tuning fork can produce note of wavelength 0.83 m and has a time period of 2.5×10^{-3} seconds. Calculate the wave velocity note and the distance covered by sound wave in 0.08 s.

Ans. Time period $= 2.5 \times 10^{-3}$ s

$\therefore$ Frequency $(f) = \dfrac{1}{T}$

$$= \dfrac{1}{2.5 \times 10^{-3}}$$

$$= 400 \text{ Hz.}$$

$\therefore$ Wave velocity $= f \times \lambda = 400 \times 0.83 = 332$ ms^{-1}.

$\therefore$ Distance covered by sound in 0.08 seconds

$$= 332 \text{ ms}^{-1} \times 0.08 \text{ s} = 26.56 \text{ m.}$$

Q. 13. The sound of an explosion on the surface of lake is heard by a boatman 100 m away and a diver 100 m below the point of explosion.
(i) Of the two persons mentioned (boatman and diver), who would hear the sound first?
(ii) Give reason for your answer in (i).
(iii) If the sound takes 't' seconds to reach the boatman, approximately how much time it will take to reach the diver?

Ans. (i) The diver hears the sound first.
(ii) It is because sound travels at 1450 ms^{-1} in water and 330 ms^{-1} in air.
(iii) The time in which sound reaches diver

$$= \dfrac{100}{1450} = 0.689 \text{ s.}$$

Q. 14. An observer A fires a gun and another observer B at a distance 1650 m away from A hears its sound. If the speed of sound is 330 ms^{-1}, find the time when B will hear the sound after firing by A.

Ans. Distance between the two observers = 1650 m
Speed of sound = 330 m/s
Time in which B hears the sound

$$= \dfrac{\text{Distance}}{\text{Speed}} = \dfrac{1650}{330} = 5$$

Thus, B will hear the sound 5 s after the gun is shot.

Q. 15. The time interval between a lightning flash and the first sound of thunder was found to be 5 s. If the speed of sound in air is 330 m s^{-1}, find the distance of flash from the observer.

Ans. Speed of sound in air (v) = 330 m/s
Time in which thunder is heard after lighting is seen (t) = 5 s
Thus, distance between flash and observer

$$= v \times t = (330 \times 5) = 1650 \text{ m}$$

Q. 16. A boy fires a gun and another boy at a distance hears the sound of fire 2.5 s after seeing the flash. If the speed of sound in air is 340 m/s, find distance between the boys.

Ans. Speed of sound in air (v) = 340 m/s

Time in which sound of fire is heard after flash is seen (t) = 2.5 s

Thus, distance between flash and observer

= $v \times t$ = (340 × 2.5) = 850 m

Q. 17. A wave has an amplitude equal to 8 cm and the wavelength of 2 m. The frequency of the wave is 150 Hz.

   (i) Draw the graph of the wave representing displacement and distance.

   (ii) Calculate its velocity.

[November, 2019]

Ans. (i) The displacement–distance graph is shown below

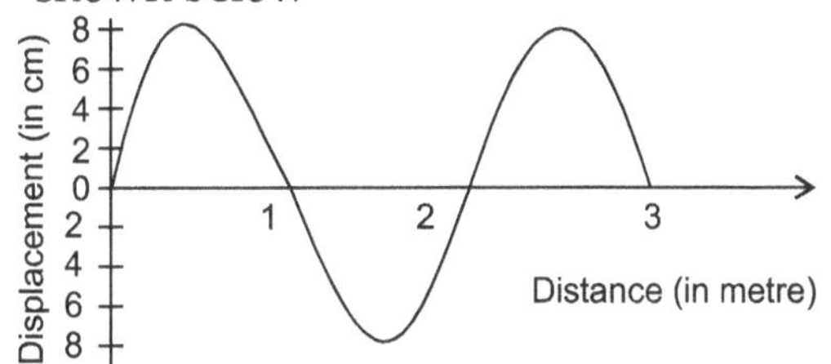

   (ii) λ = 2m, f = 150 Hz.

Velocity (v) = $f\lambda$ = 150 × 2

= 300 ms^{-1}

Q. 18. A longitudinal wave travels at a speed of 0.3 ms^{-1} and the frequency of wave is 20 Hz. Find the separation between the two consecutive compressions.

Ans. Given, v = 0.3 ms^{-1}

and f = 20 Hz

$\therefore$ $T = \dfrac{1}{f} = \dfrac{1}{20}$ s = 0.05 s

$\therefore$ $\lambda = v \times T$

= 0.3 × 0.05

= 0.015 m

Thus, the separation between two consecutive compressions is 0.015 m.

Q. 19. Speed of sound in air is 330 ms^{-1} and in water is 1650 ms^{-1}. It takes 6 s for sound to reach a certain distance from the source placed in air. Find the distance and how much times will it take for sound to reach the same distance when the source is in water?

Ans. Given,

In air, V = 330 ms^{-1}, t = 6 s

From the relation V = $\dfrac{d}{t}$

Distance travelled by sound in air,

d = V × t = 330 × 6 = 1980 m

Hence, required distance is 1980 m

And in water, V = 1650 ms^{-1}, d = 1980 m

Therefore, time taken by sound to travel the distance d in water will be

$$t = \frac{d}{V}$$

$$t = \frac{1980\,\text{m}}{1650\,\text{ms}^{-1}} = 1.2 \text{ s}$$

Hence, required time is 1.2 s.

Q. 20. Ocean waves of time period 20 s have wave velocity 25 ms^{-1}. What is the wavelength of these waves and the horizontal distance between a wave crest and its adjoining wave trough?

Ans. Given,

T = 20s

v = 25 ms^{-1}

We know, $v = \dfrac{\lambda}{T}$

$\Rightarrow$ $\lambda = v$T

$\Rightarrow$ λ = 25 × 20

$\Rightarrow$ λ = 500 m

And the distance between a wave crest and its adjoining wave trough is

$\dfrac{\lambda}{2} = \dfrac{1}{2}$ × 500 m = 250 m

Q. 21. Ocean waves of time period 10 s have wave velocity 15 ms^{-1}. Find : (i) the wavelength of these waves, (ii) the distance between a wave crest and its adjoining wave trough horizontally.

Ans. Given,

T = 10s, v = 15 ms^{-1}

   (i) From the relation,

$$v = \frac{\lambda}{T}$$

$\Rightarrow$ λ = V × T

$\Rightarrow$ λ = 15 × 10

= 150 m

   (ii) The distance between a wave crest and its adjoining wave trough

$= \dfrac{\lambda}{2} = \dfrac{1}{2}$ × 150 m

= 75 m.

Q. 22. The speed of sound in air is 330 ms^{-1} and in water is 1650 ms^{-1}. The sound takes 2 s to travel a distance from the given source in air. (i) Find the distance. (ii) How much time will it take for sound to reach the same distance when the source is in water?

Ans. Given,

For air, $v = 330$ ms^{-1}, $t = 2$ s

For water, $v = 1650$ ms^{-1}

(i) Distance travelled by sound in air

$$d = V \times t$$
$$= 330 \times 2$$
$$= 660 \text{ m}$$

(ii) Time taken by sound to travel the distance d in water will be

$$t = \frac{d}{V}$$
$$= \frac{660\,\text{m}}{1650 \text{ ms}^{-1}}$$
$$= 0.4 \text{ s}$$

Q. 23. Speed of sound in air is 330 ms^{-1} and in water is 1650 ms^{-1}. It takes 14 s for sound to reach a certain distance from the source placed in air. Find the distance and how much times will it take for sound to reach the same distance when the source is in water?

Ans. Given,

In air, $V = 330$ ms^{-1}, $t = 14$ s

From the relation, $V = \dfrac{d}{t}$

Distance travelled by sound in air,

$d = V \times t = 330 \times 14 = 4620$ m

Hence, required distance = 4620 m

And in water, $v = 1650$ ms^{-1},

Therefore, time taken by sound to travel the distance d in water will be

$$t = \frac{d}{V}$$
$$t = \frac{4620\,\text{m}}{1650 \text{ ms}^{-1}} = 2.8 \text{ s}$$

Hence, required time is $t = 2.8$ s.

Q. 24. Ocean waves of time period 60 s have wave velocity 95 ms^{-1}. Find wavelength of these waves and the horizontal distance between a wave crest and the adjacent trough.

Ans. Given,

$$T = 60 \text{ s}$$
$$v = 95 \text{ ms}^{-1}$$

From the relation, we have

$$v = \frac{\lambda}{T}$$

$\Rightarrow \qquad \lambda = vT$

$\Rightarrow \qquad \lambda = 95 \times 60$

$\Rightarrow \qquad \lambda = 5700$ m

And the distance between a wave crest and its adjoining wave tough is

$$\frac{\lambda}{2} = \frac{1}{2} \times 5700 \text{ m} = 2850 \text{ m}.$$

Q.25. If the speed of sound in air is 340 ms^{-1} and that of in water is 1360 ms^{-1}, then calculate the time taken to travel a distance of 1700 m by sound in (i) air (ii) water.

Ans. Given,

Speed of sound in air, $v_a = 340$ ms^{-1}

Speed of sound in water, $v_w = 1360$ ms^{-1}

Distance, S = 1700 m

(i) Time taken by sound in air,

$$t_a = \frac{S}{v_a}$$
$$= \frac{1700}{340}$$
$$= 5 \text{ s}$$

(ii) Time travel by sound in water

$$t_w = \frac{S}{v_w}$$
$$= \frac{1700}{1360}$$
$$= 1.25 \text{ s}.$$

Q. 26. The diagram shows a snapshot of a wave form of frequency 50 Hz in a string. The numbers in diagram represent distance in centimeters.

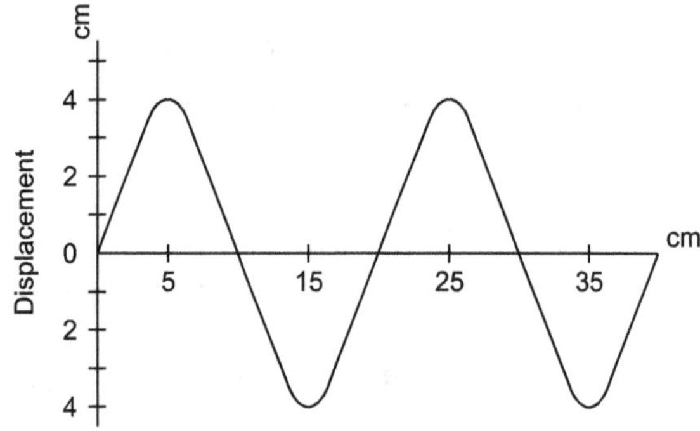

For this wave motion find,

(i) Wavelength (ii) Amplitude (iii) Wave velocity.

Ans. (i)   Wavelength = 20 cm.

(ii)   Amplitude = 4 cm.

(iii) Wave velocity $= f\lambda$

$$= 50 \times 20$$

$$= 1000 \text{ cms}^{-1}$$
$$= 10 \text{ ms}^{-1}$$

Q. 27. The figure shows the snapshot of a sound wave in a certain medium at a certain instant.

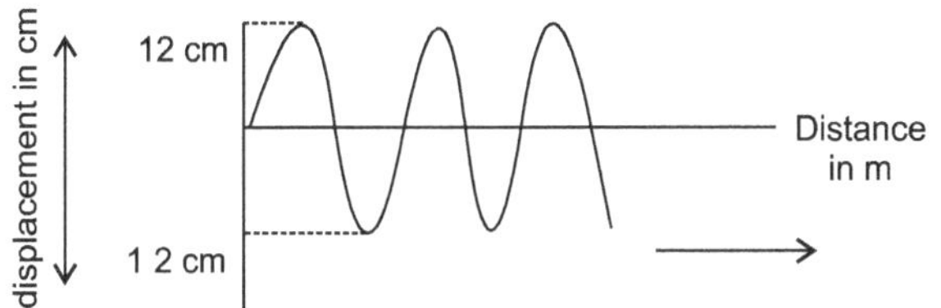

(i) What is the amplitude of the wave?

(ii) If the velocity of the wave is 4 ms^{-1}, calculate the wavelength of the wave if its frequency is 20 Hz.

(iii) If a wave of same type but with higher frequency is passed in the given medium, will the speed of the wave increase, decrease or remain the same? **[February 2020]**

Ans. (i) Amplitude of the wave = 12 cm

(ii) Given : $V = 4 \text{ ms}^{-1}$

$$f = 20 \text{ Hz}$$

$\therefore$ Wavelength, $\lambda = \dfrac{V}{f} = \dfrac{4}{20}$ m

$$= 0.2 \text{ m}$$

(iii) The speed of sound will remain the same because speed of sound in air does not depend on frequency.

Chapter 9. Current Electricity

Q. 1. A charge of 75 C is brought from infinity to a given point in an electric field, when amount of work done is 3.75 J. Calculate the electrical potential at that point.

Ans. Charge $= Q = 75$ C

Work done $= W = 3.75$ J

Electric potential $= V = ?$

We know, $V = \dfrac{W}{Q}$

$\therefore \quad V = \dfrac{3.75}{75} = 0.05$ V

Q. 2. A charge of 5000 C flows through an electric circuit in 2 hours and 30 minutes. Calculate the magnitude of current in circuit.

Ans. Charge $= Q = 5000$ C

Time $= t = 2$ hour 30 minutes

$\Rightarrow \quad t = 2 \times 60 + 30 = 150$ min

$\Rightarrow \quad t = 150 \times 60$ seconds

$\Rightarrow \quad t = 9000$ seconds

Electric current $= I = ?$

We know, $I = \dfrac{Q}{t}$

$\therefore \quad I = \dfrac{5000}{9000} = 0.555$ A

Q. 3. A charge of 8860 C flows through an electric circuit in 2 min and 40 s. Calculate the magnitude of current in the circuit.

Ans. Charge $= Q = 8860$ C

Time $= t = 2$ min 40 s

$\Rightarrow \quad t = (2 \times 60 + 40)$ s

$\Rightarrow \quad t = 160$ s

Electric current $= I = ?$

We know, $I = \dfrac{Q}{t}$

$\therefore \quad I = \dfrac{8860}{160} = 55.375$ A

Q. 4. A battery can supply a charge of 25×10^4 C. If the current is drawn from battery at the rate of 2.5 A, calculate the time in which battery will discharge completely.

Ans. Charge $= Q = 25 \times 10^4$ C

Electric current $= I = 2.5$ A

Time $= t = ?$

We know, $I = \dfrac{Q}{t}$

$\Rightarrow \quad t = \dfrac{Q}{I}$

$\therefore \quad t = \dfrac{25 \times 10^4}{2.5} = 10^5$ s

$\Rightarrow \quad t = 100000$ s

Q. 5. A dry cell can supply a charge of 800 C. If continuous current of 8.0 mA is drawn, calculate the time in which cell will discharge completely.

Ans. Charge $= Q = 800$ C

Electric current $= I = 8.0$ mA

$\Rightarrow \qquad I = 8 \times 10^{-3}$ A

Time $= t =?$

We know, $\qquad I = \dfrac{Q}{t}$

$\Rightarrow \qquad t = \dfrac{Q}{I}$

$t = \dfrac{800}{8 \times 10^{-3}} = 100 \times 10^3$

$t = 100000$ s

Q. 6. Calculate the total number of electrons flowing through a circuit in 20 mins and 40 s, if a current of 40 μA flows through the circuit. [1 $e^- = 1.6 \times 10^{-19}$ C]

Ans. Number of electrons $= n =?$

Time $= t = 20$ min 40 s

$t = (20 \times 60 + 40$) s

$t = 1240$ s

Electric current $= I = 40$ μA

$I = 40 \times 10^{-6}$ A

Charge on one electron $= 1\, e^- = 1.6 \times 10^{-19}$ C

Charge $= Q =?$

We know, $\qquad I = \dfrac{Q}{t}$

$\Rightarrow \qquad Q = It$

$\Rightarrow \qquad Q = 40 \times 10^{-6} \times 1240$

$\Rightarrow \qquad Q = 49600 \times 10^{-6}$ C

$\Rightarrow \qquad Q = 4.96 \times 10^{-2}$ C

Now, $Q = n \times$ charge on 1 electron $= ne^-$

$\therefore \qquad 4.96 \times 10^{-2} = n \times 1.6 \times 10^{-19}$

$\Rightarrow \qquad n = \dfrac{4.96 \times 10^{-2}}{1.6 \times 10^{-19}}$

$\Rightarrow \qquad n = 3.1 \times 10^{17}$ electrons

Q. 7. 4×10^{20} electrons flow through a circuit in 10 hours. Calculate the magnitude of current. [$e^- = 1.6 \times 10^{-19}$ C]

Ans. Number of electrons $= n = 4 \times 10^{20}$

Time $= t = 10$ hours

$\Rightarrow \qquad t = 10 \times 60 \times 60$ s

$\Rightarrow \qquad t = 36000$ s

Charge on one electron $= e^- = 1.6 \times 10^{-19}$ C

Electric current $= I =?$

$\because \qquad$ Charge $= Q = ne^-$

$\Rightarrow \qquad Q = 4 \times 10^{20} \times 1.6 \times 10^{-19}$

$\Rightarrow \qquad Q = 6.4 \times 10^{1}$

$\Rightarrow \qquad Q = 64$ C

Electric current $= I = \dfrac{Q}{t}$

$I = \dfrac{64}{36000}$

$\Rightarrow \qquad I = 1.77 \times 10^{-3}$ A

$\Rightarrow \qquad I = 1.77$ mA

Q. 8. What is the electrical potential at a point in an electric field when 24 J of work is done in moving a charge of 96 C from infinity?

Ans. Electric potential $= V =?$

Work done $= W = 24$ J

Charge $= Q = 96$ C.

We know, $\qquad V = \dfrac{W}{Q}$

$\Rightarrow \qquad V = \dfrac{24}{96} = \dfrac{1}{4}$

$\Rightarrow \qquad V = 0.25$ V

Q. 9. A work of 25 J and 30 J is done when 5 C charge is moved first to point A and then to point B from infinity. Calculate the potential difference between points A and B.

Ans. $\qquad W_A = 25$ J ; $W_B = 30$ J

Work done to move the 5 C charge from A to B $= W_B - W_A$

$W = 30 - 25 = 5$ J

Charge $Q = 5$ C

Potential difference between A and B

$$V = \dfrac{W}{Q} = \dfrac{5}{5} = 1\ V$$

OR

$W_A = 25$ J, $W_B = 30$ J, Charge $Q = 5$ C

Potential at point A $= V_1 = \dfrac{W_A}{Q}$

$$V_1 = \dfrac{25}{5} = 5\ \text{volt}$$

Potential at point B $= V_2 = \dfrac{W_B}{Q}$

$$V_2 = \dfrac{30}{5} = 6\ \text{volt}$$

Potential difference A and B

$= V_2 - V_1$

$= 6 - 5 = 1$ volt

Q. 10. A charge of 25 C is moved from infinity to points A and B in an electric field when the work done to do is 10 J and 10.5 J respectively. Calculate the potential difference between the points A and B.

Ans.
$$W_A = 10 \text{ J}$$
$$\text{Charge } Q = 25 \text{ C}$$

Potential at point A = $V_1 = \dfrac{W_A}{Q}$

$$V_1 = \dfrac{10}{25} = 0.4 \text{ V}$$

Also, $\quad W_B = 10.5 \text{ J}$

Potential at point B = $V_2 = \dfrac{W_B}{Q}$

$$V_2 = \dfrac{10.5}{25} = 0.42 \text{ volt}$$

Potential diffentence between A and B
$$= V_2 - V_1$$
$$= 0.42 - 0.40$$
$$= 0.02 \text{ volt}$$

Q. 11. Calculate the potential difference that will exist across the ends of a wire of resistance 2Ω when a current of 1.5 A passes through it.

Ans. Given,
$$R = 2 \, \Omega$$
$$I = 1.5 \text{ A}$$
From the Ohm's law, we have
$$V = IR$$
$$\Rightarrow \quad V = 1.5 \times 2$$
$$\Rightarrow \quad V = 3V.$$

Q. 12. A current of magnitude 0.2A flows in a wire having resistance 15Ω. What is the potential difference across the end of the wire? What is the unit of potential difference?

Ans. Given,
$$I = 0.2 \text{ A}, R = 15\Omega$$
Potential difference will be
$$V = IR$$
$$\Rightarrow \quad V = 0.2 \times 15$$
$$\Rightarrow \quad V = 3.0 \text{ V}$$

Q.13. When a car's starter motor is switched on for 3 s, a charge 36 C goes through the motor coil. Estimate the amount of current in the coil.

Ans. Given, $\quad t = 3 \text{ s}$
$$Q = 36 \text{ C}$$
We know, $\quad I = \dfrac{Q}{t}$

$$\Rightarrow \quad I = \dfrac{36}{3}$$
$$\Rightarrow \quad I = 12 \text{ A}$$
Hence, the current in the coil is 12 A.

Q. 14. A cell is bound to a bulb where a potential difference is of 36 volts across it. The current in circuit is found to be 12 A. Find the resistance offered by the filament of bulb to the flow of current.

Ans. Given,
$$V = 36 \text{ V}, \ I = 12 \text{ A}$$
From the Ohm's law, we have
$$V = IR$$
$$\Rightarrow \quad R = \dfrac{V}{I}$$
$$\Rightarrow \quad R = \dfrac{36}{12}$$
$$\Rightarrow \quad R = 3\Omega.$$
Hence, the resistance offered by the filament is 3Ω.

❑